Eighteen Miles of History on Long Beach Island

John Bailey Lloyd

A CORMORANT BOOK

Book design by Ray Fisk
Marion Figley, editor

DOWN THE SHORE / The SandPaper
PUBLISHING

For information, address:
Down The Shore Publishing, Box 3100, Harvey Cedars, NJ 08008
Down The Shore and The SandPaper, and the respective logos, are registered U.S. Trademarks.
Printed in Canada. First printing: revised, expanded edition, 1994.
10 9 8 7 6 5 4 3 2 1

Library of Congress Cataloging-in-Publication Data
Lloyd, John Bailey, 1932-
   Eighteen miles of history on Long Beach Island / John Bailey Lloyd.
      p.   cm.
   Includes index.
   ISBN 0-945582-17-X (hardcover)
   1. Long Beach Island (N.J.) — History.   I. Title.   II. Title: 18 miles of history on Long Beach Island.
   F142-L65L58   1994
974.9'48—dc20   94-29744
                                                      CIP

Photographs

Front cover: Ocean view of Beach Haven in the 1920s, showing the beach, boardwalk, and Baldwin Hotel at left, by Earl C. Roper.

Back cover: Barnegat Light, then Barnegat City, shortly after the turn of the century, with the Sunset Hotel and lighthouse in the distance, courtesy Lynn Photo.

Endpapers: Panoramic view of Beach Haven and Dock Road, circa 1900, by Robert F. Engle.

Facing page: Sailboats on Little Egg Harbor Bay near the Beach Haven Yacht club at turn of century.

A view of Barnegat Lighthouse and the keeper's house taken from the roof of the Sunset Hotel, circa 1900, showing the wood-covered acreage that would wash away within the next twenty years. Across Barnegat Inlet is north beach or "north point o' beach" as it was then called, today's Island Beach State Park.

Contents

A wrecked schooner off the Peahala Club around 1910. The Long Beach Life Saving Station at Maryland Avenue in Beach Haven Terrace shows in the middle distance. Beyond it, at far left, are the two-story Dolphin Inn at Thirteenth Street in North Beach Haven and the skyline of Beach Haven.

Preface

The history of Long Beach Island and its lost neighbor, Tucker's Island, began more than two hundred years ago when Philadelphians and West Jerseyans journeyed across the state for the pleasures of hunting, fishing and sea bathing on the barrier islands, reachable then only by sailboat. Development here proceeded slowly in the nineteenth century until the twenty-nine-mile Tuckerton Railroad on the mainland connected the coastal towns with the cross-state line to Camden and the Amboys. In 1872, steamboat service was introduced to Long Beach Island while the new resort of Beach Haven was being built. By 1886 there was a railroad bridge across the bay, and tracks were laid to Beach Haven and to Barnegat City, on the north end of the island. Though we marked its centennial in the summer of 1986, the railroad has been gone since 1935.

This disappearance of an earlier Long Beach Island is typical. After a century of growth, we find astonishingly little physical evidence of our early history. We can drive up and down the island and point out where everything once was, but that is all. Only Barnegat Lighthouse, a score of classic summer cottages in Beach Haven and in Barnegat Light, a church that is now a museum, and the former Harvey Cedars Hotel remain. Everything else is substantially altered or gone, most of it in the last fifty years.

We have become an island of lost landmarks. Fire, storm, tide and general obsolescence have claimed nearly all of them. The big hotels, the boardwalk, the gunning clubs, the train, the old causeway and even Tucker's Island itself have all vanished. All we have are photographs and the memories of those people who were here and who lived through these changing times.

These people are our greatest resource. Their observations and recollections fascinate us because the island was once so very different. Many of their interviews are on tape for future generations. Information from much earlier times must be gathered from old letters, diaries and newspaper accounts. These items exist but are hard to find. The Long Beach Island Historical Association and Barnegat Light Museum are striving to collect them. Only when they have been gathered can we continue to tell the complete story of this island and its eighteen miles of remarkable social history.

John Bailey Lloyd
Beach Haven, New Jersey
September 1986

Preface to the New Edition

When I wrote the preceding words for the first edition of *Eighteen Miles of History,* I had little expectation that I would ever find enough material or pictures to do another book on the history of Long Beach Island. But I did, and that was how *Six Miles at Sea* came to be published in 1990. It was nearly three times longer than *Eighteen Miles,* and during its research, I found that I now had more than enough material to bring the first book up to the same size as the second — but it was too late for that.

I would have given anything to completely rewrite it, but *Eighteen Miles* was still selling well, and publishers have little desire to invest in a competing duplicate which would have used most of the same pictures. The economics of the business simply do not permit that. But then something remarkable happened, a stroke of luck for an author anxious to rewrite a first work. The printer in Philadelphia declared bankruptcy and, while emptying a warehouse of unused material, accidentally tossed out the plates for my book.

Since we would have to incur the cost of another first printing, why not make *Eighteen Miles of History* an entirely new book? And so this edition, greatly expanded and added to, has been born. It contains all of the fine pictures of the first work and three times as many new ones, many of which have not been seen for nearly a century. New chapters have been added and the old ones expanded with new information. This book will now serve as the perfect companion piece to *Six Miles at Sea.*

John Bailey Lloyd
June 1994

Acknowledgements

Writers as creators come up with the ideas, do the research and sometimes take years putting the words together, but in the end, no really good book has ever been produced without a good editor to keep that writer from straying. I am indeed fortunate to have had, once more through the partnership of Down The Shore Publishing and The SandPaper, another of those good editors and perhaps this time even a great one in Marion Figley, who put me, a librarian, to shame in her tireless efforts to check meanings and facts.

Marion also knew exactly when and where to cut and, for all that, we never once had an argument over a single word. We simply strove for economy and clarity in our efforts to make the finest book possible for this time and place and possibly for fifty years to come. In that we were not alone because the final stages of this book have been a joint effort.

The production and design process has changed drastically since the first edition of this book was created; instead of using pencils, pica rulers and waxed galleys of type, it is now done on computer. Yet despite the high-tech tools, the creative act of making a physical book from a manuscript and collection of photographs is still the same complicated and somewhat indefinable process.

Ray Fisk, who sees things in photographs and their juxtaposition with text that writers and editors see in words and phrases, did the picture editing and page layouts. He oversaw the myriad production details and minutiae of this complex book, and was persistent in seeing that it is complete and of the highest quality.

Anita Josephson, despite an intense schedule meeting deadlines with other projects, made time to see that every page of type was correct and in position, and that last-minute corrections were made. My thanks also go to Leslee Ganss for her excellent cover design and graphics.

All of us owe a great debt to Jack and Virginia Lamping of Toms River. Jack has been on the scene at every major turning point in Island history for the past sixty years. It is he who was entrusted by Robert F. Engle in 1940 to care for the priceless glass negatives and other photographs that appear throughout this book. Many of them have not been seen since the early years of this century.

George C. Hartnett of Moorestown has once again been most generous in allowing the use of his splendid post card collection of Long Beach Island.

More than a decade has gone by since I first began the research on *Eighteen Miles* and some of these people have passed on, but my debt to them and to their families endures.

Robert and Margaretta Aaronson of Bordentown
Kristen Anderson of Beach Haven
Bay State Bank of Long Beach Island and Manahawkin
Beach Haven Free Public Library
John Brinckmann of Greensboro, North Carolina
Rose Britz of Beach Haven
Walter P. Browning of Devon, Pa.
Margaret Thomas Buchholz of Harvey Cedars
Benjamin Crane of Tuckerton
Joe Cranmer of Beach Haven
Walter and Helen Cranmer of Beach Haven
W. Corkran Darlington of Wallingford, Pa.
William De Frietas, Jr. of Waretown
Nils and Olga Eklund of North Beach Haven
Nathaniel T. and Betty Ewer of Beach Haven

David Lewis Eynon of Philadelphia, Pa.
Elizabeth Colmer Garrison of Beach Haven Gardens
William and Phyllis Parker Gee of Beach Haven
Phil Hart of Manahawkin
Marie Howe of Beach Haven
Walter Inman of Surf City
Olive Jones of Surf City
Adrian and Edith King of Beach Haven
Arthur Lord of Pennington
Pauline Miller of Toms River
Virginia Wilson Mollino of Beach Haven Terrace
John and Elaine Monkaitis of Wyckoff
Gregory Morris of Beach Haven
Nicholas and Peg Morris of Chester Springs, Pa.
Ocean County Library
Al Oldham of Harvey Cedars
Walter and Sara Stratton Osborn of Beach Haven
Barry T. Parker of Mount Holly
Watson Pharo, Sr. of Beach Haven
Elisabeth Powell of Haven Beach
Julius and Clara Robinson of Beach Haven

Richard Shackleton of Holgate
Carl and Carroll Sheppard of Philadelphia, Pa.
Agnes Shinn of Brant Beach
Herbert Schoenberg of Beach Haven
Robert and Joyce Stahl of Titusville
Evelyn Suter of Parkertown
Joseph Taggart of Rosemont, Pa.
Daniel and Muriel Tooker of Beach Haven
John Troast of Wyckoff
A. Jerome Walnut of Barnegat Light
Herbert S. Webster of Bryn Mawr, Pa.
Barbara Windrow of Mendham

Photographs:
Beach Haven Library Museum, Beach Haven
W. Corkran Darlington of Wallingford, Pa.
Nathaniel T. Ewer of Beach Haven
Harold Jones of Surf City
Long Beach Island Historical Museum, Beach Haven
Carl Van Thulin, Lynn Photo, Ship Bottom

Outfitted for a musical skit, Engleside Hotel guests clown on the beach for photographer Robert F. Engle in 1903. The Engles, father and son, organized dances, concerts, games, minstrel shows, costume parties and other activities at their Beach Haven hotel to keep everyone constantly entertained.

Harper's New Monthly Magazine

Surf boats much like these late 19th-century fishing boats depicted in *Harper's Monthly* were used by earlier residents of New Jersey's barrier islands for whaling. At right, an artist's depiction of one of the whale lookouts likely used at the Great Swamp, now Surf City, from the 1936 edition of *The Lure of Long Beach*.

Chapter 1

THE SHORE WHALERS

In every maritime nation of Europe since the Middle Ages, coast dwellers had hunted and killed whales from small boats launched into the surf. The huge creatures were towed ashore, cut up and rendered into oil over fires on the beach. The practice spread to the New World after early reports of the unbelievably vast herds cruising the North American coastline became just one more reason for colonization. Whale oil was such a valuable commodity that conflicting claims of who might have made the first sighting of a helpless, beached whale sometimes had to be adjudicated in the courts.

The best proof of ownership of a dead whale was to have actually killed it from a boat. On that there could be no argument, and as early as the middle 1600s, only a generation or two after the first settlements at Plymouth and the Massachusetts Bay Colony, families and partnerships were engaged in shore whaling from Long Island to the lonely barrier beaches of New Jersey, where ordinarily no other means of livelihood existed.

Shore whaling as practiced then was a seasonal occupation restricted to the bitter cold months of February and March and sometimes November, when the whales were migrating. The whales hunted off the coast were never very big,

The Lure of Long Beach, *1936*

averaging about fifty feet in length. Only occasionally did a huge creature like the sperm whale leave the Gulf Stream to enter these colder and relatively shallow waters. The species actively hunted was the North Atlantic Greenland or "right" whale.

In Colonial times there were whaling stations all along the beaches in New Jersey from Cape May to Sandy Hook. The first local whaler was a man by the name of Soper who came with his family to Great Swamp in present-day Surf City around 1690, probably because that part of the island extends farthest east and also because the swamp's tall, white cedars afforded convenient lookout posts to spot migrating whales. He was soon joined by fellow New Englander Aaron Inman, who had three sons.

By the beginning of the nineteenth century, a hundred years later, there were twelve families living in that location, nearly all of whom were engaged in shore whaling for part of the year. In addition to Sopers and Inmans there were the Cranmer, Rutter, Mullins and Stevens families. By then there were at least two whaling stations or quarters above and below Great Swamp, one at Harvey Cedars and another near Brant Beach, but these were not permanent settlements.

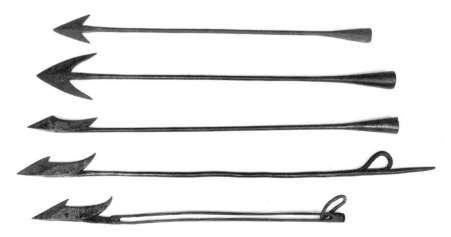

Long Beach Island Historical Museum (Hermann Koch collection, right; Helen R. Green, facing page)

Whales were hunted from shore-launched boats. Once harpooned, above, they were dispatched with a killing lance and towed to shore where they were cut up and rendered over fires on the beach in try pots for their oil. At right, harpoons found in Holgate show the development of the toggle head which secured the barb in the whale. Double-ended Beach Haven lifeboats of 1895, facing page, were direct descendants of the original Great Swamp whale boats.

It was not hard to spot whales in those early years. They could be seen as easily from a high dune as from a tree, but it was important to know which was the "right" whale, so a higher vantage point was necessary. A thirty-foot tower with a crow's nest was erected on the beachfront at Great Swamp. The whale watcher probably did not spend hour after hour in the tower exposed to the coldest weather of the entire year, since it was necessary only to determine whether the whales already spotted were right whales or the less valuable finbacks. Finbacks were more common, but they were too swift and made so little oil that they were not worth hunting.

It was only the right whale that was sought. It was so called because it delivered the most oil and the best bone. It was relatively slow, and it floated when dead. From a distance, the only way to tell a right whale from a finback was by its spout. A whale comes up to breathe about every twenty minutes, expelling moist air from its blowhole. A right whale has two blowholes and sends up a crotched spout. Only after this signal difference was ascertained would a bell be rung and the boats launched.

The really big difference between shore whaling and deep-sea whaling is the surf. The whaleboat, the tools and the methods are the same. The traditional whaleboat was twenty-eight feet in length, a little more than half as long as the average right whale hunted from it. It was six feet wide at the center thwart and sharp at both ends, with oak ribs and half-inch cedar planks. It had to be sturdy but not so heavy that it could not be gotten off the beach in a hurry. The regulation crew was six, counting all hands. Going out in the surf, the boat header in the stern was the only person facing forward and the only one who could see. He had a twenty-eight-foot tiller. The harpooner in the bow faced backward and manned a fourteen-foot steering oar until they neared the whale. With four oars, such a boat could reach a top speed of ten miles an hour. The average speed of the whales hunted off the island was five miles an hour, but if panicked or harpooned, they were capable of much greater speeds.

The harpoon was eleven feet long, eight feet of hickory and three feet of iron shank with a toggle pin that remained fixed in the blubber of the whale. It was attached to six hundred feet of line which uncoiled from a tub amidships as the whale began to run, towing the boat with it until fatigued. At this point, the men would pull the line in, hand over hand, until they were once more alongside the whale. Then the killing lance was used. It was longer and sharper than a harpoon, did not have a toggle pin and was free of a line. A good man would be able to dart a lance fifty or sixty feet and sink five feet of iron into the whale. Four strong oarsmen could row about a mile an hour with a dead whale in tow. Sometimes they were ten miles out and it took a while to bring the whale to shore.

The whale was pulled onto the beach as far as possible, and the blubber was cut into eighteen-inch pieces and boiled in large kettles called try pots. It was this process of "trying" that rendered the valuable oil from the blubber. Each whale yielded about forty or fifty barrels of oil, but the long pieces of baleen in the whale's jaws were even more prized. It was a misnomer to call it whalebone, but it was called that anyway. Flexible but strong, baleen was used for corset stays and umbrella ribs and anything that is today made out of plastic. The whale's skeleton had practically no value. If it did not lie about bleaching in the sun, it was used to make decorative garden fences and gateways. Pieces were taken home as souvenirs by the first vacationers to Great Swamp, and many a rib bone hung from a barn beam far inland from the sea.

The early families who devoted themselves to the pursuit and killing of whales had plentiful game and fish to live on the rest of the year, but it was the sighting of the first right whales in February that sent every member of the tiny community to the beaches to aid in the launching of the boats. The industry died out in the 1830s when the right whale all but vanished from these waters due to overhunting by New England whaling fleets. The last right whale taken off the Atlantic seaboard was killed six miles off Amagansett, Long Island, in 1918.

A 1925 aerial view of Tucker's Island and a dwindling Tucker's Beach looking northeast toward the Beach Haven Inlet and the southern tip of Long Beach Island. The inlet would eventually widen and drift southward, consuming all of Tucker's Island in the next twenty years. The slough, a navigable arm of the bay, is seen on the west side of the upper third of the island; it once separated Tucker's Island from Tucker's Beach, and it was here that the lighthouse and the community of Sea Haven were located.

Chapter 2

TUCKER'S ISLAND

On a 1769 survey map of the Jerseys, East and West — as the state was known in the Colonial period — Long Beach Island is identified as "Old Barnegat Beach." Its northern tip is at the Barnegat Inlet, and from there it stretches southwestward eighteen miles to another inlet, a very wide and deep one. No name is given to this inlet, but it is clearly the only entrance into Little Egg Harbor Bay and to a small seaport village known today as Tuckerton.

South of this unnamed inlet there is another barrier beach on the chart. It is some seven or eight miles in length and is labeled "Mihannan Shoal," obviously an Indian name whose meaning has been lost. Other maps of the period call it Short Beach. It was the custom then to name uninhabited barrier beaches after either the nearest inlet or some obvious physical feature; thus Barnegat Beach was also known locally as Long Beach or Eighteen Mile Beach, and its southerly neighbor, being about one-third the size, was called Short Beach.

Ephraim Morse was the first known settler on Short Beach. As early as the 1740s he was grazing cattle on its thousands of acres of salt hay and, to supplement his income, he used his dwelling on the edge of the bayside marshes as

a grocery for stormbound mariners who often sought shelter inside the inlet in the deep channel behind his island. Short Beach was also, with its easy access to splendid ocean bathing, an ideal location for health- and pleasure-seekers, making it the first seashore resort on the New Jersey coast. Morse did well for several years until tragedy struck. One winter night his house began to wash away as the bay rose in a storm tide. He fled with his wife and five small children through waist-deep, ice-cold water to the high dunes. There was no cover, and exposure to sleet and rain over the next thirty-six hours caused the children to sicken and die. Morse and his wife survived, and when finally rescued they left for the mainland never to return, although accounts say they eventually had five more children.

Except for harvesting salt hay, barrier beaches were virtually useless for farming; in those days, they often sold for a few cents an acre. In 1765 Reuben Tucker, a Quaker from Orange County, New York, bought out Morse's interest in Short Beach and settled down for much the same kind of livelihood as Morse, but Tucker took the precaution to build his house on the high north end of the island, where a lighthouse would one day be located. He enlarged the struc-

ture into a tavern and "place of entertainment." Such was Tucker's personality that his fame as a good host soon spread among watermen from Sandy Hook to the Carolinas. Tucker's Beach or Tucker's Island became a favored place to wait out an Atlantic storm.

In the years after the American Revolution, Tucker's Island continued to be very popular with prosperous Philadelphia Quakers, many of whom had established the base of their fortunes during the war by smelting bog iron and shipping timber out of Egg Harbor before moving to Pennsylvania. They were well-acquainted with the area and with Tucker and used his island and facilities for their five-day camp meetings held every summer. These gatherings of Friends were religious in purpose, but during them the men found every excuse to hunt and fish while the ladies enjoyed the sun and surf. For the young it was a time of matchmaking and courting. Many returned at other times of the year to stay with the Tucker family.

Tucker had fathered two sons, Stephen, who took the Tory side in the Revolution and died an exile in Nova Scotia after the war, and Ebenezer, who took up the Colonies' cause. At the end of the Revolution, Ebenezer entered the mercantile

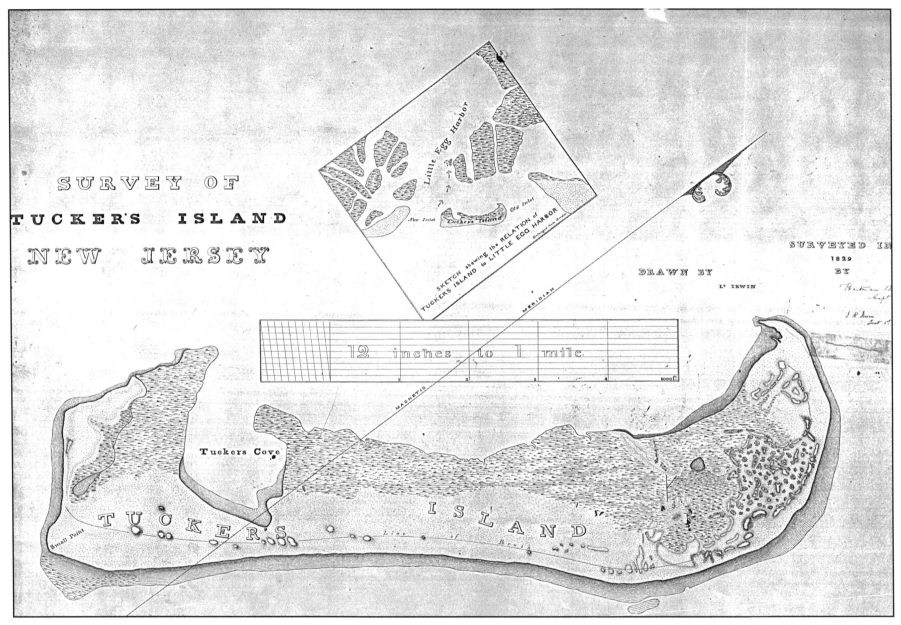

SURVEY OF

TUCKER'S ISLAND

NEW JERSEY

Little Egg Harbor

New Inlet   *Old Inlet*

Tuckers Island

SKETCH showing the RELATION of
TUCKERS ISLAND to LITTLE EGG HARBOR
Enlarged from O....

SURVEYED IN
1829
BY

DRAWN BY
Lt IRWIN

MERIDIAN

12 inches to 1 mile

1   2   3   4   5000 f^t

MAGNETIC

Tuckers Cove

TUCKER'S   ISLAND

Small Point   Line   of   Breach

Survey of Tucker's Island made by army surveyors in 1829 shows Ebenezer Tucker's boardinghouse, center right. Facing page: the Sea Haven or Little Egg Harbor Light in 1927 as the relentless sea eats away at the north end of Tucker's Island. A two-masted schooner can be seen on the horizon at left, passing the island.

and shipping business, becoming so politically powerful in the area that the mainland village once known as Clamtown or Egg Harbor voted to change its name to Tuckerton in his honor.

Meanwhile, Reuben Tucker was finding that he could turn a nice profit on his island by making the big farmhouse available to Burlington County and Philadelphia sportsmen willing to make the long, horse-and-wagon journey through the pines to Tuckerton to book "safe ferry" to the beach. Most visitors to the seashore in those early years were in the habit of setting up tents or lean-tos on the dunes, but staying at Tucker's comfortable place was the beginning of a trend which led to the development of other early boarding hotels like the Philadelphia Company House and the Mansion of Health on nearby Long Beach Island.

When Reuben died, his widow, who was known affectionately to all as Mother Tucker — not Mammy Tucker — kept the old place going for many more years. The original one-story house with its hipped roof and broad piazza became a cluster of three buildings joined together but obviously built at different times. Everywhere, the names of former guests had been cut into the boards or written on the backs of bleached clam shells and were nailed to every wall and post. The Tucker House with its three prominent cedar trees appeared on coastal charts as a navigator's landmark as late as 1845, even though it burned to the ground that very year. It had been such a familiar reckoning point that the first Tucker's Lighthouse was built on the site three years later.

Mother Tucker died around 1815 and was succeeded by her manager, Joseph Horner, who left within a few years to start his own place on the south end of Long Beach. Meanwhile, the Tucker House was run by the Rogers and Willits families right up until the time it was destroyed

by fire. Tucker's Island had by then been much reduced in size, a process that started in 1800 when a great winter storm cut a new inlet across its lower third. The portion below that inlet was forever afterward known as "Little Beach," so now there was a Long Beach, a Short Beach and a Little Beach. This "New Inlet," as it would be called for the next 125 years, became the best inlet on the coast of New Jersey. It is known today as the Little Egg Harbor Inlet.

After the New Inlet cut through on the south end of Tucker's Beach, the one on the north at last got a name, "Old Inlet." Within thirty years its entrance began to shoal up badly, and by the time a lighthouse was built on the site of the old Tucker place in 1848, it was navigable only at

high tide. Old Inlet closed completely by 1874 as great quantities of sand formed a hook around Tucker's Island, now separated from its beach by a slough or arm of the bay. The slough ran roughly northwest to southeast and was so wide on the bay or northwest side that hotel guests on the island had to cross it in a flat-bottomed boat when they went sea bathing; on the southeast or ocean end a mile away, the slough was narrow enough to have a small wooden bridge across it. A writer in 1866 noted that "the bathing ground at Short Beach is not as good as it was formerly, as sand bars have accumulated some distance from the main shore." It had been a hundred years since Tucker had bought the island and given his name to it.

Stahl family (upper left); Evelyn Suter (above and lower left)

Sea Haven Light's last keeper, Arthur Rider, who rarely left Tucker's Island, enjoyed posing with visitors and would mow hay with Harry the Horse. Facing page: the Crane family on Tucker's Beach in 1916 walking the five miles from Sea Haven to Beach Haven.

The first Tucker Beach Light, established in 1848, was discontinued after only a dozen years of operation, most likely because the Old Inlet that it guarded was now of limited usefulness while the New Inlet, several miles south of the lighthouse, was the one that provided the only safe passage between Little Egg Harbor Bay and the ocean. This was confusing to mariners, but it was also probable that funding for another lighthouse was unavailable because on the eve of the Civil War, Congress had more serious matters to consider.

Tucker's or Little Egg Harbor Light was re-established by an Act of Congress in 1865 without any provisions to have it moved because there really was no better location for a lighthouse anywhere for miles around: The high ground at the north end of Tucker's Island provided security as well as greater visibility. For the next sixty-three years its signal — six red flashes and one long white — from the tower atop the keeper's cottage could be seen twelve miles at sea on clear nights. This characteristic identified the light, 20.5 miles below Barnegat Light and twelve miles north of Absecon Light in Atlantic City. While the signal marked the entrance to the Little Egg Harbor Inlet, its red flashes cautioned mariners to study their charts because the inlet was not at all near the light. It was three miles away.

When the Little Egg Harbor Light was relit after the Civil War, it was also substantially rebuilt, with a black tower atop a white dwelling. The first officially appointed light keeper was Eber Rider, who was born at Tuckerton in 1827. He had married Mary Cranmer of Mayetta, and together they had twenty-one children, only six of whom survived to adulthood. In 1866 their eldest son, Jarvis, was appointed at the age of twenty to be the first master of the Little Egg Harbor Life Saving Station on Tucker's Island. The next son,

Anson J., became a game warden. Amanda, the only daughter, married George Penrod, who had a store at Beach Haven. There were three more sons: Eber Jr., Arthur and Hilliard.

Care of the light was a rigorous, time-consuming occupation, and each of the Rider children was pressed into it, including Amanda, but only Arthur took a liking to it; when his father retired on January 1, 1904, after thirty-nine years of service, Arthur succeeded him, staying on until the very end in 1927. Together father and son ran the Little Egg Harbor Light for sixty-three years, a remarkable record in the history of the Lighthouse Service. Arthur was assisted for awhile by Hilliard, who died in his twenties.

The Life Saving station had to be built more than a mile south of the lighthouse so the crews could get their equipment out onto the ocean beaches, where all the strandings and shipwrecks took place. A bridge was built across the slough

at its narrowest point to accommodate the vehicles used to haul the lifeboat and the surf cannon. Over the next forty-six years, Jarvis Rider and his crews logged two hundred shipwrecks.

For nearly two decades after the burning of the Tucker boarding house in 1845, there is no record of any vacation activity on the island although there must surely have been campers. Local competition may have been a factor. Bond's, across the Old Inlet on Long Beach, was flourishing. Since 1854 vacationers had been taking the Camden and Atlantic Railroad to Absecon and sailing up Great Bay to Bond's place. Nor did ship's crews come to the island anymore. Stormbound mariners purchased whiskey and groceries at Hatfield's store on Tucker's Neck, located along Shooting Thoroughfare less than a mile across the water from the lighthouse. Hatfield's became well-known enough to be on the official navigation charts of those years.

It was the arrival of the Tuckerton Railroad that finally changed the whole history of the area. The completion of a twenty-nine-mile track from Whiting in north-central Ocean County to Tuckerton in 1871 promised to bring thousands of vacationers into the area. The Camden and Amboy line, which crossed the state, passed through Whiting, and would bring many to the seashore for the first time. The round trip from Camden to Tuckerton cost $2.50. These newcomers would need places to stay, and already there was a brand

new resort starting up at Beach Haven with two hotels and many attractive summer cottages.

Inspired by this activity, Alfred Stevens, one of the Life Saving Service crew at Captain Jarvis Rider's station, supervised the construction of a four-story hotel on Tucker's Island with two outside decks or galleries. After a wing was added, there were twenty-eight rooms. It was near the Life Saving station and would provide additional income for Stevens and his wife and the men who had helped to build it. During the summer

months they were idle and were not paid when the station was closed. Stevens had backing, but the hotel was not a huge investment because, with the exception of doors and windows, there was little expense for lumber. Thrown overboard in storms or washed off the decks of ships, it was gathered up from the beaches. Stevens named his hotel the Columbia and advertised in the Philadelphia papers. Its first season was 1875, one year after the Parry House opened at Beach Haven and a year before the Engleside Hotel.

On excursions to Sea Haven at low tide, boat captains and mates often carried well-dressed and well-shod passengers across the mud flats. Facing page, a view of Sea Haven, circa 1900, shows the Columbia Hotel at far left, St. Albans Hotel at center, and Little Egg Harbor Lighthouse at right.

The island had not seen such activity since the days of Reuben Tucker. The success of the Columbia inspired Eber Rider, now in his tenth year as keeper of the lighthouse, to build an even bigger hotel nearby on the slough where boatloads of happy guests could sail right up to the front door. It was finished in 1879, and it and the Columbia were filled to capacity every summer. Rider at first called it simply "The House of Entertainment," but financial backers suggested "St. Albans" to give it a little more class. In those years when the railroad ran only into Tuckerton and had a spur track to Edge Cove for steamboat service, it was just as easy to go to Tucker's Is-

land as to Beach Haven. It was at this time that the name "Sea Haven" was given to the community to compete with Beach Haven.

It was more than just a name change. A company was formed to sell real estate. Tucker's Island, where the lighthouse, the two hotels and the Life Saving Station were, would be called Sea Haven, and all the property across the slough would still be called Tucker's Beach, which by now — since the Old Inlet had closed up in 1874 — had formed a huge hooklike beach with shoals nearly a half-mile wide around the eastern and southern edges of the island. Tucker's Beach was now part of one continuous stretch of land that

reached all the way to Barnegat Light.

In 1884 the two hotels at Sea Haven advertised access to telegraph facilities for vacationers because the Little Egg Life Saving Station had a unit of the U.S. Signal Service with a submarine cable to Tuckerton. No station on Long Beach Island had such access yet, and it was suggested that businessmen could relax a little more at Sea Haven knowing that they had instant contact with their offices in distant cities by means of telegraph. The resort was also served daily throughout the summer months by the small paddle-wheel steamer *Mary* with stops at Edge Cove and Absecon. Sea Haven had reached its zenith.

The Jones and Homer families of Tuckerton in 1912 stand before "Skeeters," their vacation cottage on Tucker's Beach. South of them, across the slough, is Sea Haven. On the facing page, a clambake put on as a fund-raiser by the Life Saving crew at Sea Haven.

The Tuckerton Railroad, backed by the mighty Pennsylvania Railroad, was building a railroad bridge across Manahawkin Bay to Long Beach Island and laying tracks south to Beach Haven and north to Barnegat City. The project was completed in 1886. There were plans to take the train the additional four and a half miles to Sea Haven, but nothing ever came of it. The project, financed as it was by the Pennsylvania Railroad, may have been dropped because of friendly connections with Charles T. Parry of the Baldwin Locomotive Works, who was the principal stockholder in the land company developing Beach Haven. He had just finished building

the Baldwin Hotel and may not have welcomed the competition from another resort. To be deprived of a railroad stop when one was so near at hand was, in those years, a serious setback, and by the 1890s Sea Haven was finished.

Besides the Riders at the lighthouse and the Life Saving station, there were in the 1890s always six or seven other families who were classified as winter residents because the men were all on duty at the Life Saving station ten months of the year. There were a dozen or so school-age children in these families, so in 1895 a school was built near the lighthouse out of the proceeds from several clambakes. Clambakes were traditional

annual fund-raisers at Life Saving stations then, and they were usually well-attended by summer people, who contributed generously.

The new schoolhouse opened its doors December 9, 1895, with Lydia Wills of Tuckerton teaching nine students in six grades. Hitherto, classes had been taught at the Life Saving station, which was on the south side of the island. Since almost all the children lived near the station, they now had to walk a mile to and from school in all kinds of weather. The school doubled as a community center and also was used as a church on Sundays. It had only one big room with a dozen double desks, a potbellied stove and an organ. It

was equipped with a belfry in the shape of a watchtower to match the architectural style of the lighthouse and the Life Saving station. The large bell could be used as a signal in fog.

By the turn of the century, fourteen years after the railroad had come to Beach Haven, tiny Sea Haven, its neighbor just five miles down the beach, was in slow decline. Only a handful of summer residents still kept cottages on Tucker's Beach near the ocean, and some were still on the island at Sea Haven, but not for long. The Columbia and St. Albans hotels were in ruins. In 1907 the Sea Haven Company mortgaged the whole south end of the island, about a thousand acres, to the company that had originally financed Rider's hotel. They planned an ambitious development called St. Albans-by-the-Sea with lots for sale on a

grid of twenty streets, all named after American lakes and intersected by three wide avenues running north and south. They speculated that the railroad might some day be extended south from Beach Haven, but that was never to happen. Finally, by 1918, they were forced into bankruptcy, two years before a fierce storm carved out Beach Haven Inlet and made any further road contact with St. Albans impossible.

There was no gravel on Sea Haven to build streets. The only roads were made of hard-packed sand and crushed clam and oyster shells atop layers of salt hay. Weekly trips were made up the beach to Penrod's General Store at the corner of Beach Avenue and Amber Street in Beach Haven, with Harry the Horse pulling the two-wheeled cart loaded with those children who

wished to go along on the shopping expedition — and most of them wouldn't have missed it no matter what the weather was like. They crossed the slough bridge at the south end of the island over onto Tucker's Beach. From that point it was a six-mile walk up to Beach Haven. These trips were always great social occasions for the shoppers to visit with Amanda Rider Penrod. Once the cart was loaded, the older children had to walk back with the adults while Harry, lent for the trip by the Light Saving station, patiently pulled his load along the rutted sand road that led south out of Beach Haven.

The families of the surfmen lived in six little clapboard-sided bungalows, each painted a different color. Inside, one half of each house was heated with a three-burner kerosene stove where

courtesy of Barbara L. Windrow (right)

The Life Saving crew at Sea Haven, with lighthouse in distance, give a visitor an awkward ride during breeches buoy practice. At right, Sea Haven students and their teacher pose by their one-room schoolhouse around the turn of the century.

Charles Edgar Nash

The last days of the Little Egg Harbor Lighthouse, in September 1927, with the ocean threatening its base.

the family cooked and ate all their meals. The other half was divided into two bedrooms, one for the parents and the other for the children. The families of the Life Saving Service were there only from September until the last of May; then they went home to Tuckerton and Parkertown for the summer. There was a food allotment from the station for each man, but it purchased little except staples, so most people on the island caught and killed nearly all their food. It was unusual for them ever to see red meat or any meat other than duck or goose. They ate fish, clams and oysters nearly every day of their lives, and sickness of any kind was rare.

Life at Sea Haven in these last nostalgic years went on. The Atlantic winds howled across the shallow, wave-washed shoals, snapping the red and black storm signal flags on the high tower of the Life Saving station. The island children, when not sitting next to the big, warm stove in their classroom doing their lessons with hand-held slate boards and chalk, were out digging clams in the flats or fishing for eels from the rickety pier of the boathouse. They climbed all the enormous dunes, played in the hulls of old shipwrecks or cautiously entered the gloomy, echo-filled hotels, on the

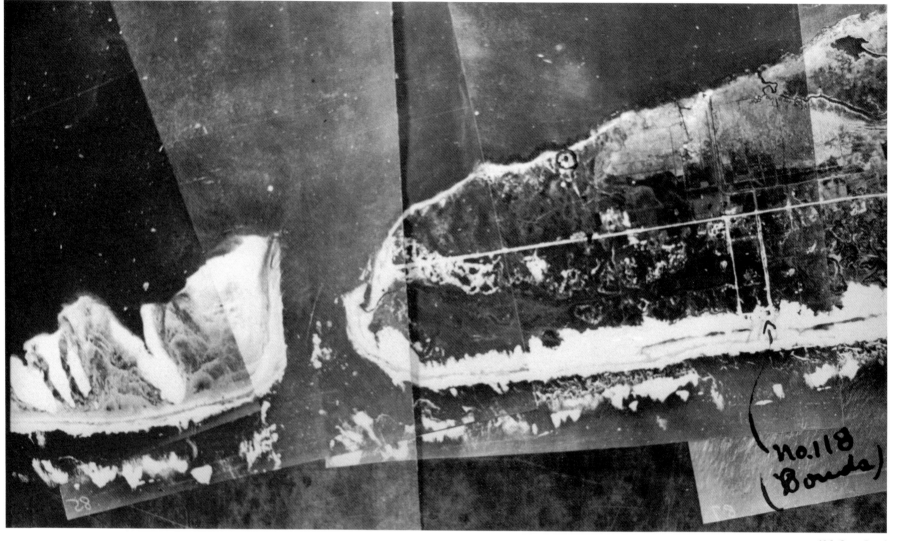

U.S. Coast Guard

This 1921 composite of aerial photographs by the U.S. Coast and Geodetic Survey shows the birth of the Beach Haven Inlet after a severe northeaster. Beach Haven and Bond's Coast Guard Station are at right; to the left, Tucker's Beach is once again separated from Long Beach Island.

lookout for ghosts. When spring finally came and hard sunlight took the chill out of the ever-present wind, they would run through the twisting trails in the high reeds and bayberry. They looked for exotic bits of flotsam washed into the slough by storm tides. Across the

slough bridge came the booming sound of the surf on stormy days.

Arthur H. T. Rider had been keeper of the light for only six years when there were demands for an acetylene-powered range light on the south end of the island to guide vessels into the New

Inlet. Tucker's Light was, after all, several miles away, guarding nothing but an inlet filled with sand; it had become a useless expense. Little was done, however, to make changes, and the daily task of running the light went on as before. In 1915 the U.S. Life Saving Service became the U.S.

Coast Guard. There were few shipwrecks then and little rescue work, but Prohibition was only five years away and then there would be work aplenty. The Little Egg unit would have its hands full all through the 1920s chasing rumrunners. By then the unit would have two major inlets to patrol, Beach Haven and Little Egg Harbor.

Beach Haven Inlet was born on the night of February 4, 1920, in a fierce snowstorm. Mountainous waves driven by northeast winds opened it up a half mile north of where the Old Inlet had closed up in 1874. Within a month it was apparent that this "new inlet" would not threaten Tucker's Island because its drift was northward toward Holgate. University of Pennsylvania professor Lewis Haupt, an expert in beach erosion, was called in to design and build two big timber jetties filled with rock and meadow sod at Cleveland Avenue and McKinley Avenue. When they were completed in 1924, they stopped the devastating erosion at Holgate and seem to have worked so well that the currents of the inlet began to wash in the other direction — toward Tucker's Island. As the Beach Haven Inlet began to widen and move southward, Tucker's Beach, Sea Haven's buffer from the sea on the northeast, began to erode at an alarming rate.

In 1925, there was a half mile of beach between the island and the sea. The next year, sand from the big dunes of the sea beach, driven by pounding waves, washed into and filled the slough. Then a series of severe storms in the spring of 1927 washed out all of this loose sand, and the ocean swirled to within three hundred yards of the lighthouse. Tucker's Island, edged only with fragile sod banks, was now completely defenseless.

On October 12, 1927, the historic house with its light tower fell dramatically into the sea while a photographer recorded the event. The Coast Guard station was a mile to the southwest and

relatively safe for another several years, but plans were being made to abandon it.

At a meeting on the evening of November 8, 1932, the governing body of Long Beach Township ordered its tax assessor to remove from the books "that portion of the Township south of the new inlet at Beach Haven known as St. Albans-by-the-Sea as it has been practically washed away by the ocean." Sea Haven was already gone; St. Albans was the last part of the island still remaining. Officially, now it had ceased to exist.

The Little Egg Coast Guard Station at Sea Haven was finally abandoned in February 1933. The crew was temporarily barracked at the Long

Robert F. Engle

Children play on one of the new Haupt jetties which stopped erosion at Holgate but greatly accelerated erosion of Tucker's Beach and Tucker's Island.

courtesy of Barbara L. Windrow (all)

This dramatic series of pictures, taken October 12, 1927, shows the Little Egg Harbor Lighthouse falling into the sea. Of importance in the days of sail...

...a lighthouse had stood on the north end of Tucker's Island, 22½ miles south of Barnegat Light and 12 miles north of Absecon Light, since 1854.

The Little Egg Harbor Coast Guard station is pictured on November 10, 1932, after continuing beach erosion and a storm brought ocean waves crashing into the buildings. It was on the south end of Tucker's Island and was one of the last buildings to go when it was abandoned by the government that year.

Beach station on Maryland Avenue at Beach Haven Terrace until November, when they were moved into a big houseboat at Tucker's Neck on Shooting Thoroughfare to await the building of new quarters nearby. Their former station on Tucker's Island washed away the next year.

The last of the landmarks to go was the little Sea Haven schoolhouse, which Captain Rider had bought and moved to the extreme southwestern edge of the island so it could be used as a summer house for the old Sea Haven families coming over from Tuckerton. It was often visited but seldom used and lasted into the war years, when it ended its days ignominiously as a brig for hardened disciplinary cases among the troops stationed on Long Beach Island in 1942 and 1943. "Bad soldiers," these prisoners were called by the local people. The historic old building, damaged and defaced beyond repair, finally vanished in a winter storm after the war. Little remained of the island itself anymore.

In the late forties, along the edge of the deep, new Beach Haven Inlet, flocks of seabirds stood at low tide on a long sand bar, all that was left of what had once been a five-mile island with trees, ponds, a lighthouse, a Coast Guard station, a school, two hotels and a proud little community. It had been New Jersey's first seashore resort. By 1952 even the birds had no place to stand. Tucker's Island had disappeared into history.

Chapter 3

TOWN ON THE EDGE OF GREAT SWAMP

Surf City, in 1919, had no houses north of Twelfth Street. From there to the Harvey Cedars Coast Guard Station there was not a single building in the miles of vine- and grass-clad dunes. Only a narrow, rutted, sometimes flooded wagon trail ran along the edge of the railroad track north to Barnegat City, and the only cross street running from ocean to bay in all of Surf City was at Ninth Street. Anticipating a postwar boom in real estate, the town looked to its unused northern half and began to level a great ring of sand dunes that had formed the rim of a low, craterlike area once known as Great Swamp.

When the work crews had finished, all of the land from Twelfth Street north to Twenty-fifth Street on the edge of the Frazier Tract (North Beach), a distance of nearly a mile, was as flat and treeless as a prairie. Great Swamp, with its stagnant bogs, twisted red cedar and tall bayberry, was gone forever. But today, deep down in the mud, beneath the streets and all the houses, lie thousands of stumps of white cedar, like ancient bones.

In 1919, however, the true Great Swamp had been dead for nearly a century. It had once covered all of the northern half of Surf City and extended into parts of North Beach. Its great size,

nearly two hundred acres, made it a phenomenon for a barrier island. Ringed by mountainous, protective dunes and fed by fresh water from the same aquifer that lies under the Pine Barrens, it was amazingly fertile. It was a leafy, shady spot filled with wild birds from far inland, an enchanted place, a forest where the melody of meadowlarks merged with the crash of the sea.

Its tall stands of Atlantic white cedar could be seen from the mainland and from far out in the ocean. Great Swamp had been attracting visitors for over a century. As early as 1690, shore whalers from Long Island and New England established stations on its northern and southern edges, and in the years after the War of 1812 it was a favored summer campsite for West Jersey vacationers. By 1821 a group of prosperous Burlington County farmers formed a stock company and began to build the first big boarding hotel on the New Jersey coast. They would call it the Mansion of Health.

The year the hotel was born the swamp died. Roaring up out of Virginia, a hurricane of incredible ferocity struck Long Beach Island on the afternoon of September 3. The powerful surge of the ocean, with its wind-lashed waves, crashed over and through the wall of dunes around the

swamp and turned it into a marsh. This storm, known as the Norfolk and Long Island Hurricane of 1821, was unique. It continued northward toward Sandy Hook and crossed into western Long Island in the vicinity of today's Kennedy Airport, making it the only hurricane in U.S. history to have its eye or center pass over a part of New York City.

The hurricane destroyed the swamp. The big trees were uprooted, and those that weren't soon turned into skeletons in the tidal salt water. The new hotel, well inland at what is now West Seventh Street, survived the storm and opened for business the next year. With Great Swamp gone, the area came to be called in the 1830s and 1840s "Buzby's Place" after the most famous of the owner-managers of the Mansion of Health, Hudson Buzby.

In 1854 a railroad was completed from Camden to Atlantic City and the Mansion of Health went into decline as traveling across the state to the seashore by stagecoach fell quite out of fashion. By the late 1850s the Mansion was deserted and had acquired the reputation of being haunted by the ghosts of shipwreck victims. The area around it took on the name of "Mansion" or "Old Mansion" after the picturesque ruin which eventually burned down in 1874.

The twenty or so members of the area's permanent population felt that their little community needed a real name, and in 1875 they chose to call it Long Beach City even though they had no political independence and were still a part of Stafford Township on the mainland. In 1894, following the example Beach Haven had set four years earlier, Surf City and Harvey Cedars both declared their independence. The name Long Beach City, however, had become over the years so often confused with the more populous and better-established Long Branch up the coast in Monmouth

County that the United States Postal Service demanded a name change before the town could incorporate.

A decade earlier, in 1885, a New York real estate lawyer named Weeks W. Culver and his partner, Benjamin Wright, bought up three hundred acres in Long Beach City as well as several other big parcels on the island as far south as the Peahala Club. They were determined to create a popular resort, and if the name had to be changed they would call it "Culver."

Culver and Wright began to advertise it as such, but the name never became official because both partners died within months of each other in late 1894. No one really wanted to call the town Culver, and while title to Culver and Wright's extensive holdings was being cleared in the courts — a process that took twenty-five years and greatly impeded the growth of the town — Henry McLaughlin, a Philadelphia lawyer and bank trust officer who was assigned to work on the case, suggested "Surf City." That appealed to residents and visitors alike, and that was the name that stuck.

Beach Pavilion   Surf City, N. J.

The 1898 Surf City pavilion on 11th Street was an attempt to spur development and attracted a party in Victorian finery one summer Sunday, facing page, bottom. At top left, 19th Street and the north end of Surf City, once the heart of Great Swamp, remained undeveloped in 1935.

Surf City's other names have faded into history. But the ruins of Great Swamp still lie under the town, and some say that thousands of cedar stumps can be found on the ocean floor as far as a half mile off Surf City, the remains of a much earlier forest that may have been cut in the 1600s and later inundated.

The Mansion of Health survives in a good regional ghost story. Buzby and Culver are footnotes in county histories. But there is one name still in use that most certainly recalls the town's early history. It is not on any map, but ask any old-timer in Surf City and he will tell you that the cove at the foot of South First Street on the bay is called "Mansion Cove." In the years from 1820 until 1850, Mansion Cove was the boat landing for guests of the Mansion of Health. It was from this cove that they rode carts a half mile along the edge of the meadows to West Seventh Street.

Harper's New Monthly Magazine

Like the Philadelphia Company House at Holgate, every 19th-century seashore boardinghouse had a bar where male guests spent most of their time when not fishing or gunning.

Chapter 4

THE PHILADELPHIA COMPANY HOUSE

Philadelphians who could afford to go to the seashore in the 1820s had to spend a full day crossing the New Jersey forests and plains in a stagecoach that cost them as much as $2.50 one way. If it was their first trip, they were always agreeably surprised when, at dusk, the stage finally rattled into Tuckerton.

"Clamtown," as it had been called in Colonial times and until 1790, had grown up. Straight, tree-lined streets, handsome houses, a mill pond and two well-lit, nicely appointed hotels to accommodate the tide of vacationers heading to and from the surf in bathing season made it an exciting and even a sophisticated place to be passing through in those years. The place hummed with activity, and it belonged to the Quakers whose characteristic broad-brimmed, white beaver hats were everywhere to be seen. Tuckerton was a hub of commerce in the region.

Seven miles from town, out the creek and across Little Egg Harbor Bay to the southern tip of Long Beach Island was a newly refurbished boarding hotel called the Philadelphia Company House, managed by Captain Joseph Horner. The Company House was formerly Horner's own place, and so well-known was he that the whole southern end of the island was called "Horner's Beach." In 1821 he had sold out to a group of Philadelphia gentlemen, his former guests, and he wound up staying on as manager. The group's investment capital expanded the hotel into one of the best-known watering places on the New Jersey coast, rivaled only by the larger Mansion of Health ten miles up the beach at Great Swamp.

The vacationers, after a night in Tuckerton and a hearty breakfast, went down to the Green Street wharf, where they boarded Captain Horner's sloop, big enough to hold twenty people. If the tide was against them, two men with a long rope towed the boat from a footpath out the winding salt creek to the flat, grassy meadows along the edge of the bay. Here they set sail, tacking to stay in the channels around the low islands, heading ever eastward toward the tall old ship's mast in the distance. At its base they could now see the dark silhouette of the Philadelphia Company House. In front of it, dozens of rowboats bumped at the spidery pilings of a long dock and several sailboats swung at their moorings.

The Company House, with its barnlike roof, many windows, and rough, unplaned siding, had one feature essential to all seaside boardinghouses then, a wide, wraparound, covered porch or piazza lined with rocking chairs and strung with hammocks. The long building, outlying sheds and summer kitchen stood all alone on the edge of the meadows exactly three miles south of the center of what is now Beach Haven. Cattle and horses roamed at will in the treeless sand dunes. With the additions to Horner's old place, the lodging could now accommodate one hundred people at the rate of four dollars per week. Most guests stayed two weeks or longer.

Newcomers were greeted at the dock by these "old-timers," who had been there already a week or two, some looking for familiar faces among the passengers. Philadelphia was a small town then. "Did you bring any sand? We got everything over here but sand" was the standard jest greeting arrivals. Civility and good humor were the order of the day, as was informality of dress. City folk tried to look like farmers in flannel and calico. The new guests were led into the well-stocked bar for a midmorning social drink to get acquainted. Perfect strangers, in the manner of shipboard life, became fast friends overnight.

Harper's New Monthly Magazine

Asking newcomers if they had brought any sand or lowering a sleeper into a tub of water were two of the typical jokes pulled by the guests at early shore hotels like the Philadelphia Company House.

At the beach, the women would sit under parasols and umbrellas or gather shells; on windy days they sat in the swales or valleys between the several ridges of dunes. It was the custom then for the sexes to be segregated on the strand because the men usually swam naked or with little clothing. The men went ocean bathing as a group early in the morning and spent the rest of the day gunning, fishing and sailing. Other guests preferred to sit in the bar and play cards or simply stroll around the broad piazzas, waiting for extraordinary meals of fresh fowl, apple dumplings and tarts, and plenty of eels, clams and oysters. Fresh produce was in abundance. It was brought over from the mainland almost every day by hawkers who sold the guests ears of corn, quarts of fresh blueberries and bushels of apples.

Every evening after dinner the trestle tables in the dining room were cleared out and there was dancing to fiddle music under a big, wooden chandelier festooned with holly and bayberry. Candles burned brightly in reflectors of bone-white clamshell. At the end of a full day of activity, all the guests agreed that it was salt air that made people sleepy.

This narrow section of Long Beach Island owed its popularity not only to its closeness to Tuckerton, but also to the unusual abilities of three men who dominated the area for nearly sixty years. They were jovial, entertaining and practical. They were natural-born innkeepers.

First, of course, was Joseph Horner, who had learned his trade as manager of the old Tucker place on nearby Tucker's Island. It was he who built the first boarding hotel on the south end of Long Beach that within a few years became the celebrated Philadelphia Company House. Horner and members of his family managed it successfully until 1847, when it was purchased by Lloyd Jones of Tuckerton, who added greatly to it. One of Jones' favorite guests, Thomas Bond of New York, became the hotel's next owner in 1851. It was he who changed its name formally to the Long Beach House and made it into the most famous hostelry on the New Jersey coast in the 1850s, 1860s and 1870s.

The original Philadelphia Company House remained as one wing of Bond's Long Beach House until 1909, when the rambling complex, long abandoned and ruined, was torn down. The lumber was rafted across the bay to West Creek, where it was cleaned up and resold. Some of it found its way back home and is now part of several vintage houses around the island.

In the roughly seventy years that Horner, Jones and Bond were in charge, it was the custom for every departing boatload of guests to receive a jug of whiskey and a rousing three cheers. The cheers would be repeated at intervals as they sailed away. Out past Goose Bar and Barrel Island, out beyond Story Island when the spires of Tuckerton appeared in the distance, faintly over the wind would come a "Hip, hip, hooray!" Guests went home with fond memories and returned year after year.

Ruins of the east wing of Bond's Hotel in 1910 show the original structure of the Philadelphia Company House built nearly a century earlier. The doors led to another wing that had been added in the 1840s by Lloyd Jones of Tuckerton, who owned the hotel before Bond.

Chapter 5

THE MANSION OF HEALTH

When women went sea bathing early in the 19th-century on Long Beach Island, their hotels provided them with ox carts for the ride to the beach, the soft sand being impassable for a horse-drawn carriage. The women could have walked to the beach, but the ox cart rides made the return trip more bearable. The trek over several ridges of sand hills in a sodden wool bathing dress and often in clouds of mosquitoes and flies could be unpleasant. But there was more to it than that. The cart ride was fun. From all accounts, it was a social occasion and the women loved it.

The men walked to and from the surf. Wet bathing attire did not present a problem because most men did not own any bathing suits. They swam just as they had since they'd been boys, in the buff, and it was for this reason that sea bathing at coastal watering places in the early nineteenth century was segregated. Red flags for men and white flags for women were flown to indicate whose turn it was at the beach.

The most famous of the New Jersey watering places north of Cape May was the Mansion of Health, built in 1821 on the southern edge of Great Swamp. The Mansion was located on the north side of today's West Seventh Street be-

tween Barnegat and Central avenues in Surf City. It opened in 1822, the same year as the newly organized Philadelphia Company House thirteen miles down the beach, but the Mansion was bigger and within the next two decades would become very popular as it prospered under the management of Hudson Buzby. The whole area of what is now Surf City came to be known simply as "Buzby's Place."

The well-known engraving of the Mansion (shown here), with its stylized, unnaturally flattened landscape was done by T. H. Mumford to illustrate a journey made to Long Beach Island in 1823 by Philadelphia historian John F. Watson. *Watson's Annals*, the short title for his book not published until 1857, provides the earliest description of the Mansion of Health. Watson was staying at the Philadelphia Company House in present-day Holgate when he made a sailing excursion up the bay with several friends to see the new hostelry, which he described as 120 feet long and a tenth of a mile from the surf. Mention was made of the powerful Hurricane of 1821, which had destroyed the wildly beautiful Great Swamp, and he wrote about the families of shore whalers living permanently in the area.

As early as 1815 there had been regular summer visitors in the area, mostly prosperous Burlington County farmers and their families from around Pemberton and Wrightstown. For a few weeks each August before harvest time, they made the daylong, arduous journey through the pines with horses and wagons. Leaving their teams to be cared for at the creeks on the mainland near Barnegat and Manahawkin, they sailed out around the Bonnet Islands to Great Swamp.

They set up tents in the dunes and fished, hunted, dug clams and oysters, and picked berries much as the Indians had done in the centuries before them. The change in diet and routine, the sunshine and the sea bathing proved healthful. A local resident named James Cranmer had a tavern well-stocked with rum and whiskey at twenty-five cents a gallon and an assortment of rare wines gathered on the beach from shipwrecks. Cranmer, for a fee, also allowed campers the use of the kitchen.

But the rough accommodations became less satisfactory each year, and the Burlington farmers decided they needed a place of their own. With more and more people being at-

An artist's conception of the Mansion of Health on the south edge of Great Swamp in 1823, at what would now be west Seventh Street in Surf City.

Buzby advertised his place in the Philadelphia papers as "the perfect spot for gentlemen fishers and fowlers." For the ladies there were "pleasant and safe aquatic excursions," which meant a ride through the dunes to the beach in an ox cart. For the next fifteen years the Mansion prospered as the most famous resort up and down the coast.

There was great camaraderie among the men. They fished and gunned all day, chewed a lot of tobacco, drank a lot of whiskey, shot up a lot of little shore birds and in general acted like schoolboys on holiday. The ladies conversed under parasols or read novels in the big chairs on the piazza.

Bad times befell the hotel after the death of Hudson Buzby and the building of a railroad from Camden to Atlantic City in 1854. Travel through the pines by stagecoach to the seashore lost its allure. After a succession of bad managers and a rumor that the place was haunted by the ghosts of shipwreck victims, the hotel ended its days as shelter for occasional campers and harvesters of salt hay. But its former glory was slow to die, and the area came to be known as "Old Mansion," which, for a time, even became the mailing address used by descendants of the old whaling families who still lived in that part of the island once known as Great Swamp.

In 1874, when local residents were calling the area Long Beach City, the Mansion burned to the ground. A new but smaller hotel called Mansion House was built atop the old foundation. After the railroad came to the island in 1886, the hotel was moved three blocks to the ocean side of the tracks at Eighth Street. Mansion House, after the turn of the century and under new owners, became the Marquette Hotel and eventually the Surf City Hotel.

tracted to the island, they figured they might try to make a profit out of it as well. They had as their example the success of Joseph Horner's small boardinghouse at the inlet. On a trip down there they learned that a group of former guests of Horner's had plans to sell shares to expand it into a boarding hotel to be called the Philadelphia Company House. The Burlington farmers, inspired by this, formed the Great Swamp Long Beach Company and, when they had sufficient capital, began to build what was to become the first really large boarding hotel on the New Jersey coast.

The Mansion of Health was slow getting started, but its greatest years began after 1825. The charge to stay there was five dollars a week, which many felt was exorbitant, but they came anyway. Big stagecoaches drawn by four horses rattled into Manahawkin three days a week in July and August, and there were many private equipages owned by wealthy Philadelphians. Their teams and carriages were left at the dock and picked up a week or two later. With city people willing to spend five dollars a week for a vacation, the whole area, from fruit and vegetable hawkers to gunning and fishing guides, flourished.

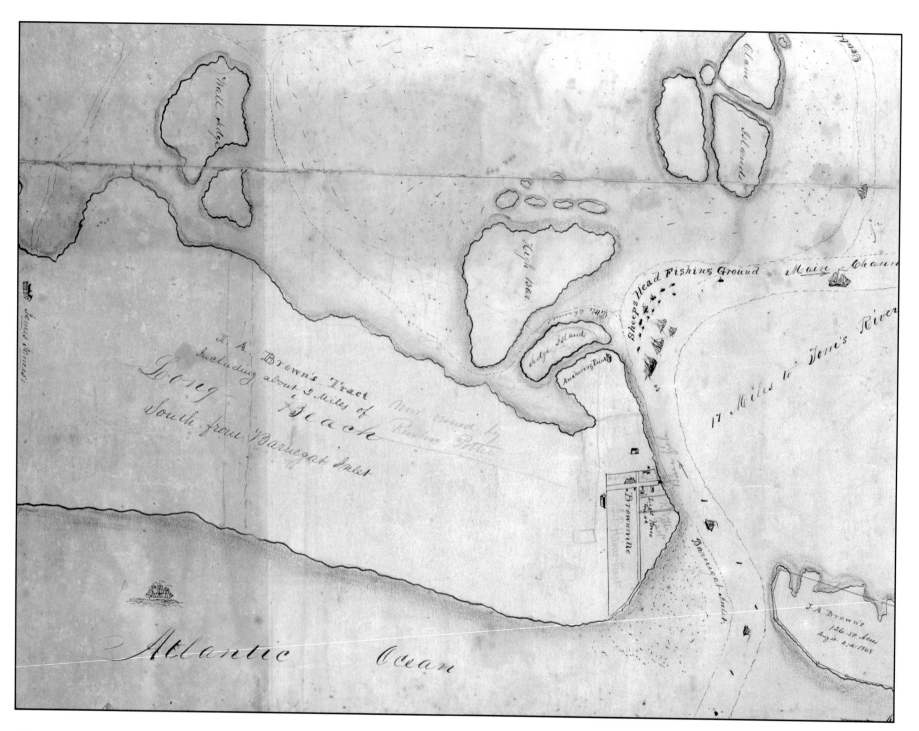

Chapter 6

WHEN BARNEGAT LIGHT WAS BARNEGAT CITY

"Atlantic City will never make it. It's too far from Tuckerton." This old saying, current around the time of the building of the Camden and Atlantic Railroad in the 1850s, sounds facetious, but there was an element of truth in it. Tuckertonians, whose own railroad would not be built for another twenty years, were smugly recalling an earlier day when their town was important enough to be declared by President Washington the third port of entry in the United States — after New York and Philadelphia.

Eastward, nearly six miles across the bay from Tuckerton, lay the barrier island called Long Beach, its southern end a wearying sameness of treeless sand hills, bogs and coves, bathed in harsh sunlight. It seemed of little value to coast dwellers in the early nineteenth century, but its very nearness to Tuckerton was the factor that brought it more summer visitors in those years than would ever venture onto the spectacularly beautiful north end of the island, where shady groves of red cedar and steep, sandy bluffs fronted the Barnegat Inlet. That part of the island was too far away for Philadelphia people, who looked to Tuckerton as their gateway to the shore.

Barnegat Light Museum (both)
The keeper's house in the 1890s, at the foot of Barnegat Lighthouse. Facing page, an 1869 survey calls the inlet area Brownsville a generation before it became Barnegat City.

Philadelphia and Tuckerton had strong Quaker ties. It was a relationship that began early and carried over into the first days of the young nation. Many a newly prosperous city merchant was able to trace his roots back to Egg Harbor and the Tuckerton area, where fortunes had been made before and during the American Revolution. Tuckerton, in Colonial times, was a major seaport, an exporter of lumber and bog iron, and a mart for shipwrecked goods and the plunder of privateers.

As early as 1750, annual summer meetings of Quakers, members of the Society of Friends, were being held at Short Beach at the southern end of Long Beach Island, directly across from the village that was to become Tuckerton. When Reuben Tucker, a Friend himself, bought Short Beach in 1765, he also built a boardinghouse to accommodate the summer visitors and renamed his property Tucker's Island. It was already New Jersey's first seashore resort. Joseph Horner established a similar place a few miles away on the south end of Long Beach in 1815. The boardinghouse concept never got started at the Barnegat Inlet until after 1820, and the people who came to stay there were not Philadelphians. They were New Yorkers.

Barnegat Light Museum (this page)

Above, a panoramic view of sparsely settled Barnegat City in the 1930s after the Sunset Hotel had burned. Below, the Social, a boardinghouse owned by the Kroger family. Facing page, the keeper's cottage was undermined by the ocean, but Barnegat Lighthouse flashed its beacon until 1925.

Mere distance from Tuckerton may not have been the only factor inhibiting development of the area at the northern inlet. There was the nature of the inlet itself. Barnegat Inlet, originally "Barendegat" or "Inlet of the Breakers," was so named in 1609 by the first Dutch explorers for its turbulent channels and foaming shoals. It was never so reliable a haven in storms as the wide, safe inlet eighteen miles to the south opposite Tuckerton. Barnegat Inlet became even less important after 1750 when the Cranberry Inlet opened up ten miles north, opposite Toms River, making Island Beach a true island and keeping it separate from Squan Beach for the next sixty-five years. This inlet was a great boon to maritime activity in the whole Barnegat Bay area, lasting until the winter of 1815, when it suddenly

Long Beach Island Museum

closed up. At least two efforts were made by local dredgers to reopen it, once in 1821 and again in 1841, with no success.

Cranberry Inlet had been vital to the continuing prosperity of Toms River. Without it, the merchants and farmers had no choice but to send all their cargo schooners through the Barnegat Inlet, another ten miles to the south. Most of their trade went to and from the port of New York. If fewer Philadelphians ever made it to the north end of the island, the difference was made up by the increasing numbers of New Yorkers who were seeing it for the first time and spreading the word. The south point of beach of the Barnegat Inlet, where the lighthouse would eventually be built, had superb physical advantages. It was several feet higher above sea level than the rest of the island and covered with shady oak and cedar. Behind a beautiful, thirty-acre crescent of wooded land along the edge of the sea lay a broad, shallow bay teeming with fish and wildfowl of every description. It was a sportsman's paradise.

Jacob Herring opened a boardinghouse at Barnegat Inlet in 1820, several hundred feet inland from the spot where the first Barnegat Lighthouse would be built in 1834. The Herring House was immediately popular with gunners, who hunted in all seasons then. They were almost entirely a New York crowd of sportsmen who liked Herring and who always affectionately referred to the place as the "Jakey Henny," based on Herring's pronunciation of his own name in a thick German accent. Herring became well-established over the next twenty years, and his son, Garret G. Herring, was one of the early keepers (1839-41) of the lighthouse.

Thirty years of Atlantic storms had taken their toll on the old place by the time Herring elected to sell out to Captain John M. Brown in 1855. Brown, a salvage operator and former wreckmaster, moved down from Squan with his wife and four sons and bought not only the Herring House, but sizable parcels of land on both sides of the inlet as well. His purchase included nearly two miles of beach south to James James' ("Double Jimmie's") Club House at present-day Loveladies. Brown and his sons so dominated the area for the next twenty years that everything outside the government property at the lighthouse was called Brownsville. That name for the area appears on an official state survey map drawn by Samuel Downs in August 1868.

Brown and his sons completely rebuilt and enlarged the old Herring House, painting its exterior walls white, unlike all other New Jersey buildings of the day, which were left to blacken in the sun and weather. It was apparently done to match the base of Barnegat Lighthouse, then under construction. Brown renamed the newly furbished place Ashley House, using his wife's maiden name. The Ashley House became more popular than ever, not only with the old New York sporting crowd, but also with the crowds of sightseers sailing over to marvel at the massive structure of the lighthouse, which flashed its first bright beam twenty miles out into the dark Atlantic in January 1859.

When Captain Brown's eldest son, Ashley, drowned at sea around 1865, Brown sold everything the family had owned on Long Beach, including a tract across the inlet on Island Beach, to Reuben Potter. The Ashley House was bought by Charles Martin, an experienced innkeeper known to all as "Uncle Charlie," who, with the aid of his daughter Elizabeth, made the place famous for its excellent cooking and good service. The last owner of the sprawling, whitewashed hostelry was J. Warner Kinsey, who ran it until 1884, when he left to manage the new Sunset Hotel built by

Richard Plunkett (above); Robert F. Engle (facing page)

Across the street from the Oceanic Hotel in this 1906 snapshot, John W. Haddock faces his ornate house on East 4th Street. After a winter northeaster in 1920 undermined the Oceanic, the Haddock House was saved by moving it to East 7th Street, and the badly damaged hotel was torn down. On the facing page, children play on an eroding beach east of the lighthouse in 1918, as attempts are made to save the doomed keeper's house.

an investment group developing the area into Barnegat City. Brownsville was fading into memory, and the historic old building that had served three generations of New Yorkers was torn down in 1887.

From 1762, when the lighthouse at Sandy Hook was built to mark the entrance to New York Harbor, there were no other lighthouses or warning lights on the whole 127-mile sea-

coast of New Jersey until the 1820s. The toll of shipwrecks was mounting year after year. In 1823 the entrance to Delaware Bay was marked with a gray tower and light at Cape May. That same year, to back up the very limited range of the sixty-year-old light at Sandy Hook, a pair of powerful lights was installed in twin towers on the Highlands at Navesink with a range of twenty-five miles at sea. In

1834, Barnegat Light became the fourth light on the Jersey coast.

The lighthouse built at Barnegat Inlet was only forty feet high with a white, fixed light. Its range was less than ten miles in clear weather, and since it did not flash or blink, it was often mistaken by ships at sea for the light of another ship closer to shore. It never did enough to prevent wrecks, which continued in spite of the light. Attempts were made to put in a brighter beacon, but by 1855 it was obvious that what was needed was a new lighthouse. Besides, swift currents were eating away at the south side of the inlet, and the 1834 light was about to topple into the water. Plans for a new and much bigger tower were made, and construction began immediately at a site nearly a thousand feet back from the first tower. It would serve mariners well for the next sixty years.

The only way to get to the lighthouse or any part of Long Beach Island for most of the nine-

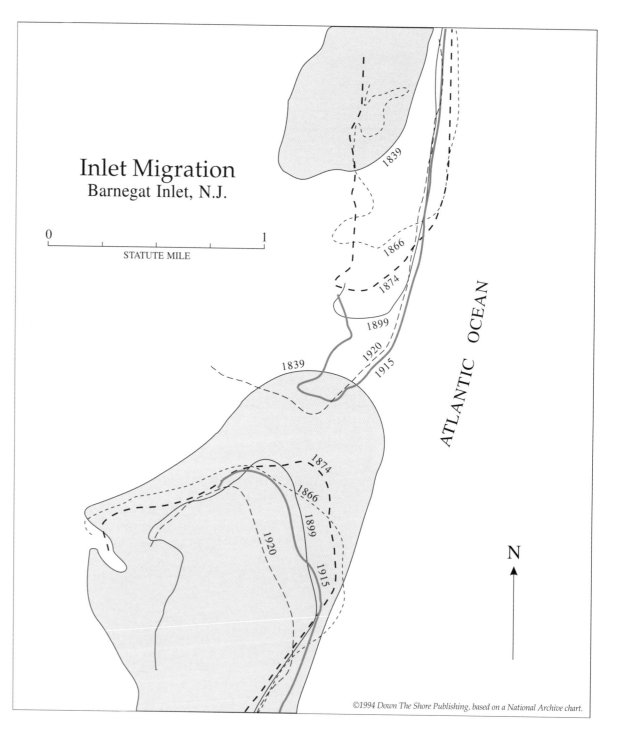

Inlet Migration
Barnegat Inlet, N.J.

0   1

STATUTE MILE

ATLANTIC OCEAN

1839

1866

1874

1899

1920

1915

1839

1874

1866

1899

1920

1915

N

©1994 Down The Shore Publishing, based on a National Archive chart.

Barnegat Light Museum (photographs)

The Oceanic Hotel and the lighthouse keeper's house were so damaged in the February 1920 storm that they were torn down, above. On the facing page, an oceanfront cottage on East 4th Street is a victim of the same storm. The inlet migration chart at left shows the erosion at Barnegat City between 1839 and 1920.

teenth century was by boat, but around the 1850s the railroad started improving transportation on the mainland. Since 1854 Philadelphians had been taking the Camden and Atlantic Railroad to Absecon and sailing up to the southern end of Long Beach. New Yorkers could take steamboats from Manhattan to Sandy Hook and then take a train to Long Branch; after 1863 the Long Branch and Seashore Railroad ran to Toms River, where boats could be hired to sail toward the lighthouse and popular boarding hotels like the Ashley House, Double Jimmie's and the Harvey Cedars Hotel.

In 1871 the Tuckerton Railroad connected Tuckerton with Whiting in north-central Ocean County, where connections could be made with the Camden and Amboy Railroad, which crossed the state; within a year there was a spur to Edge Cove, southeast of Tuckerton, where there was steamboat service across the bay to the new resort of Beach Haven. The north end of the island was still served by sailboat and from the Barnegat pier located on the south bank of Toms River, where there was a terminal of the Pennsylvania Railroad. After 1881, train passengers here could board a paddle steamer called the *Hesse*, which made regular runs in the summer months across the bay to Seaside and the new resort of Barnegat City.

Calling a tiny new resort a "city" in those years was an obvious attempt to capitalize on the success of Atlantic City. It was done with Long Beach City, which later became Surf City, and there were other examples up and down the coast with names like Neptune City, Sea Isle City and the like. The only objection to the name Barnegat City came from those who felt that there were already too many other "Barnegats" in the area, including the town on the mainland, the bay and the inlet, but Barnegat City was the name the town kept until 1948, when it was officially changed to Barnegat Light.

When Barnegat Light Was Barnegat City   **47**

Seen here from the top of the lighthouse, the Sunset Hotel, above, dominated the bay side of town until it burned to the ground in 1932. Barnegat City, with its one-room schoolhouse showing on the left in the bottom photo, remained sparsely settled until after World War II. On the facing page, a view from the town's secluded dunes during those same years shows the southern tip of Island Beach across the inlet.

Between 1881 and 1883 two splendid hotels were built at Barnegat City, the Oceanic at East Fourth Street on the oceanfront and the Sans Souci, later to be renamed the Sunset. The Sunset was on the edge of the bay and stayed open all winter to accommodate the gunning crowd, who spent freely. Beautiful summer cottages were rising among the tall cedars south of the lighthouse. A railroad bridge was being built across the bay from Manahawkin to Long Beach, and tracks were being laid up the island to Barnegat City. The year was 1886, and from all appearances the little resort was beginning to boom.

But the boom did not last even a decade. Devastating erosion ate away at the oceanfront, so severely that the huge Oceanic Hotel had to be moved back. Several fine oceanfront houses were lost, and investment in the area slacked off. By the time the eagerly anticipated Long Beach Railroad got to the island, it was too late for Barnegat City. The only major improvement in the area after the arrival of the railroad was the building of the expansive, three-family keeper's house at the base of the light in 1889. Barnegat City hardly got started before it had passed its prime. All rail traffic coming onto the island now was heading to the new big hotels in Beach Haven. However disappointing that may have been to the developers of Barnegat City, it seems not to have affected the vacationers who preferred the north end.

Train traffic to the north end of the island was never as regular as it was on the south end, and it stopped altogether in 1923, more than a dozen years before it ended on the rest of the island. By 1923, almost nine years after the automobile bridge was built across the bay, a road was finally run to Barnegat City, but the magnificent old Oceanic was gone. Half of it had washed into the sea in 1920 and the rest had been torn down. The Sunset burned to the ground in 1932. Throughout this long period until after World War II, Barnegat City enjoyed a peace and quiet that few resorts ever do. Being too far from Tuckerton seemed to matter not at all.

Cresson Prichard

Chapter 7

THE POWHATAN, THE MANSION, THE MONUMENT

Saturday, April 15, 1854, was a day of unnatural stillness. Under a sky of slate, the temperature dropped hourly. The wind began to blow just after midnight with roaring gusts that shook the frame houses in the tiny community in the sand hills around the Mansion of Health in present-day Surf City. Then the windowpanes began to tick with sleet. A violent northeaster and a late-season blizzard had combined into what would be one of the storms of the century.

By dawn the freezing salt spray and snow were flung across Long Beach Island with the force of gun blasts. The ocean churned like boiling milk. In the gathering light, those who could get to the beach saw a stranded, three-masted ship out on the sand bar just off what is now Seventh Street in Surf City.

To the 350 passengers and crew of the *Powhatan*, an immigrant packet ship forty days out of Bremen, Germany, it was a nightmare. Their ship shuddered in every wave, sinking deeper into the sand. Above the tilting deck, torn sails flapped like pistol shots in the screaming wind. Some passengers clung to the rigging. Most huddled along the rails waiting for rescue. The hull was filling with water.

There would be no official Life Saving Service anywhere on the Atlantic coast until the early 1870s. In 1854, rescue equipment was provided by the federal government and kept at newly established "government houses" that had been built every ten miles or so along the beach. There were, however, no paid crews to maintain this equipment or even use it. All the work was done strictly by volunteers, local fishermen and baymen who were experienced

in the use of the surf boat and line gun, a small cannon used to shoot a line to a faltering ship.

The nearest government house was at Harvey Cedars, where a crew was hastily gathered. It was low tide, but ice and deep snow made footing extremely difficult. In a valiant attempt to haul the heavy surf cannon down the beach, the exhausted crew nearly froze to death and had to turn back.

All that Sunday the passengers and crew of the *Powhatan*, clearly visible from shore, huddled along the railing of their ship and watched the snow-covered, utterly desolate coastline, their first and last view of America. No rescue would ever come. The tide was coming back in. The ship had swung around on the bar and was now pointed south, parallel to the beach. At 5 P.M. one huge comber washed them all overboard.

No one survived the freezing water. Forty bodies came ashore on the island; others came in at Brigantine and Absecon, and many were never found. They had all been, it was later discovered, well-to-do Germans of the farming class.

After the local wreckmaster had gathered the bodies that came ashore at Long Beach, he declared that none of them bore any identification or valuables. How he could have done this without the aid of confederates is unclear, but that is how the local account goes. At any rate, his announcement of the lack of identification, money or jewelry on any of the drowning victims was an astonishing piece of news since most immigrants to America in those days wore money belts. The victims of the *Powhatan* were buried in a common grave at the Baptist Church on Route 9 in Manahawkin. But the lack of identification of the passengers buried there puzzled local residents, and ugly rumors began to spread.

It so happened that the wreckmaster, Captain Isaac Jennings, a public appointee, was also the current manager of the Mansion of Health. In time, the missing money belts were found buried at the base of an old cedar stump near the beach, but before the dishonest manager could be arrested, he had fled. The rest of the story is part of a legend passed down through generations of old Surf City families. As a result of the crime, the Mansion, which had seen its best days and was now abandoned, came to be haunted by a ghost. Those who chanced to climb to the upper floors at night swore they saw, standing in the moonlight, the figure of a young woman with a baby in her arms. She was always staring out to sea from one of the balconies and always quickly disappeared.

In 1904, fifty years after the wreck of the *Powhatan*, the state of New Jersey erected a monument over the common grave in Manahawkin. The inscription on the monument reads: "To the Unknown from the Sea."

Ray Fisk

The *Powhatan* grounded and broke apart off Surf City in 1854, killing all aboard. A monument at the old Baptist cemetery in Manahawkin, above, marks the common grave of the unidentified victims.

TO THE RESCUE!—HURRYING WITH A SURF-BOAT TO THE SCENE OF A WRECK.—Drawn by Schell and Hogan.—[See Page 393.]

An engraving from a late 19th-century newspaper captures the perilous duties of the U.S. Life Saving Service, forerunner of today's Coast Guard.

Chapter 8

THE RED HOUSES OF LONG BEACH

All through the nineteenth century, accounts of shipwrecks fill the pages of eastern newspapers. Big storms, fog and navigational error caused so many vessels to run aground each year off the uninhabited Atlantic barrier beaches that government intervention finally became necessary. The movement began in New Jersey with its 127-mile coastline, where a combination of heavy traffic on the way to and from the busy port of New York and frequent northeast storms had made it a highly dangerous lee shore. New Jersey also lay directly in the path of the sea lanes from Europe.

Low-lying, nearly invisible barrier beaches were a considerable hazard in themselves, but what posed the real danger to wayward sailing ships was the system of continuous, submerged sand bars which lay anywhere from one hundred to four hundred yards in front of the beaches along the coast from Sandy Hook to Cape May. It was on these sunken and sometimes shifting reefs that most ships grounded and then broke apart before anyone aboard could be saved. Except at the highest tides or in natural cuts near inlets, sand bars and shoals were a constant menace to mariners in the coastal trade.

Many a fine ship, its sails blown to shreds, its hull and masts leaning, was discovered in the first light of a winter dawn settling into the sandy ridges out beyond the breakers. The faint cries of doomed passengers and crew rose and fell on the howling wind. There seemed to be no well-conceived plan in those years to get people safely from ship to shore without a boat, and usually the right kind of boat was not available. Those on the beach had no choice but to stand by and watch the ship break up in the crashing waves of the next high tide. Then the bodies would wash ashore. Some means, it was agreed, must be provided to get wreck victims safely through a quarter mile of churning surf before they drowned or froze to death. Not even a strong swimmer could survive a distance of three hundred yards in forty-degree water.

Aside from better lighthouses, perhaps, there really was not much that could be done in those years to prevent ships from running aground in foul weather. There were, however, ways and means to save lives when a ship became stranded. Volunteers could operate surf boats, and there was no shortage of local men who knew how to use them. There were other devices, too. Around 1840, a small cannon called a line

gun had been perfected to shoot a projectile with a thin line attached, from the beach out to the stranded vessel. If properly aimed, the line fell across the rigging where a crew member could seize and use it to pull toward him a much thicker "hauling" line. When this was secured to the ship, a block or pulley and a cork ring called a breeches buoy could then be hung from the line to travel back and forth between ship and shore until everyone was safe. There was also a cumbersome and new torpedo-shaped device called a "life car" that could bring in several people at one time in its nearly airtight compartment.

What was needed along the nearly deserted barrier beaches, then, was a way to store the surf boat and all the other heavy and complex equipment so that they could be gotten to by volunteers and dragged down the beach to a site opposite the ship in distress. Such a building could also be used to temporarily house survivors until they could be taken to the mainland. Early in the century, the state of Massachusetts had experimented with this concept with shelters provided by the Humane Society.

Shipwrecks went on each year with a mounting loss of life and property. The winter of 1847 was so bad that Congressman William A. Newell of New Jersey was able to push through the first federal appropriation for lifesaving. It was only ten thousand dollars, but it was a start. Newell took the money provided by a reluctant Congress and in 1850 was finally able to buy boats, rockets and other newly invented rescue apparatus to be stored in several so-called "houses of refuge" which were to be built all along the Atlantic coast.

The first such house went up at Sandy Hook, and in a very short time there were others built, usually at intervals of twenty miles as they were in New Jersey where there were more ship strandings. There were two on Long Beach Island, one at Harvey Cedars and the other at the south end near Bond's Hotel. Each unit was placed in the charge of a responsible local person, and each small, wooden building was stocked with the best modern equipment for lifesaving. Volunteers turned out in the event of an emergency. There was no provision for salaried keepers or crew; that would not be for another twenty years.

In case of washout, each house of refuge was built atop sunken pilings, and the building's frame was strong enough to withstand relocation in case the pounding surf altered the shape of the beachfront. These early houses were not painted and had to be fairly close to the water so that they could be seen. Each house was about fifteen feet high, covered with cedar shingles on the roof and sides, and had big, barnlike doors on the lee side of the building so that equipment could be taken out quickly. Inside each building was a fully equipped boat on a wagon, a mortar apparatus with its lines, powder and shot, and the life car.

Long Beach Life Saving Station, Beach Haven, N. J.

U.S. Life Saving Service crews like the one above were drawn from shore natives with lifelong experience on the water. Rescue boats were double-ended and stored in Life Saving stations much like the Long Beach station on the facing page. Largely unchanged, the building still stands today on Maryland Avenue in Beach Haven Terrace.

When there were no volunteers present, these early houses of refuge were not easy for shipwreck survivors to find. Signboards were placed at intervals in the dunes to aid them and were printed in several languages. Those who managed to get ashore in foul weather might have perished had they not been able to find these houses. There was straw in the bunks, wood for the stove, matches in a tin case, a barrel of hard bread, coffee, a cask of fresh water, salted meats, blankets and warm clothing. All of this was in addition to the equipment used by the volunteers in rescue work.

After the wreck of the *Powhatan* off Long Beach Island in 1854 with the loss of more than three hundred lives, it was clear that the volunteer system was not always dependable. The closest house of refuge at Harvey Cedars had not been close enough for the volunteers to drag the heavy equipment through deep snow in time to get opposite the wreck, several miles to the south. But Congress, facing the coming Civil War, was unwilling to spend any money to build more houses of refuge and nothing was done until 1870. It was then that Sumner Kimball, a lawyer from Maine, became chief of the Revenue Marine Service of the United States Treasury Department.

Kimball was in charge of all the houses of refuge then in existence, and he ordered an immediate in-

Robert F. Engle (facing page)

Crew members at the Harvey Cedars Life Saving Station, above, drill with a breeches buoy. The rescue device, facing page, was a pair of breeches or "britches" sewed into a ring buoy which ran on a line fired from the beach. In their laced-up puttees, the Ship Bottom Station crew wheel out the mortar cart and fire away.

vestigation of them. There were only twenty-four on the whole coast from Maine to Florida, and they had been in use for twenty years. Kimball made an inspection down the coast and found the buildings neglected and dilapidated and much too far apart to be useful. Apparatus was rusty or broken, and portable items had been carried off. He persuaded Congress to vote twenty thousand dollars to reequip them and to enroll permanent crews who, he said, "would sleep

right beside the boats the way firemen sleep next to their engines." This was the beginning of the United States Life Saving Service.

The newly formed Life Saving Service provided for each station to be manned by six men and a keeper who lived in the stations from September through April, when there was the most danger from storms. Each was paid forty dollars a month, which was a good wage then for a bayman whose income was seasonal. The keeper

got sixty dollars. These men had fished, clammed and gunned in local waters all their lives, and they knew how to operate boats in the surf. Besides their skills, they were chosen for their resourcefulness, courage and integrity. It was a proud service.

Along the desolate barrier beaches from Sandy Hook to Cape May, forty-one units were placed approximately three miles apart. These new station houses were of uniform design, eigh-

teen feet by forty feet and windowless on three sides. They were painted reddish brown and, devoid of any ornamentation save a cupola, lightning rod and large white numerals on their seaward walls, they resembled big barns or garages in the dunes. Locally they were called "red houses."

Inside the two-story, cedar-shake buildings there were a boat room, a mess room and a bunk room. The doors of the boat room always faced southwest so they could be opened easily in a howling northeaster. The boat room contained the boat and gun carriages and other equipment used in rescue work. Behind it on the same floor was the mess room with a big iron stove. Here the crew cooked, ate and lounged. Upstairs under the eaves was the long bunk room with one end partitioned off for the keeper or commander of the station.

When the Life Saving Service was active, from 1871 until 1915, there were six stations on Long Beach Island. They were Barnegat Inlet, Loveladies Island, Harvey Cedars, Ship Bottom, Long Beach at what is now Beach Haven Terrace, and Bond's at what is now Holgate. Three miles south of Bond's there was a seventh station on Tucker's Island, the Little Egg Harbor Station. Of these stations, Loveladies Island, Harvey Cedars and Long Beach Station still stand today in their original locations. All the rest have been moved or torn down.

The exact distance from the Long Beach Station at Maryland Avenue in Beach Haven Terrace to Bond's in

Holgate was determined in 1910 with a huge, twelve-foot measuring wheel and proved to be three and three-fourths miles. This was when Bond's Life Saving Station was still on the oceanfront at Inlet Avenue in Holgate at a spot that is now underwater. It had had an artesian well since 1887 when the station was rebuilt, and today the cap for that well sometimes appears out near the sand bar at extremely low tides. The original station, built in 1871, was a hundred yards farther east of that bar before it had to be abandoned: There is no clearer evidence to show how much the beaches of the south end have eroded in the last hundred years. Bond's Coast Guard Station east of Inlet Avenue was moved in the 1920s a quarter mile south to Janet Avenue on the bay. It is now a private dwelling.

In all but one of the forty-two stations along the coast the government was a squatter on beach land which was becoming increasingly more valuable, and owners were, with some justification, asking to be compensated. But many of these titles were cloudy. Releases had to be obtained from heirs who had moved to distant western states. The title to Loveladies Island was never obtained.

For most of the men in the Life Saving Service on Long Beach Island in the 1870s and 1880s, it was a lonely existence and often a very dangerous one. There was monotony, but the men were seldom idle. They had their nightly watches to perform. Every four hours two men left the station house. One would walk north on the beach and the other south, meet the patrols from the adjoining station houses, exchange a brass token and leave. Then there were routine drills and the maintenance of buildings and equipment as the crews waited and watched. Living at the stations

Long Beach Island Historical Society Museum (right)

Beach Haven druggist A.J. Durand published this 1912 post card of the Long Beach Life Saving crew. At right, a Life Saving crewman sits for a picture.

was very much like living in a firehouse. And just as old-time firehouses traditionally kept a Dalmatian dog for a mascot, the Life Saving stations had their Newfoundland retrievers, who often accompanied the night watches on their lonely beach patrols. In the nineteenth century the Newfoundland became the symbol of the Life Saving Service.

In foul weather it was impossible to see the entire beach from the tower, and patrols sometimes had to be run throughout the day as well as the night. The meeting and exchange of tokens was required only on continuous beaches. In a snowstorm all that could be seen to guide the patrol might be the blurry edge of gray water or white, churning surf or the hard sand at low tide. Many an obstacle — a ship's mast, lumber, an old wreck, a huge dead fish — caused a patrolman to stumble in the dark.

For nineteenth-century vacationers who watched crews practice, launching a surf boat in heavy seas was a stirring sight. The two-wheeled boat carriage was backed into the breakers as far as possible with two men already aboard, the coxswain and the bow man. As the carriage was tipped, the four oarsmen, in knee-deep water, gripped the sides and ran with the boat, bow first, straight into the surf, swinging themselves aboard the moment it began to glide. Then, seizing their long oars, they pulled furiously with all their strength as every wave threatened to roll the boat back onto the beach. They kept their eyes on the coxswain, who was steering and giving commands.

Communication among the six stations on the island was by telephone, a welcome improvement over the old wigwag semaphore used in the early years. The single cable was strung on iron poles which ran along the sand hills on the oceanfront. Each pole was about eight to ten feet high and was usually sunk

DRILL AND EXERCISE IN THE SURF-BOAT.

Scribner's *Magazine, January 1880*

about three feet into the sand. There were crosspieces on each pole and glass insulators. It was a party line, and each station had a certain number of rings on the bell to indicate who was to answer it.

There were many happy times. In calm weather, families and friends of the men at the stations would sail over to the island for a surprise party, bringing with them cakes and pastries and good things from home. On these occasions the boat room would be used for dancing, but the watch was never neglected, and the surfmen would make their rounds accompanied by their wife or sweetheart. Weather permitting, every holiday was celebrated, especially Christmas, when all of the children would show up. The men in the service at the island's six stations in the 1890s were all from the oldest families in the region: Perrine, Soper, Ridgeway, Inman, Truex, Cranmer, Sprague, Rider, Rogers, Birdsall, Gaskill, Shinn, Parker, Hazelton, Crane, Falkinberg, Pharo, Rutter.

In the early years of the Service, the men wore civilian clothing, dressing much like the fishermen and baymen that they were. In 1899, right after the Spanish-American War, the Service adopted a naval uniform, largely as a consequence of the recent role they had played in coastal defense acting as sentinels looking for the Spanish fleet. It was not that the enemy fleet was ever much of a threat, but the public perceived it as such.

By the middle of the 1880s, the railroad had come to the island and with it more people. The simple "red houses" became more ornate. There were overhanging eaves, fancy scrollwork and observation decks, and the buildings were painted with popular colors to blend in with the summer cottages. New stations built in the 1890s were required to have a seventy-foot flagstaff and a four-story tower.

All of this was happening just as the need for the Service was declining. It was the age of the steamship, and the old barks, brigantines and schooners were being phased out and turned into unrigged barges. They occasionally parted their hawsers and drifted ashore, but there were seldom any lives to save. Yet many old surfmen refused to retire and stayed on at the station, full of honor and stirring tales of the old days of thudding surf cannons, sleety gales and grateful survivors. With the formation of the United States Coast Guard in 1915, they, like the sailing ships they once rescued, became reminders of a passing era.

Lynn Photo (facing page)

In 1915, the U.S. Life Saving Service became the U.S. Coast Guard, as seen in this sign change at the Long Beach station, above. Steam-powered ships helped shift the organization's focus from saving lives in coastal waters along barrier beaches, right, to a wider range of duties on land and at sea.

Chapter 9

DOCK ROAD: FIRST ENTRANCE TO BEACH HAVEN

The typical midnineteenth-century seashore resort on Long Beach Island consisted of little more than a solitary, porch-encircled boardinghouse designed almost exclusively for the convenience of sportsmen. There were several such establishments on the island, with names like the Ashley House, the Club House, the Connahassett House, the Mansion of Health and the Philadelphia Company House. All of these "houses"

were many miles apart, completely independent of each other and usually a long hike to and from the beach. None was part of a community or town. That kind of resort with shops, cottages, pavilions, bathhouses and more than one hotel was at least a generation away and would not be seen until the founding of Beach Haven in 1874. All of the old-time hotels were built much closer to the bay than the ocean to have easier access to waterborne

goods and supplies. Fishing and hunting were best on the bayside, but it was transportation that was the key.

Southern Ocean County at midcentury lacked rail connections with any major lines across the state, and this factor slowed development on Long Beach Island until after the Civil War. The best-known resort on the island in the 1860s was Bond's Long Beach House at the south end. Formerly the Philadelphia Company House,

Beach Haven's Dock Road once ran along the canal that was Mud Hen Creek, the town's original and only tie to the mainland before the railroad was built. Towed on a barge from Harvey Cedars in 1873, the Hotel DeCrab, foreground above and facing page, served boat captains carrying materials and ferrying passengers to the new resort town.

now was a resort on the order of Cape May or Long Branch where vacationers could enjoy the sun, surf and fresh air and, in time, build cottages of their own. As early as 1867 Pharo had purchased 670 acres two and a half miles north of Bond's. It was a barren strip of bogs and huge sand hills less than a quarter of a mile wide and fronted on the bay with marshes almost twice that wide, a place altogether useless as the location of a gunning and fishing hotel, which is why the land had never been used.

The area did, however, have a distinct advantage over other parts of the island as far as Pharo was concerned, and that asset was a natural waterway. The wide meadows were crossed by a navigable creek nearly a half-mile long called Mud Hen Creek. Pharo saw it as a perfect way to float all his construction materials to the solid, buildable land without having to drag them across the meadows. He would use the creek, and, near it, he would start his new resort. This place was still so remote that in order to get people to come to it he would capitalize on a tried-and-true selling point — health.

Pharo had a wife and daughter who suffered from hay fever, then, as now, a common complaint. On the island he had found out what many had known before him: that when the wind blew in off the sea or across the broad salt marshes, the air was so free of pollen that allergy victims were immediately relieved of their symp-

Bond's was enjoying its best years, drawing many successful Philadelphia business and professional men and their families, many of whom sailed up from Absecon, where there was a train to Camden. Among them was Archelaus Ridgeway Pharo, whose fortune had been made in Tuckerton years earlier in ship building and lumber. He was a frequent summer guest at Bond's in the late 1860s while he and his friends were planning to build the twenty-nine-mile

Tuckerton Railroad through the pines from Whiting in north-central Ocean County to Tuckerton. At Whiting there was a connection with the cross-state Camden and Amboy line. This new road would at last make the island easily accessible to city people seeking relief from the summer heat and physical ailments.

Old-style boarding hotels like Bond's were not expected to handle the crowds the railroad would be bringing to the shore. What was needed

In the 1890s, a view from Dock Road looking east shows the towers of the Engleside and Baldwin hotels separated by the wooden water tower. Mud Hen Creek, bulkheaded now, was along the south side of the road; at high tide, barges could be towed all the way to Bay Avenue.

toms. Pharo's daughter, exploring the sand hills and beaches of the proposed site, was so delighted with it that she wanted to name it "Beach Heaven." Pharo considered this but chose instead to call it Beach Haven. His decision took place on November 19, 1873, when he deeded his parcel of land to the newly formed Tuckerton and Long Beach Land, Building and Improvement Company. That was the beginning of Beach Haven, and construction of a magnificent new hotel on Centre Street, a block east of the head of Mud Hen Creek, began at once.

The Tuckerton Railroad to Whiting had been completed in 1871. The next year Pharo added a

two-mile spur track out to the edge of the bay near Tuckerton and started running a shallow-draft steamboat called the *Barclay* from Edge Cove out to the island. For two seasons it delivered passengers to Bond's, but this was not to last, for Pharo and his partners had their new hotel at Beach Haven ready for occupancy in June 1874. It was named the Parry House after Charles Parry of the Philadelphia firm of Burnham, Parry and Williams, later to become the Baldwin Locomotive Works. Parry was also one of the principal shareholders in the Tuckerton and Long Beach Land, Building and Improvement Company, and he and Pharo and the other partners

had by now built big summer cottages of their own and had laid out a grid of wide streets with big lots for sale. Beach Haven became the first formally organized town on Long Beach Island.

The logistics of this operation were immense. All building materials and supplies for the new resort had to be towed across the bay from the spur track at Edge Cove. The proper term for this boating maneuver was "scowing," whether the goods were towed by sail or by steamboat. At Beach Haven there was the problem of getting these heavy loads across the broad meadows onto the solid land where the buildings were under construction. It would have been very diffi-

Robert F. Engle

Catboats hoist sail near the Beach Haven Yacht Club in 1883. At the end of Dock Road, the club and its dock were the center of social activities. At left is the trestle for the Hotel Baldwin's rail line. Built initially to haul building materials, it later carried guests and fishermen between the bay and the Pearl Street hotel.

cult were it not for the existence of Mud Hen Creek, which cut through the marsh and meadows all the way to the first ridge of sand dunes alongside today's Bay Avenue. Sailing craft and barges were able to get in at high tide, unload their supplies onto ox carts and get back on the next tide.

In a short time a bumpy corduroy road of cedar logs was laid, the logs placed edge to edge and solidly bulkheaded to form a road along the northern bank of Mud Hen Creek. The bulkheading was extended for some distance out into the bay, where the water was deep enough

to build a wharf for the steamboat. Small boats were tied up along the full length of it. At first this road to the dock served as a simple tow path, and as it was improved it became a road substantial enough to have horse-drawn wagons meet the larger boats that no longer needed to come up the creek at all. From the very beginning the path alongside the creek was called Dock Road.

In the next fifteen years before there was a train to the island, Beach Haven became a thriving resort with summer visitors supporting three major hotels, some smaller ones and a score of sprawling summer cottages. Dock Road was the

only way into the new resort, and up this creek or along this road were carried every board foot of lumber, every foundation stone and brick, and every sack of cement for the Parry House (1874), the Engleside (1876) and for every cottage and smaller hotel built before 1886. The only exception was the Hotel Baldwin (1883). Materials to build it were landed at Dock Road, but they were hauled away from there in a southeasterly direction by a horse-drawn rail car along tracks built across the meadows in 1882.

Beach Haven did not open as a resort until the spring of 1874, when the Parry House was completed. But for at least two years before that, there was so much activity along the creek that Tilton Fox, a former captain in the coastal trade, seeing a business opportunity, bought a decommissioned "government house" at Harvey Cedars and had it towed to Beach Haven on a hay scow in 1872. The building had been built in 1847 to store lifesaving equipment and to serve as a house of refuge for shipwreck survivors. It had been one of the first of its kind on the New Jersey coast, but it had become outmoded with the formation of the U.S. Life Saving Service in 1871. Fox had the house set up on pilings a few hundred feet in on the north side of the waterway. He and his wife opened a boarding hotel for party boat captains and named it Hotel Crab, but his patrons suggested that the name lacked elegance, so he frenchified it into the Hotel DeCrab.

The colorful and canny Captain Tilton Fox ran the Hotel DeCrab from 1872 when he floated the former "house of refuge" to the Beach Haven bayfront until 1917 when he sold it to Sarah Cranmer for $650.

While there were many houseboats on the bayfront, the Hotel DeCrab was, for nearly ten years, the only permanent structure on Dock Road until the Beach Haven Yacht Club dock and clubhouse were built on the very edge of the bay some several hundred feet to the west. Fox's place, with its pilings driven deep in the bay mud, stood most of the time above the swirling tides. As a precaution, his floorboards were underlaid with crisscrossed railroad ties of thick cedar designed to rise inside his hotel just like a raft when storm tides flooded the meadows. Crab lines hung off the front and side porches, and from the railings dangled the bow lines of numerous small craft, which carried in the captains from the much-larger boats anchored in deeper water.

Captain John Tilton Fox, known to all as "Tilt," was born on Christmas Day 1836. Only five feet tall, Tilt had been captain of a three-masted schooner out of Barnegat and had served as first mate on a schooner during the Civil War. He came to work for Charles Parry in 1872 when the Parry House was being built. In 1884 and 1885, before the train came to the island, he sailed three days a week to Tuckerton to pick up the mail for Beach Haven, which he took from the dock to the Engleside lobby in his big wheelbarrow called "The Crab." It was always loaded with fish, crabs and oysters, and the mailbag sat on top.

Tilt's long rides across the bay must have stimulated his thought processes because when he got ashore he never stopped talking. It took

him literally hours to get uptown — longer, it was said, than it did to get to Tuckerton and back. He sold candy at the Hotel DeCrab and had a water cooler in the main room, where everyone gathered to swap fishing yarns and hear Tilt recite poetry, of which he had a limitless store. Captain Tilt ran the Hotel DeCrab on Dock Road for forty-five years, from 1872, when he brought the building down from Harvey Cedars, until September 1917, when he sold it to Sarah Cranmer for $650. She was the wife of John Cranmer of the Acme Hotel, and she wanted to have a little restaurant of her own. Fox was secretary of the Kynett United Methodist Church and for twenty-five years, until his death in 1919, he taught Sunday school at the Pennsylvania Railroad station on Third Street.

In a photo taken from the top of Beach Haven's water tower around 1910, parallel "mosquito ditches" run across the meadows between the Baldwin horsecar line and Dock Road. For a decade, the horsecars, below, carried passengers between town and bay.

The Parry House burned to the ground in August 1881, and Charles Parry undertook the building of a new hotel several blocks to the south between Marine and Pearl streets. To transport building materials, he constructed a wooden trestle with narrow-gauge railroad tracks to run diagonally across the meadows from the steamboat wharf at Dock Road right up to the entrance of what would become the Hotel Baldwin. For two seasons after the hotel opened, a small, specially made locomotive transported guests for two seasons, but it was replaced by a horsecar which ran fishermen back and forth for at least a decade after the railroad came to Beach Haven in 1886. There was a small drawbridge built where the narrow rail trestle crossed the entrance to the canal. It was lifted when boats sailed in and out, and was kept open all winter when the hotel was closed and the line was not in operation.

In 1896 Dock Road was officially dedicated as a borough street. Until this point it had been in the care of the Tuckerton and

Long Beach Building Association. Now it was widened to twenty feet, and railings were put up as a safety measure. The canal remained open, but once the drawbridge for the old Baldwin railway across the meadows had been removed, the seldom-used track itself was abandoned. The iron rails were salvaged, but the long row of pilings remained in the meadows for many a year, a curiosity to new visitors. In 1899, there were still only two buildings on Dock Road, the Hotel DeCrab and the Beach Haven Yacht Club.

At the turn of the century, John Cranmer, brother of Mose Cranmer, the caretaker of the Peahala Club, moved with his family to Beach Haven and bought the Phillip Dunn cottage on Third Street. Cranmer wanted to live on the bay, so in 1901 he had the building moved out to Dock Road about a hundred feet west of the Hotel DeCrab and converted it into a hotel for fishermen. The following year he bought another cottage on the south side of Centre Street between Beach and Atlantic avenues and also moved it to Dock Road, attaching it to the Dunn Cottage for a bar. Cranmer's business was a success, and he at once started work on a much larger building on the next lot to the west. This became the Acme Hotel, and it was ready for business in 1904. The Dunn Cottage and its addition were torn down in 1910 to make room for a clubhouse for the Fraternal Order of Elks; it was later to be known as the Antlers Grill, a very popular place during Prohibition, as was the Acme in those colorful years.

Captain Cranmer continued to expand his place. In 1913 he added four more bedrooms and a large veranda enclosed in glass. He installed a new café, or grill room, and hired an artist to paint panels with Swiss mountain landscapes.

Beach Haven's salt meadows and marshes underwent dramatic changes in two decades. In 1912, facing page, the wetlands west of Bay Avenue are relatively untouched. By 1934, above, buildings sprouted on both sides of Dock Road, a broad new Centre Street leads to the bay, and filled wetlands await development.

Cranmer's place was already very popular with fishermen as he got ready for the automobile age.

By March 1915, the old canal was filled in with dredged mud and sand; the railings, no longer needed, were pulled down. One block away, Centre Street was being graded to run all the way to the bay. Now that Dock Road was ten feet wider to make room for cars, Captain Cranmer bought himself a new Oldsmobile for $350. Mud Hen Creek was gone forever, along with thousands and thousands of little, clicking fiddler crabs.

Because crabs, fish and waterfowl were still plentiful, no one worried about a marsh creek filled in here or there. But there were game laws, and Captain Cranmer always took the side of sportsmen. He disliked J. Hamilton Evernham, the Ocean County game warden, as much as they did. Around 1918, when the game laws were getting really strict and "Hammy" was making life miserable for every gunner on Little Egg Harbor Bay, Cranmer would hang a sheet from a west window on the top floor of his hotel to warn all the boatmen far out on the bay that the game warden was snooping around. Gunners with illegally shot birds either wouldn't come ashore or would hide excess birds on marsh islands until the sheet was pulled in. It took some time, but the wily J. Hamilton Evernham caught onto the sheet trick. Cranmer was a step ahead of him, though. He started leaving the sheet out morning, noon and night. Then, as soon as he got word from the tender at the drawbridge that Hammy was on the island and headed for Beach Haven, he took it in.

Cranmer was popular, and it was to the Acme that everyone went to sit at the bar and hear good stories about fishing and hunting. But the best was yet to come. Prohibition became the law of the land from 1919 until 1933. Nowhere was it more disregarded than at Beach Haven, where the rum fleet was only twelve miles off the coast

Iced-in sneakboxes, neat rows of decoys in their sterns, indicate the popularity of gunning on the island. By 1915, this Dock Road canal had been filled as Beach Haven began drawing more and more vacationers.

and any young bayman with a boat was willing and able to get cases of whiskey in burlap bags from the drop-off points at the Beach Haven Inlet. In 1925, Cranmer sold his place to Gustave Tueckmantel. Illegal booze was brought into the Acme, but not through the famous trap door in the floor. That wasn't necessary, and no boat could even get under the hotel at any tide. But it was a good story, and celebrities flocked there even when Prohibition was long over. They liked the Tueckmantels and the whole atmosphere.

In June 1917, "Uncle Joe" Schonders bought the Elks clubhouse and converted it into the Antlers Grill. It, too, ran as a speakeasy all during the twenties and remained a popular bar, especially with the college crowd in the forties and fifties while Dock Road was slowly filling in with houses on both sides of the street.

In August 1930, after a dispute over riparian rights that had lasted several years, the New Jersey Supreme Court ruled that the Beach Haven Yacht Club had been, since its founding in 1882, only a squatter on marshland belonging to the Joseph Taylor estate. The club would have to move the building within six months or purchase the land in question for ten thousand dollars. The yacht club members chose to move and bought a strip of land along West Avenue between Centre Street and Engleside Avenue. In January 1931, the fifty-year-old structure was dragged two blocks across the meadows to its new site.

The Hotel DeCrab, the oldest building in Beach Haven and in great disrepair, was torn down in August 1984 after it had been condemned by the borough. The Acme Hotel has been substantially rebuilt into a bar-restaurant called The Ketch. The original corduroy road is still there, four feet down under the asphalt of the present Dock Road.

Chapter 10

THE HARVEY CEDARS HOTEL

Along the coast of New Jersey in late Colonial times, few residents of the little towns on the mainland creeks would have chosen to live all the year around on Long Beach. Unless one owned a tavern at one of the inlets or was engaged in shore whaling, there was no way to make a living on a desolate, nearly treeless barrier island. There was just enough fresh water in ponds to raise horses and cattle, but the animals could fend for themselves as they fed on the salt hay which grew abundantly in the wetlands on both sides of the bay.

Both salt hay and seaweed were of some importance to the local economy. Salt hay is a type of cordgrass related to sweet hay in the uplands. As early as 1800 it became an important source of winter silage for mainland cattle and was harvested on the meadows of the barrier islands every summer by work crews. It was cut by hand with scythes and heaped into huge, mushroom-shaped haycocks, which appear in many nineteenth-century paintings of coastal marshes. It was then scowed to the mainland and sold.

The men who did this work were often far from home for days and weeks at a time and had to stay in temporary shelters called quarters or — in the case of their particular occupation —"harvest quarters." Any quarters or shelter for the crews who worked in the meadows had to be located on an elevated piece of ground called a hummock or hammock. At high tide, when the meadows are often under water, a hummock will resemble a small island in the marshes. A hummock makes an excellent place to pitch a tent or build fires for cooking. They vary in size, but one of the largest of these hummocks on the New Jersey coast was on Long Beach at a point opposite the town of Barnegat. Almost six acres in size, it was partially covered with a thick growth of cedar trees that, too twisted and stunted to be cut for lumber, were nonetheless high enough to be visible from the mainland three miles away. This particular stand of trees was distinctive enough to be identified locally as "the harvest cedars," but that combination of words was never easy to pronounce, so it was better known as Harvey Cedars.

On the oceanfront, not far from the "harvey" cedars, was another type of quarters or temporary shelter. This was a whaling quarters used overnight or longer by those who

were then the only permanent residents of Long Beach, the whaling families of Great Swamp, now known as Surf City. The men who hunted whales from shore had several work stations up and down the beach. It was never certain where they might land a slain whale, but wherever it was, they had to go to work immediately. Doubling as part-time shelters, these stations were also called "quarters."

Much confusion has arisen over the origin of the place name Harvey Cedars. As the years passed, no one remembered that there had been a harvest quarters at the harvest cedars in this part of Long Beach, and it got mixed up with the nearby whaling quarters on the beach. There also was talk of a person named Harvey. In one book of local history, Harvey even acquired the first name of Daniel, and it was said that he lived in a cave on the hummock that was the future site of the Harvey Cedars Hotel. It was not explained why anyone would have a whaling quarters on the bay side of the island. The truth is, of course, that Harvey is a myth.

There were a few souls who eked out a precarious living on the barrier islands and who lived in caves and lean-tos. They were called "beachers" and their principle source of revenue was the trove of shipwrecks. Whatever they found they sold or traded at one of the local taverns. They lived off the half-wild cattle and all the game and fish they could catch; some were more ambitious than others and in time acquired property.

Just after the War of 1812, Sylvanus Cox, a beacher turned farmer, built a house on the six-acre hummock known as the harvest cedars. It had certain advantages in that it was separated from Long Beach Island by a narrow creek over which Cox built a bridge. The hummock was high enough to garden and, being nearly surrounded by the creek on three sides and the bay on the west, was ideal for keeping chickens and small livestock from wandering. It still had the clumps of cedar that had given it its unusual name.

In 1841 Cox sold his place to Samuel Perrine of Barnegat, who rebuilt and enlarged the old structure, converting it into a boarding hotel for sportsmen and for their wives, who enjoyed a vacation too. He called it the Connahassett House at Harvest Cedars in all his letters and advertisements.

In the 1850s and 1860s there were several fair-sized boarding hotels to choose from on the island. What had once been the fanciest, the Mansion of Health at Great Swamp, was now in decline. Bond's Long Beach House, at the southern end near the inlet, was the exclusive hideaway of upper-class Philadelphians, who made a great pretense of roughing it on vacation. The Oceanic at Barnegat Inlet and its companion, the Sunset, were not yet built, but the Ashley House was there, and there was "Double Jimmie's" at Loveladies, which both attracted the New York crowd, but popular choice fell on Perrine's Harvey Cedars Hotel. It became the place to visit even if one did not plan to stay; Perrine's register was always filled.

The hotel's biggest attraction was its public dance hall on the south side of the main building. Sailing parties from other hotels went there on summer evenings for the lively square dances and reels. The scraping of fiddles and chanting of the caller could be heard far out on the water. For many years, before a long dock was built there, sailing parties arriving at low tide had to wade ashore, the men carrying their ladies piggyback through the shallows up to the dance hall.

Captain Sammy Perrine was a very entertaining and genial host. Like Thomas Bond of the equally well-known Long Beach House, he

" A SHIP ASHORE !"

Harper's New Monthly Magazine, *February 1878*

This illustration, from a reporter's account of a visit to the shore in 1878, shows revelry at the Harvey Cedars Hotel dance hall when it is announced that a ship is aground and all race to the beach to the rescue; Samuel Perrine, the proprietor, was also the first captain of the Life Saving station at Harvey Cedars.

Captain Samuel Perrine Jr., seen above around the turn of the century at the wheel of the luxury schooner *Sans Souci*, and standing in the center of his crew, was a nationally known hero of the U.S. Life Saving Service. Perrine's father built the Connahassett House, later called the Harvey Cedars Hotel.

was keenly interested in shipwrecks and the plight of their victims. He was in the forefront of every volunteer rescue effort, so when one of two government houses on the island was erected near his hotel in 1848, Perrine was placed in charge. Government houses were manned only by volunteers and used to store a boat and other rescue equipment. A generation later in 1871, when the U.S. Life Saving Service

was formed, Perrine became the first captain of the unit at Harvey Cedars.

Perrine, who died in 1881, was succeeded by Captain Isaac S. Jennings, who brought the hotel into a new era. Jennings was born in Manahawkin in 1821. He went to sea early, principally in the coasting trade, and captained his own vessel before retiring from ocean life in 1858. A man of strong physique and cheerful disposition, he

became a surveyor, a freeholder and a justice of the peace. Jennings' wife, Mary, made the kitchen and dining room of the Harvey Cedars Hotel the equal of any of the palatial new places that had sprung up at Barnegat City and Beach Haven. There was a long bar facing the bay with a big fireplace, and there was plenty of whiskey served, especially in the gunning season. The whole complex was nearly self-sufficient, with big vegetable gardens, fruit trees, cows, pigs, chickens and a never-ending supply of fish, clams, crabs and duck. The Jenningses were famous for the abundance of seafood served. Turtle soup and broiled sheepshead were their specialties.

Mary Jennings had a brother, David M. White, who took it upon himself to give the Harvey Cedars Hotel a distinctive flavor that became the talk of the region. An insatiable beachcomber and magpie, he was out every morning with his horse, wagon and saw, looking for fresh wrecks and castoff cargo of any kind. In time the grounds took on the fantastic appearance of a ship's graveyard, with carved figureheads, spars and masts strung with miles of cordage, flags and lanterns. Much of the wood was meant to be cut for fuel, but White was also an avid collector of nameboards, which every ship bore then. Many of them were beautifully scrolled and carved. White nailed them up everywhere. The once-proud names of wrecked vessels were affixed to every outbuilding on the place, including chicken coops, pigpens and doghouses.

At the age of seventy-four, Captain Jennings died January 10, 1895, at his home in Harvey Cedars, just a month after taking office as the town's first mayor. He had been proprietor of the Harvey Cedars Hotel for fifteen years; his wife had died two years earlier. William Thompson of Gloucester, New Jersey, became the new owner.

The place had slowed down following Mary Jennings death in 1893, but Thompson, known to all as the "Duke of Gloucester," was an ener-

The original architecture of the Harvey Cedars Life Saving Station, above, has been largely preserved as the present Long Beach Island Fishing Club on Cape May Avenue.

getic, colorful character, and he soon had it going again. Within eight years he was confident enough in the future of the hotel to undertake massive renovations. He spent large sums to raise the hotel one floor off the ground to make it taller, and he added more rooms, giving it the appearance that it bears today.

But it was all for naught. The whole north end of the island had been eclipsed by the attraction and splendor of the big hotels at Beach Haven. The old places at Barnegat City and Harvey Cedars began to fade. Most of the decline had to do with the lack of transportation; train service to the north end was very poor. But there simply was no money to be made in hotels or real estate. Miles and miles of rolling dunes and broad meadows lay virtually untouched until the 1950s, when they suddenly became ripe for development after the building of the Garden State Parkway.

An 1870 print shows the Harvey Cedars Hotel, with its dance hall on right, as published in the 1936 edition of *The Lure of Long Beach*. This last remaining Long Beach Island hotel from the 19th century survives as a Bible conference today.

of two or three weeks at a time, there were always at least a hundred or more young, single workingwomen ready to participate in a fun-filled, well-organized vacation. Most of them still lived at home with their parents, which was the custom then, and Camp Whelen was a new experience and a chance to socialize and share ideas. They returned year after year.

The camp had two buses for runs to the movies at night or to Beach Haven for weekly boat trips to Atlantic City. The "girls" went in small groups to the dances at the Baldwin and the Engleside, and there were frequent beach parties in Harvey Cedars with plenty of hot dogs and marshmallows. There was a piano in the camp's dining room, and singing and amateur shows were very popular. Visiting speakers were welcome, and camp directors placed just enough emphasis on religion and sound Christian principles to make the vacation spiritually as well as physically rewarding.

By 1935, the camp had been in operation only fifteen years, and the nation was in the depths of the Great Depression. Workingwomen were concerned with holding onto their jobs, and there was neither time nor money for vacations. Camp Whelen closed its doors.

The old hotel was vacant once more, but this time it was in terrible condition, having been vandalized repeatedly. Then one summer on the eve of World War II, a young evangelist named Jack Murray and his friend Bill Ritchie saw it while they were fishing. Intrigued by the building, they

Thompson held on until 1914, the year the automobile causeway was completed, but it did him no good: There would be no road on the north end until 1920. Thompson sold to Daniel B. Frazier, a Philadelphia real estate broker who had the entire hotel repainted and made extensive improvements to the old place, but he, too, was to be disappointed. Train service was down to one run a week, and there was no automobile road. On the whole north end there were few

passable side roads, and at high tide the bay came to the very edge of the boulevard. It was as much a wilderness as it had been in the nineteenth century. Frazier sold out in 1921 to the Philadelphia YWCA, and the old hotel entered another era. It became Camp Whelen.

Camp Whelen was particularly successful because it was housed in the historic, former Harvey Cedars Hotel. Each summer, all during the 1920s and until 1935, for successive periods went in and decided then and there that it would make an ideal religious retreat for young people. They located its owner, Mabel Bayard, in the Germantown section of Philadelphia, offered all they could afford to raise, $7,500, and it was accepted. It took an incredible amount of hard work to restore the old hotel, but with lots of help they did it, and the Harvey Cedars Bible Conference opened in August 1941. The Reverend Al Oldham has been its director since 1951, and improvements to the place never cease. As the last of the great nineteenth-century hotels on the island, it is in better condition than it was a hundred years ago.

The Harvey Cedars pavilion at Passaic Avenue was built in 1898 to attract developers. To the left of the pavilion is the home of Francis Fenimore, founder of the Harvey Cedars Gun Club. As the Philadelphia YWCA's Camp Whelen, facing page, top, the Harvey Cedars Hotel gained new life as a vacation spot for young women. The hotel's long wooden walkway, facing page, later became Camden Avenue.

Bond's Long Beach House, romantically depicted in this illustration from Woolman and Rose's *Atlas of the New Jersey Coast*, 1878.

Chapter 11

CAPTAIN BOND'S LONG BEACH HOUSE

Of the eight major hotels built on Long Beach Island before the coming of the railroad in 1886, all but one, the Harvey Cedars Hotel, are gone. The others — the Sunset, the Oceanic, the Mansion of Health, the Parry House, the Hotel Baldwin, the Engleside and the Long Beach House — were all torn down or destroyed by fire. Historically, the most significant of these old hotels was the famous Long Beach House of Thomas Bond. Out of it and the influential men who stayed there over the years came the genesis of Beach Haven.

The Long Beach House, on the island's south end at what is now Holgate, became for a few dozen years before and after the Civil War the best-known hostelry on the New Jersey coast. It attracted men of wealth and influence from Philadelphia and New York. Railroad magnates, lawyers, judges and doctors came to Bond's in the summer to relax with their families and in the winter months to hunt birds with their genial host.

Thomas Bond had not planned to be an innkeeper. Born in Boston in 1799, he had been, in the first half-century of his life, a successful owner of a New York jewelry firm that made expensive watchcases. Owning and managing the Long Beach House became one of his two second careers. The other was his interest in lifesaving, which had obsessed him ever since he witnessed the wreck of the brig *Ayrshire* in January 1850 off Squan Beach. The Francis Life Car was first used to rescue lives in that wreck, and all the crew and passengers but one were rescued. Bond was a close personal friend of the life car's inventor, fellow Bostonian Joseph Francis, born in 1801, and the two corresponded all their long lives.

In the years Bond had his business in New York, his avocation was gunning. He hunted in the marshes east of Brooklyn and Flushing, and in New Jersey around Paterson and Jersey City, but he was always in search of better and more remote areas. He started sailing down to Squan and Toms River, and on a trip aboard the schooner *Wissahickon* in February 1846, Bond saw his future Long Beach House for the first time. He recorded in his diary that on his first outing he killed twenty-one ducks, but that had been a bad day, one without wind. The next day he shot fifty ducks and twelve geese and decided that he liked this island called Long Beach.

He became a regular guest of Lloyd Jones, the proprietor of the Philadelphia Company House, as it was then still called. By 1851, Bond had purchased for three thousand dollars several buildings and one hundred acres of dune and marshland from Jones, who had been improving the property for the previous five years. It was never really Bond's intention to be an innkeeper. He simply wanted to have the place properly managed and make the main building a private hunting lodge for himself and his friends but, unable to find a competent manager for it, he decided to retire and take it over himself. He applied for a hotel service license, sold his business in New York and moved to Long Beach Island, where he would spend the next forty years.

Bond renamed the place Long Beach House when he opened as innkeeper on July 4, 1852. At the end of the season he purchased more land, one thousand acres south to the edge of the Old Inlet where Tucker's Beach began. Included in his purchase was a very valuable ice pond which for many years supplied not only his own place but also the big hotels in Beach Haven. Since the early 1820s, when the Philadelphia Company House began, this area of Long Beach had had a good reputation and it was now up to Bond, using the strength of his personality and generous spirit, to build it up, and at this he succeeded.

For the next twenty years, until the coming of the railroad to Tuckerton, the only way to get to this remote area other than by a two-day stagecoach trip across the state was to take the Camden and Atlantic Railroad to Absecon and sail up from there by one of the "Long Beach packets," thirty-one-foot cat yachts. Many a lasting friendship began on those two- to six-hour trips aboard Captain Billy Gaskill's *Eliza* and Captain Morford Horner's *Mary Jane*. The length of the journey depended on wind direction and tide, but Bond supplied the whiskey to ward off any possible chill. In time, these old packet boats were replaced by steamers, including the paddle wheeler *Mary*, which also went to Sea Haven on Tucker's Island.

In keeping with his interest in lifesaving, Bond had, from his very first days as proprietor, a "Government House" near his property to aid shipwreck survivors. The federal government had set up these houses of refuge all along the Atlantic coast sometime in the 1850s, at least twenty years before there was an official lifesaving service. The government paid for the house and the equipment, but all the dangerous rescue work was done by volunteers, of whom Bond was one of the most dedicated. He kept the key to the Government House in the barroom of his hotel and often recruited his guests if there was a wreck. As often as not, he would bring the survivors into his place, where he would feed, clothe and entertain them, all without compensation. This was Bond's way; he was generous to a fault. He wrote many letters to the government asking to be reimbursed, but for naught.

Thomas Bond never married and generally avoided the company of women, although it was said he had impeccable manners in their

An artist's rendition of Bond's Long Beach House, above. In the 1872 photograph, facing page, Thomas Bond had enlarged his rustic seashore boardinghouse, anticipating waves of vacationers steaming in on the new Tuckerton Railroad. Those vacationers, however, flocked to the classier Beach Haven hotels.

presence. He preferred to be with men in the thick of the action, shooting on a cold rainy morning on the bay or directing a rescue in a howling blizzard. He was also an inveterate cardplayer and a skilled musician. To spend an autumn evening in Bond's bar and billiard room by a crackling fire with some of his fun-loving cronies was one of life's great pleasures. The whiskey and cigars were the very best, and the food was always excellent. Bond would allow no stinting on these matters.

Today, some tend to think of the old nineteenth-century "sportsmen's hotels" on Long Beach Island as being exclusively for men when, in fact, they were not. Certainly all that incredibly abundant fish and game drew plenty of "gentlemen fishers and fowlers" to places like the Mansion of Health, Double Jimmie's, the Ashley

House and Bond's, just as the old accounts say, but most of them were well-established, married men. Along with their sons, they brought their wives and daughters with them or chances are they couldn't have come at all.

Many of the women were adept at fishing and enjoyed shooting at small birds quite as much as the men. Some of them were remarkably fine shots and have left records of their scores in old hotel ledgers. Bond's was very informal in those years before and after the Civil War, and if the men dressed like farmers, the ladies wore calico and gingham. They were taken to the beach in mule-drawn hay wagons, and Bond did everything he could to make them comfortable. He was astute enough to realize that if they weren't happy, the men would never get back.

There was a cost to all of Bond's marvelous hospitality, which could not last forever. As meticulous as Bond was about his account books and keeping his daily journal, he constantly allowed money to slip through his fingers. By the late 1860s, the place was in such a state of disrepair that newcomers were shocked. Once they registered at the desk, they were asked to go and pick out a room, and by default it became their responsibility to assign tasks to the domestic staff — what there were of them. All of this greatly amused Bond's regulars, who were quite used to it. Bond often seemed to be a guest in his own place, where social pretensions were banished. Casualness was the order of the day. It was like a big, happy fraternity house.

From Bond's well-preserved records it is interesting to see what was or what should have been available to his guests. Each room contained one carpet, an iron bedstead and mattress, two sheets, two pillows and two cases, one counterpane, a washstand with bowl and pitcher, a chamber pot, one soap dish, two quilts and two chairs. There was a lot of "borrowing" and rearranging as items vanished from one room and appeared in another. There were so many practical jokes going on all the time that no one could be sure of anything, but eventually everyone got settled and joined in the fun.

The years after the Civil War were the beginning of what has been called the Gilded Age in America, when the display of wealth was equated with social prestige. Bond failed to realize women's needs and especially their power. As much fun as it was to go to Bond's, the place was going out of style. Roughing it at the seashore belonged to the old days. Women wanted to dress up on vacation, and they wanted silver, crystal and elegant cuisine. All of this and more were soon to come to Long Beach Island.

Among Bond's oldest regulars, going as far back as 1856, was Archelaus Pharo of the Tuckerton Railroad. In 1872, just after his railroad on the mainland had opened, Pharo started regular steamboat service across the bay in the summer months to pick up the crowds from Philadelphia. He brought them straight to the Long Beach House, and this was Bond's most profitable year. The place was packed all summer, but it would not last. Unfortunately for Bond, his old friends, Pharo and Charles T. Parry, were planning a new resort on a grand scale just two miles up the beach at a place they had already named Beach Haven.

With his hotel free of debt for the first time in years, Bond was filled with enthusiasm and he began, at the age of seventy-two, to invest heavily in improvements. He added another wing, bringing the total to 102 rooms, and put in new carpets and furnishings throughout the hotel. He bought more livestock and trees for his orchard. By the winter of 1873, he had borrowed and spent fifteen thousand dollars. It should have been obvious to him what was going to happen at Beach Haven, but he had a stubborn streak.

The spring of 1874 saw the opening of the Parry House in the new resort of Beach Haven. All of Bond's former loyal guests, including Pharo, Parry and Ashhurst, had moved there and were building cottages. They also took the steamboat service along with them, and Bond

Bond's, above, was empty for 20 years before it was torn down in 1909. The gentlemanly and aging Bond, facing page, lived near his old hotel in a small cottage and was cared for by the Holgate and Horter families who had bought up most of Bond's land holdings. Bond died at the age of 93 in 1892 and is buried in Tuckerton's Greenwood Cemetery.

would go into debt to Charles Freeman of the Camden and Atlantic Railroad paying for steamboat service from the rail terminus at Absecon. But the times were against Bond, and the new arrangement did not work. He had a very poor season until August, when he recorded 178 guests.

Even Lloyd Jones, Bond's old friend, who had sold the Long Beach House to him back in 1851, was building a new place of his own at Beach Haven called the Bay View. The Long Beach House would never recover from all this competition. Bond accepted it philosophically and began a third career, devoting all of his energies to the new U.S. Life Saving station that had been erected on the oceanfront near his property in December 1873. He was made master of the station at a salary of eighty-five dollars a month and took the title of Captain Bond, with a paid crew of six men under him.

At Beach Haven, the first manager of the Parry House, Robert Engle, left after two years and built an even bigger and grander hotel just two blocks south called the Engleside. Bond sank deeper into debt with each passing year as fewer and fewer vacationers wanted to stay at a place that had become old-fashioned and out-of-date. By 1883, Bond's principal creditor, Charles Freeman, bought the buildings at foreclosure proceedings. He closed the Long Beach House for good three years later when the railroad arrived in Beach Haven. There was a big farewell party at the old place, and many former guests, some of whom had cottages in Beach Haven, came to talk about old times and take home a souvenir or two.

In 1883, an aging Bond retired from the Life Saving Service. He was eighty-four and was still taking his boat *Fashion* out to the is-

lands for gunning or fishing. There was no pension for him. He spent his last days in a little cottage near the ruin of his old hotel. Cared for by the Holgate and Horter families who had bought up most of his former land holdings in the area, Bond was never in need. He had outlived all of his contemporaries, but many young people came to see him to talk about the old days, and he remained alert until his death in 1892 at the age of ninety-three.

One profoundly sad incident occurred in his last days that recalled an event nearly sixty-five years earlier. Bond, the confirmed bachelor, once had a sweetheart and planned to marry her until they had a quarrel. Bond's stubborn streak prevailed over his usual jovial manner. He refused to reconcile with her and left. She apparently was the same sort and eventually married someone else. When Bond was ninety-two and she was

eighty-seven, he received a letter from her. Alone and widowed, she was dying in a hospital in New York, and Bond was too ill at the time to travel.

He died in Mays Landing, and his remains were brought to Beach Haven for a viewing at the Ocean House Hotel on Centre Street, where on a rainy October day both young and old came to talk and hear about the old times on Long Beach before there were trains and telephones. Bond was buried in Tuckerton's Greenwood Cemetery in a grave unmarked until 1938. It was through the unflagging efforts of Jessie Coole of *The Beach Haven Times*, who had transcribed his diary for that paper in the late thirties, that a marker was finally placed. The flat, gray stone bears the simple inscription "Thomas Bond — Pioneer. 1799-1892."

Bond had a favorite poem, one he was so fond of quoting that many who heard him recite it thought he had written it himself. The poem was actually written by Hannah Flagg Gould, and it seemed to embody much of Bond's philosophy about life, a darker side that few people ever saw in this outgoing and generous man.

A Name in the Sand

Alone I walked the ocean strand
A pearly shell was in my hand
I stopped and wrote upon the sand
My name, the year, the date.

As onward from the spot I passed
One lingering look behind I cast
A wave came rolling high and fast
And washed my lines away.

So shall it be, with every trace on earth of me.
A wave from dark oblivion's sea
Will roll across the place where I have trod
And leave no track or trace.

The old hotel remained a picturesque ruin for another twenty years in the sand hills about a hundred yards south of today's last street in Holgate. In 1909 it was torn down, and all the lumber was rafted over to West Creek for resale. Much of it found its way into old houses around the island and the mainland. Not even a foundation stone remains of the old place. In February 1920 a violent northeast storm cut a new inlet through the former site, acting out in a haunting fashion the last lines of Bond's favorite poem.

This 1878 etching from *Woolman and Rose's Atlas of the New Jersey Coast* took artistic license, flattening the landscape and moving the hotel to the oceanfront.

Chapter 12

THE PARRY HOUSE

each Haven was born out of the incorporation of the Tuckerton and Long Beach Building, Land and Improvement Association. Awkward though the name might have been, the men who formed it that early spring of 1873 had one clear purpose in mind, and that was to build a resort community unlike any ever seen on Long Beach Island. Its centerpiece would be a magnificent new hotel two and one half miles north of Bond's Long Beach House. The site they chose for it was an undeveloped tract of land to be deeded over to them later that year in two large parcels amounting to a thousand acres.

The men behind the association had, for many years, been regular guests at Bond's. They knew and loved the island and had every reason to believe their enterprise would succeed. They had the money and the power to back it. Among them was Archelaus Pharo, who owned the Tuckerton Railroad, the steamboat line and most of the land that would one day be Beach Haven. There were lawyers, judges and doctors. Another of the big shareholders was Charles Thomas Parry of the Philadelphia firm of Parry, Burnham and Williams, later to be known as the Baldwin Loco-

motive Works. Parry wanted a hotel that would be without rival anywhere on the island and, as he was its principal investor, all agreed it should be called the Parry House.

An army of carpenters went to work at once. Throughout the mild winter and spring of 1874 the sand hills north of Bond's rang with the buzz of saws, the slam of new lumber and the staccato clatter of hammers as the imposing Parry House rose to its full four stories in a graded lot along the north side of Centre Street between Beach and Atlantic avenues. It would be two hundred feet by thirty-two feet with room for more than three hundred guests, making it easily twice the size of Bond's. A fleet of sailboats and the paddle wheeler *Barclay* towed countless barges and scows piled high with boards and beams, plaster and nail kegs, and windows and doors from the train stop at Edge Cove to the canal along Dock Road, where all cargo was unloaded into wagons pulled by oxen through the soft, rutted sand.

The Parry House was ready for occupancy by June 25, its first guests a group of Haverford College students celebrating their graduation.

They were delighted to have nearly the whole place to themselves. Work had been completed in an astonishingly short time, but it must be remembered that there was no heating or electrical work and only minimal plumbing to contend with. There was stonemasonry, but once the foundations were laid, ninety percent of all the work was carpentry. Carpenters were paid $1.50 for a twelve-hour day, and lumber, nearly all of which came from South Jersey sawmills, cost only pennies a running foot. The principal builder and contractor at the new resort was George S. Butler of Tuckerton, aided by his son William L. Butler, who was to become Beach Haven's first mayor in 1890.

Elsewhere in Beach Haven graceful summer cottages on big lots sprang up here and there in the six-block grid of wide, sandy streets from Third on the north to Coral on the south. The first two houses in town were built by Archelaus Pharo on the north side of Second Street only a block away from the Parry House. One was for his own use and the other was for his friend Dr. Albert Smith of Philadelphia. Smith had been one of that group of wealthy sportsmen who stayed at Bond's in the previous decade.

Just a block to the west of the Parry House, on what is now the northeast corner of Bay Avenue and Centre Street, Lloyd Jones of Tuckerton was building a small hotel of his own to be called the Bay View House. The Bay View was a duplicate of Bond's, which Jones himself had once owned and improved before he sold it to Bond back in 1850. Jones' new place was close enough to the head of Mud Hen Creek that at high tide the bay washed under his porch and boats were able to tie up to his railings. In October 1874, their first year of operation, both the Parry House and the Bay View House were open for gunners, and the steamer *Barclay* was still carrying excursionists across the bay until late November.

The Parry House's first manager was an enterprising Mount Holly Quaker and one-time farmer named Robert Barclay Engle, who within two years would, with the backing of his cousin Samuel T. Engle, build a palatial new hotel of his own one block to the south called the Engleside. When he left, two other Burlington County men, named Darnell and Buzby, took over the job of running the Parry House and started to advertise in Philadelphia for business.

Running at right angles to the ocean, the Parry House afforded the occupant of every room a sea view. There was a broad piazza around three sides at ground-floor level, but most guests preferred the upper-level decks to get away from the mosquitoes. The enclosed observatory deck on the top floor was a favorite spot for socializing. In an 1878 lithograph, pictured on page 84, the artist — who, it is certain, never visited the location, for he put the hotel too close to the ocean — also took great license with the landscape. Not at all so flat as he depicts, the whole area was scattered with bogs and bayberry and high, grass-clad sand hills. There was no gravel for roads, and oxen were the only beasts strong enough to pull the heavy wagons. Narrow boardwalks ran along every street.

Even on the bayside the dunes were enormous and much effort was soon expended in leveling them to fill in the bogs for roads and lots.

In 1876, after the completion of the Engleside, there were three major hotels in Beach Haven. Fresh ocean breezes and a nearly six-mile distance from the woods of the mainland seemed to provide such a relief from hay fever symptoms that Beach Haven backers billed it as "the only practical seashore resort in America." However, a travel writer for *Harper's New Monthly Magazine* visiting the resort in 1877 described the hotels as "three overgrown caravansaries on a flat and verdureless shore under an intolerably glar-ing sky. In storms the hotels are bleak and unsheltered and, in calms, filled with mosqui-toes." Despite the writer's low opinion, Beach Haven and its hotels were becoming more popular each summer.

Then, on August 10, 1881, at four A.M. the Parry House, filled nearly to capacity with two hundred persons, caught fire. An alert minister, visiting from Moorestown, was either up all night or at work very early preparing a sermon. He smelled smoke and roused the guests in time so that no lives were lost.

The Parry House fire began when Mr. and Mrs. Buzby were in charge. It apparently started in the flue of the bakery which was part of the hotel. There was no fire apparatus. In the darkness and smoke, guests stumbled in the hallways. Big Saratoga trunks were tossed out windows, but few guests were able to save anything. Townspeople quickly organized a bucket brigade with buckets on ropes hauled up to the higher places, all to no avail. Within two hours the hotel and nearby drugstore were completely gone. There were twenty thousand dollars in damages, and the place was insured for only fourteen thousand dollars. From time to time, it had been suggested that a big tank of bay water could be used to keep freshly caught fish alive for a little while to save ice. Such a tank could have been used in case of fires, but it never got built.

On Sunday, with all the survivors of the fire packed into the Engleside, the Rev. James Lamb, who had become an instant hero, presided over a nondenominational service of thanksgiving in the lobby. Mrs. Parry, who had been staying at the hotel at the time of the fire, was so moved that she gave money to begin construction of an Episcopal church. It would be called Holy Innocents after one of her beloved daughters, who had died the previous spring at age nineteen, and for all other departed children. The building, which still stands at the corner of Beach and Engleside avenues, now houses the Long Beach Island Historical Museum.

It was the Parry House fire that inspired the creation of the Beach Haven Fire Company on April 28, 1883, with Charles T. Parry as its first president. With the loss of the Parry House, the land association chose a site four blocks south between Marine and Pearl streets to build a new hotel on a much grander scale. It was to become one of the great symbols of Beach Haven's Victorian era, the Hotel Baldwin. Nearly eighty years later, it, too, would be destroyed in a spectacular fire.

The Parry House graced Beach Haven for only seven years, but out of the blaze that destroyed it came the first fire company, a landmark church and the resort's other major hotel, the Baldwin. The Parrys' summer cottage, owned by their descendants, is still standing at 127 Coral Street. The summer cottage that was built by Parry's partner, Dr. Edward Williams, and known as Portia Cottage remains at 123 Coral Street. Williams was the principle benefactor of the Kynett United Methodist Church and parsonage, which now occupy part of the former site of the Parry House on Centre Street. The home of Parry's other partner, William Burnham, at Atlantic Avenue and Coral Street, later became known as the "Baby Hospital" because it was purchased and operated as a summer place by Children's Hospital of Philadelphia. It was destroyed in the Hurricane of 1944.

Robert F. Engle (both)

Two legacies of the short-lived Parry House include the Archelaus Pharo home, above, and Holy Innocents Episcopal Church, facing page. Pharo was one of the principals in the Parry House, and his home was Beach Haven's first summer cottage. Mrs. Charles Parry donated the funds to build the church, now the Long Beach Island Historical Museum.

Chapter 13

THE ENGLESIDE: 1876-1943

Built by prosperous Quakers in 1876, the Engleside Hotel, above, was the more staid of Beach Haven's two biggest hotels. Properly dressed Engleside guests walked from the hotel to the beach on a narrow boardwalk placed over flattened dunes that later became the hotel's tennis courts.

In 1875, at the end of Beach Haven's second full season of operation as a resort, it was clear to its founders that their investment was paying off. As soon as the ice had begun to melt in the mainland creeks and the winds of early spring drove the first flock of white sails out onto the bay, the traffic never ceased on the five miles of water between the rail terminus at Edge Cove near Tuckerton and the crowded entrance to Beach Haven's Mud Hen Creek. Many of the larger catboats towed barges piled high with building materials and supplies. In the heat of summer, every eastward trip of the paddle wheeler *Barclay* brought more and more city folk in quest of relief from hay fever to this remote strip of sand "as free of pollen as a ship in midocean," according to its promoters. Health was the founders' trump card, and they continued to play it.

But Beach Haven had only two hotels and fewer than a dozen summer cottages. They seemed to have risen overnight out of the treeless sand hills on a grid of six wide streets running east and west and bisected by two avenues, all of which were no more than rutted sand roads barely passable by ox cart. The bigger of the two hotels, the 150-room Parry House, stood at the northeast corner of Beach Avenue and Centre Street, taking up most of the north side of the block with a commanding view of the ocean from its top floors. The other hotel, the Bay View, true to its name, looked out over the wide marshes toward busy Dock Road and the steamboat wharf. It was only a third as big as the Parry House.

No one had a keener perception of the potential of Beach Haven than the Parry House's personable and hardworking manager, Robert Barclay Engle. Born in Mount Holly in 1834 of old Quaker stock, he had been a farmer by trade but was also extremely shrewd in business and

politics. By the end of the century he would become a state senator from Ocean County, but in 1875 at the age of forty-one, he was a skilled manager with a major decision to make. Two seasons of full bookings at the Parry House had convinced him he ought to build a resort hotel of his own in Beach Haven and so, with the financial aid of his cousin Samuel T. Engle, he quietly purchased one whole block of land between South and Amber streets, a block below Centre. (South Street is now called Engleside Avenue.)

Robert Engle broke ground on January 1, 1876. Fortune favored the project with a mild winter, and by the end of February, just as an army of fifty carpenters had set up the hotel's huge wooden skeleton, the lumber for the sides

arrived by schooner from Virginia. Windows and doors and the frames for them were made at mills in Camden and shipped to Tuckerton by train, then "scowed" across the bay on flat barges towed by sailboats from Edge Cove. Upon arrival at the "landin'," everything was loaded into wide-tread wagons and hauled to the construction site by oxen. It was only a short distance, but horses could not have pulled that weight in the soft sand. The job was nearly all carpentry with some masonry. With no electrical, plumbing or heating work, it was not difficult to build a hotel of that size and have it ready for occupancy in six months.

Engle, in yet another clever move, chose to call his new hotel the Engleside, a play on words using his own name and the Scottish word "ingleside," which means fireside. It is a word rarely seen or heard now, but in nineteenth-century America it was familiar enough to readers of Robert Burns and Sir Walter Scott. Ingle derives from a Gaelic word, "aingeal," meaning light, fire or the sun. As a name for a hotel, the word had good connotations. To offer a guest a

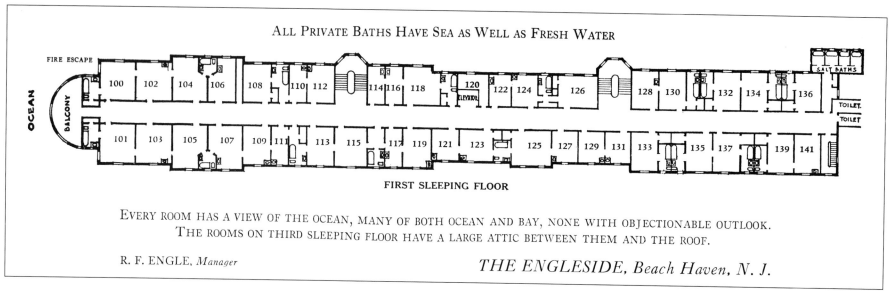

ALL PRIVATE BATHS HAVE SEA AS WELL AS FRESH WATER

FIRST SLEEPING FLOOR

EVERY ROOM HAS A VIEW OF THE OCEAN, MANY OF BOTH OCEAN AND BAY, NONE WITH OBJECTIONABLE OUTLOOK. THE ROOMS ON THIRD SLEEPING FLOOR HAVE A LARGE ATTIC BETWEEN THEM AND THE ROOF.

R. F. ENGLE, *Manager*

THE ENGLESIDE, Beach Haven, N. J.

seat at the ingleside, the best spot in the house, was a gesture of hospitality.

The Engleside was ready to welcome its first guests by June 6, 1876, the year of America's centennial, and despite all the activity in Philadelphia that summer, there was no slowing of business in Beach Haven. Engle had been right. The two big hotels facing each other across an empty lot of sand and bayberry could coexist.

They were, after all, much the same. In those early days there were no elevators, electric bells, artesian wells or bathrooms. Water used for cooking and drinking had to be brought over from the mainland in barrels to supplement rainwater, which was caught whenever possible. Ice was cut in the winter months out of huge, freshwater ponds in Holgate. It was kept packed in sawdust in well-insulated icehouses and normally lasted all summer.

The Engleside and the Parry House, representing the ultimate in seashore hotel construction in the 1870s, were similar in appearance. Each was built at right angles to the ocean to provide every room with a view, and each had a capacity of just over three hundred. There are no photographs of either of them from that first decade of the town's history, but an artist's highly stylized lithograph done for Woolman and Rose's *Atlas of the New Jersey Coast,* published in 1878, depicts them with similar glassed-in, rooftop observation rooms, multilevel balconies at their ocean ends, and broad piazzas around the lower level. The famous Engleside tower, five stories tall with an ornamental belfry atop its great conical roof, was added within a few years. The tower never contained anything but four levels of breezy porches full of wicker rockers, but it was a most charming place to be. On clear summer days in the 1890s it was not uncommon to see one hundred to one hundred fifty fore- and aft-

On a folding screen, Robert F. Engle's latest photographs were always displayed in the Engleside lobby, above. The hotel's promotional literature, facing page, included a view of three-masted schooners from the east-facing balconies and a sleeping floor plan to choose rooms.

rigged sailing craft off Long Beach Island and a continual parade of small coasters. The big tower's outward appearance, however, was what gave the building a grace and majesty beyond compare.

The Engleside was a success from the start as Engle used his religious and social connections to draw upon Philadelphia's upper-middle-class Quaker and Episcopal population. Then, and at

least for another generation, it was very much the tradition for families, with maids and nannies in tow, to spend the entire summer in a suite of rooms at the hotel. A month was considered a short stay. Engle courted families at his place. Before the railroad came to the island, the hotel maintained a "Baby Dairy" with three Guernsey cows to provide fresh milk for the children. The Engleside vegetable gardens were just to the

Earl C. Roper

In crisply starched uniforms, Engleside waitresses served elaborate dinners such as that shown on the menu from July 4, 1902, on the facing page.

south of the hotel, taking up the whole block between Amber and Coral streets from Beach Avenue to the edge of the bay meadows. Because of all the children, there was a special dining room for the infants and toddlers who, by the time they were five or six and had good manners, would graduate to the main dining room, where they could eat with their parents.

The Parry House burned in 1881, and for the next season the Engleside took up the slack until Parry's new place, eventually to be called the New Hotel Baldwin, was completed in 1883. The Baldwin was in a new location, two blocks south of the Engleside, and with two hundred rooms it was half again as big as the Engleside. A lot of money had been spent on it, and Parry was anxious to start getting it back.

The old friendly rivalry was gone. Parry began to compete for guests with the delightful novelty of a small locomotive that ran across the meadows from the steamboat wharf to the front door of the hotel. It was soon replaced by a horsecar on the same track, and when the railroad came to Beach Haven in 1886, the Baldwin laid tracks for a new route from the train station on Third Street to the hotel. These tracks ran in an easterly direction up Third Street to Atlantic, where they turned south.

The ride down Atlantic was purposely designed by the Baldwin owners to give newly arrived guests a view of the ocean as they rode in comfort to the hotel. The only problem was that the new route of the Baldwin horsecar passed directly in front of the Engleside tower. Robert Engle got a court injunction to stop it, claiming that it was a traffic hazard for his guests, who, he said, had to cross the tracks to get to the beach and might get run over or trampled by the horses. Engle won and the Baldwin Horsecar Line — which, in reprisal, refused to carry Engleside guests — was forced to tear up the

DINNER

EGG HARBOR OYSTERS, HALF SHELL
LITTLE NECK CLAMS
GREEN TURTLE SOUP, MADEIRA   CONSOMMÉ A LA MACÉDOINE
BAKED BLUE FISH, SAUCE PIQUANTE
POTATOES DUCHESSE   CELERY   OLIVES

BOILED HAM, GLACÉ

ROAST PRIME RIBS OF BEEF, AU JUS
ROAST CAPON, OYSTER FILLING
LONG ISLAND DUCKLING, APPLE SAUCE
SWEETBREAD PATTIES   PINEAPPLE CHARLOTTE

CHERRY SHERBET

CAULIFLOWER IN CREAM   STRING BEANS   RICE
PEAS   MASHED POTATOES   ONIONS
SAUTÉ OF SQUABS ON TOAST, WITH MUSHROOMS

TOMATO CHUTNEY   COLE SLAW   CELERY SAUCE
PEARL ONIONS   CHOW CHOW   GHERKINS
SWEET MIDGETS   INDIA RELISH

GREEN APPLE TART   CUSTARD PIE   CHARLOTTE RUSSE
MONTROSE PUDDING, FRUIT SAUCE
ORANGE JELLY   PEACH ICE CREAM
ANGEL CAKE   ASSORTED CAKES
WATERMELON   RASPBERRIES   APRICOTS
ORANGES   BANANAS
RAISINS   MIXED NUTS   SALTED ALMONDS
EDAM, ROQUEFORT OR AMERICAN CHEESE
BENT'S CRACKERS
COFFEE

FRIDAY
JULY 4TH, 1902

tracks and move them to Beach Avenue out of the view of the Engleside.

Winning this court case was just one more example of Engle's growing political influence that, by 1896, got him elected to the state Senate. In the summer of 1897, there were so many distinguished guests staying at both hotels that the Pennsylvania Railroad ran a Pullman car down every evening from Camden. It went back every weekday morning. The following year an oceanfront boardwalk was built to accommodate guests who exchanged visits with each other at the two big hotels.

Senator Engle, who loved beauty and comfort, lavished great care on his guests. He was very fond of flowers and had a long row of sweet peas planted along the fence which bordered the Engleside lawn. He always had bowls of fresh

flowers in the Engleside office and in the big, high-ceilinged sitting rooms. The hotel was now kept open until October 1 when the cool weather and first frost would finally make it safe for hay fever sufferers to return to the city.

The food at the Engleside was excellent and unbelievably abundant. The lightest meal of the day was breakfast, and typical choices in the 1880s and 1890s were fruit, clam broth, hot cereal, fish, steak, lamb chops, liver, creamed codfish and griddle cakes. There was a "fishermen's breakfast" every morning at six so that the men could get off to the docks at the Beach Haven Yacht Club. For those who did not wish to go out for the day, there were morning piano and violin concerts in the big, oceanfront assembly room with its gentle sea breezes. There was horseback riding on the beach, and there were numerous excursions. The little steamboat *Haven Belle* still ran for at least fifteen years after the coming of the railroad, with trips across the bay for picnics on Tuckerton's Lake Pohatcong and ice cream at Blackman's.

Robert B. Engle died in 1901, but he had a son, Robert F., ready to take over and continue all the fine traditions. That there were two Robert Engles who ran the Engleside Hotel for sixty-four years has been a source of confusion. They were father and son, but they were not senior and junior, and it helps to keep their middle names in alphabetical order. Robert Barclay Engle built the Engleside and ran it until his death. At that point his son, Robert Fry Engle, abandoned a career in photography and took over the hotel.

Robert Fry Engle was born at Mount Holly on February 4, 1868. Both father and son were enthusiastic sportsmen. Robert B. especially enjoyed gunning, and in his day the marshes were thick with shorebirds, but he never encouraged the shooting crowd to stay at his hotel, probably because so many of them were heavy drinkers:

Robert F. Engle (both)

Women's tennis whites brushed the oceanfront courts at the Engleside which had a windmill, seen at left of picture, to pump its well water. The Engles planned a constant round of activities for guests, from classical concerts to potato-on-a-spoon races, facing page.

They made the Baldwin their headquarters. Both Engles remained steadfastly dry all their lives, and the Engleside was what was known then as a "temperance house." Unlike the Baldwin, the Engleside was dry before, during and after Prohibition. Guests may have smuggled in bottles to drink in their rooms or procured them from bellhops, but the two Robert Engles did not approve and did not want to know about it. They advertised the wonderful drinking water.

Robert Fry Engle graduated from Friends Boarding School in West Town, Pennsylvania, in 1891 and went into the dry goods business in Philadelphia before taking up photography seriously. His interest in the subject led him all over the nation and into Mexico and Europe. He was a protégé of photographer Burton Holmes, the most famous travel lecturer of his day, and had Engle stayed with photography he may have become equally well-known. Fortunately for local historians, he took hundreds of photographs of Beach Haven around 1900, and virtually all of his glass negatives have been preserved.

Like his father before him, Robert F. was a great believer in health and exercise, emphasizing outdoor sports, physical activity and fun.

Guests of all ages took part in the track and field events held on the beach. Four or five times a summer on Sunday afternoons in the street in front of the Engleside there were games of "ladies softball." The men could participate, but only if they dressed in long skirts as a handicap. These were great social occasions in the years before World War I, and the Baldwin took them up, too.

Robert was a tennis enthusiast, and he built five dirt courts across Atlantic Avenue within a hundred yards of the ocean on the site of the present-day Engleside Inn. Until then, the

Engleside courts had been on Amber Street south of the hotel near Beach Avenue. Tennis stars loved to come to the Engleside, where they were accorded first-class treatment by Engle and where there was never any great shame in losing: The courts were very windy.

There were at least five tennis tournaments a summer at the Engleside. They weren't always very important, with names like the Central Jersey Championship and the Beach Haven Championship, but Engle loved the game, and many a professional stayed at his hotel at reduced rates just because Engle saw them as a drawing card. Bill Tilden, an ardent cup-chaser in those years,

started coming to Beach Haven as early as 1920, and people gathered along Atlantic Avenue to watch him play at the oceanside courts.

Tilden, tall, graceful and arrogant in his baggy sweater, usually strode onto the courts carrying several rackets in a deliberate attempt to cow his opponent. He really was, in his day, the greatest tennis player in the world, winning six consecutive U.S Tennis Championships, and then, in 1929, at the age of thirty-six, taking a seventh. The following year he won at Wimbledon for the third time. In his lifetime Tilden won seventy American and international tournaments. He never threw a tantrum, but he was always

dramatic. If a ball was miscalled in his favor, he would hit the next one out. He was tennis' first millionaire, but his lifestyle was so lavish that when he died in 1953 at the age of sixty, he was almost broke.

The Engleside Hotel was being modernized even before Robert B.'s death. An elevator had been installed in 1890, and gaslight and electric bells in 1895. Also in 1895, when the town drilled an artesian well and built a water tower, every floor on the Engleside had baths. They were located at the west end of the long hallways, and guests had the option of taking "hot seawater baths" if they wished. Every room had spring

beds and hair mattresses, and in some of the suites there was running water for toilets and sinks. By 1908, Beach Haven had a new acetylene streetlighting plant costing ten thousand dollars. When it was turned on, sixty-five street lamps illuminated the resort as it had never been lighted before. The Engleside itself had five hundred lights throughout the building, a far cry from the old days when guests had to light their way to bed with small kerosene lamps set up for them in the lobby by the porters.

Several years before there was a causeway bridge to the island, both hotels had motorized vehicles, and there were also horsecars. No one walked anywhere for a purpose, especially if transportation was available; it was considered déclassé to do so. The Engleside used horse-and-buggy transport until 1905, when Robert Engle purchased an Autocar bus with seats running lengthwise under a bright green canopy. It was the first motorized transport in Beach Haven.

The competition between the hotels now became a matter of pure showmanship. Each hotel employed a uniformed porter to ride to the station to meet the incoming trains. Each man was black, as big as any of today's linebackers and gifted with a magnificent voice.

Woody of the Baldwin, in a deep bass, called out, "Baldwin. Baldwin. Bald - win!" to the crowds debarking from the train. Miles Carey of the Engleside stole the show with his great baritone as he bellowed out, "EEEEENGLE - SIIIIDE," measuring and stretching out every syllable. In between his mighty delivery, the other fellow was able to get in at least seven or eight sharp blasts of "Baldwin. Baldwin. Bald-win!" They were enjoying the show every bit as much as the arriving guests. It was a performance that lasted nearly twenty seasons, and although frequently mentioned in letters, diaries and newspaper ac-

In 1905, uniformed porters helped passengers and carried baggage from the Engleside's Autocar bus, above, the first motorized transport on the island. A frequent guest, world tennis champion Bill Tilden, facing page, drew big crowds at the hotel's oceanfront courts.

counts of the day, it is now an all-but-forgotten piece of the town's social history.

The Philadelphia papers called the season of 1915 the best ever at Beach Haven. The Engleside, packed to its very doors, was the scene of continuous gaiety and jollity. There was something going on at every hour of the day. The fishing was marvelous. There were croquet and tennis tournaments, concerts and games, masquerade balls and the latest fad, moonlight swimming. Robert Engle had installed a diving float in the ocean in front of his hotel. Morning and afternoon dips in the ocean were a must for all young men, no matter how cold or how rough the surf

or bad the weather. It was a point of pride. The beaches were never closed.

The summer of 1916 was expected to be even better, and there was excitement in the air. Plans had been made to widen and lengthen the boardwalk after Labor Day. Two hundred shade trees had been planted all around town, and there was now express train service from Philadelphia to Beach Haven, shortening the travel time to just under two hours. The Engleside and Baldwin opened on schedule the third week of June and were already fully booked for the biggest weekend of the year, the Fourth of July, which would fall on a Tuesday. It would be a long, fun-filled holiday.

Earl C. Roper

On hot summer days, swimming solved the heat problem for hotel guests. Although each hotel employed a "bathing master," part of whose duties included lifeguarding, beaches were usually unprotected until the early 1920s. The Engleside's open air, oceanside balconies, facing page, were favorite gathering places.

On Saturday afternoon, the first of July, the Beach Haven express left Camden at 3:35 and arrived in Beach Haven at 5:30 — about an hour before dinner, but there were two sittings at the big hotels then, the latest at eight o'clock. It was the tradition in those years for young men to take a dip in the ocean immediately upon arrival, and Charles VanSant, age twenty-four, a Philadelphia stockbroker, always did this. He left his parents and two sisters in their rooms at the Engleside to unpack while he dashed for the bathhouses on the boardwalk to change into his bathing suit.

It had been hot all day and the sun was still high in a cloudless sky. The water temperature was a comfortable sixty-eight degrees, and there were still many bathers at this late hour. VanSant waded into the surf with a big Chesapeake retriever. The dog stayed in the deeper water with him for about ten minutes and returned to the beach. VanSant took a vigorous swim for a short distance and then, floating on his back just beyond the breakers in chest-deep water, he began calling to the dog by name, but the dog refused to get back in the water. The shouts continued.

No one paid particular attention to VanSant even when he let out one great shout different from all the rest and began a frantic splashing toward shore. They thought he was still calling the dog. Only when his cries became a series of shrieks for help did other bathers turn to the young man. As he approached them they saw that the water around him was filling with blood. Two had the presence of mind to seize his arms and drag him up on the beach.

When VanSant was out of the water, they saw to their horror that all of the flesh along the back of one leg from hip to knee had been ripped away right to the bone, and there was a large gouge out of the other leg. His blood was pumping out onto the sand. Three doctors were there within minutes, including the young man's own

father, Dr. E. I. VanSant of Philadelphia, and Dr. Herbert Willis, who was later to be mayor of Beach Haven. There was no room for a tourniquet and no compress could stop the bleeding. It was clearly the work of a big shark, but VanSant was never able to tell what had happened to him because he had already lapsed into unconsciousness.

He was taken to Robert Engle's office in the hotel, where plans were made to transport him to Toms River, but he had lost so much blood it was not possible. Charles Epting VanSant was dead in two hours, the victim of the first shark attack ever recorded in the eastern United States. There were some who, from the higher vantage point of the boardwalk, claimed to have seen a dorsal fin, but no one could be sure. It was presumed that only a predator the size of a great white could have done it, and it was also presumed that the presence of the dog and its scent in the water may have been what provoked it to attack a man, something hitherto unheard of.

The following week Robert Engle announced that Beach Haven would be protected by a heavy wire netting, extending three hundred feet into the sea and along the whole length of the beach. Cottagers had subscribed to a fund to buy and install the net, but the pilings which were put up by the local pound fishermen and from which the net hung lasted only until the first northeast storm.

The New Jersey Courier noted in August that Beach Haven bathers need not fear sharks. "The resort authorities have made the bathing beach one of the safest along the Atlantic coast by the installation of a net similar to those used at many of Europe's famous summer watering places. There is now a jetty with piling closely wedged, about 150 yards from the shore and stretching for 350 yards along the beach. From it they have hung a steel net similar to those used on torpedo destroyers."

Sharks had always been around, but suddenly everyone was extremely conscious of them. Other nets were put up at Wildwood, Bay Head, Spring Lake, Asbury Park, Allenhurst and Ocean Grove. When the Engleside closed in September, all agreed that the season of 1916 had been absolutely dreadful. It began with the shark attack and ended with a quarantine for polio in August during which no child was allowed into Beach Haven. As if this were not enough, there were several cases of typhoid and a threatened railroad strike which sent everyone home a full week before Labor Day. There was a war in Europe, and the National Guard had been sent to the Mexican border, but Robert Engle, ever the optimist, declared, "We will pull through."

Dancing was a popular activity at the Engleside, especially in the twenties and thirties. Al Myers, whose four-piece orchestra played at Philadelphia social functions all winter, entertained nightly in the Assembly Room. He played all the current favorites, often picking up the pace with a fast number, what was called in those days "snappy music." Cottagers and island residents were always welcome at the dances, but there was a bouncer at the door, and deportment and the dress code were rigidly enforced. Men wore white flannels, blue blazers and neckties.

There was a big porch on both sides of the Engleside, and the younger crowd drifted outside between the dances to sit on the railings and smoke. There were hydrangeas all around the porch. Passersby often took seats on the porch rockers to watch and listen to the goings-on, which usually ended around eleven. Al and his band would then go down to the Acme Hotel on Dock Road where they could have a drink and relax while they played requests.

Right next door to the Engleside on the Beach Avenue corner was Spackman's Seaside Pharmacy, famous for its long, marble counter and big ice cream sundaes. Everyone gathered there after the dances. The older crowd would head down the boardwalk to continue the evening's fun at the Baldwin, which always stayed open later and also served drinks, even during Prohibition. There was never any such carrying on at the Engleside. The doors were locked after midnight, and a watchman would let guests in.

Behind the Engleside stables between Amber and Coral streets were the hotel's vegetable gardens, above. At right, hotel staff rinse their hair in rainwater. Flowers bordered the broad south lawn, facing page, where a big purple martin house was the centerpiece.

The year 1926 was the fiftieth anniversary of the Engleside. To commemorate the event, hotel guests were met at the train station by an old Autocar that had been taken out of storage for the event. But the highlight of that day was a baby parade with 125 children ranging in age from eleven months to nine years. Lines formed at the Baldwin and stretched along the boardwalk to the Engleside, where awards were presented. Elizabeth Stratton, age two, was voted queen of Beach Haven, and the king was Frank Dease, age three. Drawn as they were from families staying at both hotels, there were children in the parade from all over the country. The two winners, however, were Beach Haven natives.

Nearly all of the waitresses at the Engleside came from Boston, where Engle advertised for help. Their good looks, humor and lilting Irish accents were as much a part of dining there as the clatter of heavy china and silver. Most of them were still in school, some in college, usually living at home with their parents in the winter months, so they welcomed this chance to get away, and many came back

In the winter of 1942-1943, Coast Guardsmen stationed on the island during World War II drilled in front of a shuttered Engleside Hotel which the borough had acquired for payment of back taxes.

year after year. They lived in a three-story building on the northeast corner of Beach Avenue and Amber Street, and they dated the local boys when they went out at night.

In the twenties, waitresses at the Engleside were paid $22.50 per month with a bonus of five dollars per month if they stayed on through the season. The hotel also paid their round-trip fare. The girls wore blue chambray with white collars and cuffs at breakfast and lunch, and white uniforms at dinner.

One of the things that long-ago beachgoers remember are the bathing habits of the Engleside's Irish chambermaids, who were a little older than the waitresses. There was not one of them who could swim, and their long-skirted bathing suits were at least a generation out of style. They would wade out into the water in a big chain, holding hands. Then they would bounce up and down in the waves and laugh and scream so loudly when they all fell

down that they attracted the attention of everyone on the beach. Their fun was infectious, and anyone who watched came away smiling and happy.

All of the enchantment of the Engleside started to unravel in the late thirties. Engle was heavily in debt, but he refused to change his rates. Weekly room and board with three unbelievably good meals a day could be had for about thirty-five dollars per person. Engle was in his seventies and didn't care about profits; he seemed to be simply winding down in his last years. He owed fifteen thousand dollars in taxes, and, in addition, the hotel needed repairs. Rescue efforts were attempted by friends who suggested that the hotel obtain a liquor license like the Baldwin, but Engle refused. He was as dry as his father had been. When there were no bidders at the tax sale, the property was taken over by the borough of Beach Haven.

The 1940 season was the last time the place was open. It was sixty-five years old and still operating pretty much the way hotels did in the 1890s. Only a few rooms had running water. The beds were of iron and painted white. All guests shared a bathroom at the end of the hall, but that's what everyone was used to. The hotel did not open for the 1941 season.

By the summer of 1942, the United States was at war and the island was swarming with military personnel in need of lodging. There was federal defense money available. The St. Rita Hotel, the Anchor Inn, Wida's, Noonan's Colonial Court and others on the island took advantage of the situation. Ironically, this is exactly what might have enabled Engle to keep the place going. The Army National Guard needed a place to stay and had to bivouac the soldiers in tents on the baseball field between Pearl and Ocean streets. They could not use the Engleside; in the year that it had been closed, the hotel had been repeatedly vandalized and plundered to the point of being unusable.

A wrecking company was called in to tear down the Engleside in August 1943, salvaging every stick of lumber for the war effort. First to go was the big round tower, taken apart piece by piece until the prime architectural symbol of Beach Haven's golden age was gone from the skyline. There was an emptiness. Standing all alone now, in the middle distance toward the bay, was the Engleside tower's strange post card companion since 1914, the town's old knock-kneed, Chinese coolie-hatted steel water tower.

To the young servicemen stationed at Beach Haven at the beginning of the war, performing their drills on the street in front of the hotel, the Engleside was a ruined barn of a place. To the locals, it was a veritable mother lode of copper, lead and brass. When the place was being dismantled, workmen soon discovered that each of the tall, graceful windows — and there were hun-

There were no bids when Beach Haven auctioned off the Engleside in 1943 for back taxes. By August, cottagers posed in front of the 69-year-old hotel as demolition began.

dreds of them — contained long, thin sash weights of solid lead, which, during the war, was nearly as valuable as gold. Before their bosses found out, many of them profited greatly.

Robert Fry Engle never knew that and may not have cared. He did not witness the demolition of the hotel that had been his father's and his for sixty-four years. He died in late December 1943 in Pennsylvania at the age of seventy-five, leaving behind a wealth of good memories and hundreds of priceless photographs from an era when he and Beach Haven were young.

Chapter 14

THE HOTEL BALDWIN: 1883-1960

The Parry House had been in operation for only eight seasons as Beach Haven's first major hotel when it caught fire in the early morning hours of August 12, 1881, and burned to the ground. The Tuckerton and Long Beach Land, Building and Improvement Association, with Charles T. Parry as its principal stockholder, needed to rebuild as soon as possible. The nearby Engleside Hotel, now five years old, had become a formidable rival.

Of primary consideration was the transport of building materials for the new hotel. There was a railroad on the mainland, but there would be none on the island for at least another three years. Everything had to be scowed across the bay from the rail terminus at Edge Cove. The paddlewheel steamboat *Barclay* and its successor, *Pohatcong,* made towing barges much simpler, but once they got to the landing at Dock Road there was the problem of getting the cargo to the construction site. A decade earlier, when the Parry House and Engleside had been built, it could be done with ox carts, but Parry's new hotel was to be built on a lot that was more than a quarter of a mile further south.

The land transport problem was solved by building a narrow-gauge railway from the steamboat wharf at Dock Road diagonally across the meadows to the edge of the building site on Pearl Street. The ties and tracks were laid on crossbeams bolted to solid cedar pilings sunk deep into the mud of the tide-washed marshes and continued over the sand up Pearl Street. A single horse could now pull a fully laden rail car along steel tracks in a fraction of the time needed by a team of oxen pulling the same load in soft sand.

On a lot between Pearl and Marine streets, the architectural firm of Wilson Brothers of Philadelphia patterned the new hotel after an English country house in an "L" shape, putting a big wing on the oceanside and giving the hotel half again the capacity of the former Parry House. The huge, four-story structure was embellished with six tall minarets, each roofed with a pointed, red cone, giving the place the look of a storybook castle. When it opened in June 1883, it was named the Arlington Inn.

There was a reason that what most people remember as the Hotel Baldwin was at first called the Arlington Inn. Wilson Brothers was the leading architectural firm in Philadelphia in the second half of the nineteenth century, and John Wilson's creations were famous. He had already designed a Hotel Baldwin in Bryn Mawr and did not consider it appropriate ever to use that name again. Certainly Baldwin would have been a suitable name for the Beach Haven hotel. Its principal financial backers manufactured locomotive engines and would soon change their corporate name to the Baldwin Locomotive Works, after Matthias Baldwin who had built the first successful such machine in Pennsylvania. But Arlington was the name suggested by Wilson, and they went along with it until something unexpected happened.

Wilson's original Hotel Baldwin in Bryn Mawr burned down in 1885. To his chagrin, he did not get the contract to redesign it, and the project went to his biggest competitor, the firm of Frank Furness. Only then did Wilson feel free to use the name Baldwin for his classic Beach Haven design, and still he hedged by calling it the "New Hotel Baldwin." That was always its official name, but over the years it simply became easier to drop the "New" and say Hotel Baldwin. The other Hotel Baldwin, the one rebuilt in Bryn

Minarets added gracefulness to the overwhelming size of the New Hotel Baldwin, located between Pearl and Marine streets. John Wilson, whose Philadelphia architectural firm designed the hotel, was an early resident in the booming resort and designed the nearby Holy Innocents Church and other summer cottages.

Mawr by the Furness firm, is now a part of the Baldwin School, a private academy for girls.

Parry had a small, specially made locomotive built at his plant in Pennsylvania. It was named the Mercer B. in honor of his twelve-year-old grandson, Mercer Baird. The train, consisting of one passenger car with a solid wooden roof and a flatcar for baggage, was named The Beach Haven Flyer. The little Mercer B. blew its first whistle in front of the Baldwin on June 9, 1884. The Beach Haven Flyer used the tracks and trestle of the earlier horsecar line that had been set up to transport lumber to build the hotel. Its route took it from Pearl Street to Bay Avenue and out across the meadows to the wharf where guests boarded the steamboat over to Edge Cove near Tuckerton, where the train was waiting for the run to Whiting and across the state to Camden. At Camden, passengers took the ferry to Philadelphia.

Baldwin guests rode in canopied rail cars in grand style across the meadows to their destination. The locomotive, however, could not take the salt air, and the coal that it used to keep its boilers fired up was an extravagance. It was all for show anyway, a promotional device for the new hotel, and within two seasons the little Mercer B. wound up in the mountains of Cuba hauling iron ore. The Beach Haven Flyer was replaced by slower, quieter and more reliable horse-drawn cars which actually had been in use all along.

Another factor ending the need for the showy locomotive and the steamboat it met at the bay was the arrival of the railroad in Beach Haven in 1886. A train trestle had been completed across Manahawkin Bay out to the island and tracks had been run south into Beach Haven. In 1887 the Baldwin Hotel began operation of a street rail-

In 1884, young Mercer Baird stood next to the little engine named for him that pulled a train from the steamboat wharf to the hotel. Two years later, the Baldwin horsecar line replaced the train.

way with two gaily decorated horsecars running from the train station up Third Street and down Beach Avenue to the hotel. At first, it ran down Atlantic Avenue, passing in front of the Engleside tower until a court injunction in favor of Robert Engle stopped that route.

The horsecar service continued to take Baldwin guests to the Beach Haven Yacht Club for fishing trips and other events until 1896 when Dock Road was widened. Years later, in 1912, when construction of the massive Ostendorff's Garage began at Pearl Street, visitors would puzzle over the trestle and inquire about "that long line of posts out in the meadows" and "what they had ever been built for." They can be seen — like archaeological evidence of an earlier time — in the first aerial photographs ever taken of the town.

Despite the competition for guests, the Baldwin and Engleside hotels drew entirely different crowds. The Engleside sought out the staid and very proper family-oriented Philadelphian. The Baldwin clientele may have been equally patrician, but they were sportier and a bit looser. They were looking for fun and excitement, and they were sure to find it at the Baldwin. There was always a bar there, and wine was served at all meals. There were a billiard room and two bowling alleys. Gunning enthusiasts converged on the Baldwin, and every other Saturday morning in the summer there was trapshooting sponsored by the Corinthian Yacht and Gun Club in the open fields south of the hotel.

The New Hotel Baldwin, as it was now being called, was in its fourth year when Charles Parry died in 1887. When his will was admitted to probate in July, it was learned that he had left an estate of one million dollars. His son, William, and his daughters, Adelaide and Ellie, each got two hundred thousand dollars and an annual allowance. His widow got thirty thousand dollars which at her death would go to the children and grandchildren. The executors named in the will were his son and his son-in-law James Baird, who had married Ellie. Little Mercer Baird, the boy for whom the locomotive had been named, was their son.

In 1909 Mercer Baird, now age thirty-seven, defeated William Butler for mayor of Beach Haven in spite of the fact that Butler had served in that office for nearly two decades. Baird was reelected to a second term but resigned in the fall of 1912; he was grooming himself to take over the Baldwin, and he had some grandiose plans. He loved parties and entertainment and had a large following willing to take advantage of his largesse. His father,

Lynn Photo

The L-shaped Baldwin, its servants quarters and kitchen at the rear and bathhouse in the upper right, had greater capacity than its rival, the Engleside. In the foreground is the Corinthian Yacht and Gun Club.

James Baird, was still nominally in charge but was ailing and would die in April 1914.

In 1912 the causeway bridge for automobiles was still under construction across Manahawkin Bay, and it was the biggest topic of the day since the railroad. All the hotels were preparing for the influx of new people, and Beach Haven already had automobiles that had been brought in on the train. Ostendorff's Garage was ready and waiting; it cost fifty cents a night to keep a car there. The Baldwin was refurnished and modernized throughout, with running water in most of the rooms. In fact, it had its own water supply from an artesian well six hundred feet deep and a water tower to provide pressure. It also had its own electrical lighting plant, a hydraulic elevator, and hot and cold seawater in all the baths. The hotel even had its own cold storage and ice plant.

The completion of the causeway was one of the major turning points in the history of Long Beach Island. Like the coming of the railroad to Beach Haven a generation earlier, it was eagerly

Grand seashore hotels like the Baldwin, here in the early 1920s, built waterside bathhouses for a practical reason: to keep lobbies and plumbing free from sand.

anticipated, especially by the owners of the big hotels, who saw it as an unlimited source of revenue. They were wrong about that.

The era of the big hotel was ending — not all at once, but certainly by the mid-1920s people were buying and building cottages of their own. But in 1912 no one expected this. There was excitement in the air, and nowhere was this more apparent than at the Baldwin. There was one last great fling, a party to end all parties that was to last nearly three years.

At the center of it all was Mercer Baird, the sullen little boy for whom the special locomotive had been named back in 1883. He had grown into a fat, self-indulgent adult with "great expectations." His father was ill and had loosened much of the control he once held over the Baldwin, leaving it more and more in Mercer's charge. Mercer loved parties and began to spend money. He could be charming, but much of that charm came from throwing money around, which was how he got to be mayor of Beach Haven. He bought the office just as if it were a toy he could discard, and when he won a second term, he announced he was tired and resigned. Now he was about to do the same thing with the Baldwin, the hotel his grandfather had built and his father had nurtured. It would be his new toy.

In 1914, the Grill Room was kept open from eight A.M. until midnight to provide à la carte service to the hungry automobile wayfarer and fisherman alike who might desire a "snack" at odd hours. There were tea dances every Monday, Wednesday and Friday afternoon at which cake, punch and tea were served. Dances were also held nightly at the Baldwin, and there were female instructors on hand every afternoon teaching large classes how to do the latest ragtime steps like the Grizzly Bear, the Turkey Trot and the Bunny Hug. Every Saturday dance had a theme. In August 1914, the Poverty Party was a

At 40, Mercer Baird decided to try politics. From 1910 to 1912, he was mayor of Beach Haven and was reelected but chose to resign.

great social success. Guests came dressed as derelicts, and Eleanor Blood of Philadelphia won first prize attired as a newsboy. The following week there was a Baby and Sailor Party and then a Desert Island Party. Something was going on at every hour of the day.

Bridge and whist parties filled hours not devoted to bathing, boating and fishing. Both the Engleside and Baldwin buses ran from morning to night, hauling guests to and from the Beach Haven Yacht Club Dock. Boats were constantly in demand, and guests who had never met before formed themselves into fishing parties; later in the day they would gather at the Baldwin Grill over German beer and thick pretzels from the Reading Terminal as if they had known each other all their lives.

The cottage colony came to the dances, and the only time the pace ever slowed at the Baldwin was on Sunday nights, when most of the staff had the evening off. Although there was no dancing, there was a buffet in the dining room followed by a concert of semiclassical music in the ballroom. Afterwards everyone took a stroll on the boardwalk and went to bed early.

All of the Baldwin bellhops and porters were black, and, unlike those at the Engleside, so were the waiters until about 1930. Most of them came from Maryland and returned home every September. Beach Haven had a sizable black servant population then. In every summer cottage in south Beach Haven there were maids, cooks, housemen and chauffeurs. When they went to the beach to swim, they all went to the "colored beach" between Amber and Coral streets. It was never officially segregated, but they all preferred to go there to be by themselves. The local lifeguards taught lifesaving techniques to the best swimmers among them, and they were pretty much on their own.

There was no other place for blacks to socialize except at Sunday evening church services at the Baldwin servants' dining room in back of the hotel on Marine Street. Once a summer there was a "colored folks ball" held in the servants' dining room, and hotel guests were invited to come and watch.

The Parry estate was rumored to total around two million dollars. It was, of course, nowhere near that, but the rumors did no harm to Mercer

In 1930, the Baldwin dug up its tennis courts, built one of the first miniature golf courses on the island and opened it to the public. At the top of the photograph are the municipal ballfield and the Little Egg Harbor Yacht Club.

Baird's credit rating. While in control of the Hotel Baldwin, he entertained lavishly. He also spent nearly one hundred thousand dollars in 1915 on improvements, including large open fireplaces in the Exchange and in the Casino, a steam heating plant, and radiators throughout the entire structure. He put in sun parlors, engines to run the electric light plant, a new barber shop, a new kitchen, and made many other changes. The Baldwin now had every modern convenience.

In August 1915 Baird gave a "Night in Paris" party with prizes for novel costumes. His Halloween, Thanksgiving, Christmas and New Year's parties that year required special train service from Philadelphia for all his invited guests. On Christmas Day he entertained seventy-five schoolchildren from the mainland and the island. Each child got ice cream and cake, candy and three or four presents from the many toy dolls, cradles, balls, and horses and wagons under the tree. For Baird, a child at heart, it was the last party he could really enjoy. He had been operating the hotel for about three years and had spent a fortune, not all of it real money. He was being dunned by contractors and vendors from all over the East. Daniel Frazier of Philadelphia, the owner of the Harvey Cedars Hotel, picked up the Baldwin and immediately resold it.

Each year there were doubts that the Baldwin would open by the end of June, and every year it opened on time but under a different manager. By now the war was on and poor train service made things even more difficult. In 1920 the hotel was bought and renovated extensively by a Mr. and Mrs. Warrington of Saint Petersburg, Florida. Running water was installed in many more of the rooms. There was the new black-and-white ballroom and, out on the verandas, the massive pillars were covered with new shingling. The Warringtons bought a new piano for the ballroom and were all ready for the 1920s, the decade that, in retrospect, would be the twilight for the big, old, seashore hotels. The Friday evening dances at the Baldwin were resumed because, except for special parties, it was the Engleside's Saturday dances that were always at the center of the resort's social life. Many cottagers attended both dances.

Baird, who had loved the high life, died in the middle of the Roaring Twenties. In a January 1924 issue of *The Philadelphia Inquirer*, his obituary read: "W. Mercer Baird, former mayor of Beach Haven and grandson of Charles Parry of the Baldwin Locomotive Works, died December 29, 1923, in Philadelphia. He was 52. Divorced since 1912, he had been living for the past seven years with a Mrs. Mary Frances Schlicutes of Akron Street in Philadlephia, to whom he left everything he had and made her executrix. To his only son, J. W. Mercer Baird, he left the sum of five dollars, stating, 'By his attitudes and actions he desires to free himself of all ties and relationships to me.' " It was a dreary ending for the self-indulgent Baird, who would have enjoyed the 1920s in Beach Haven.

Prohibition did nothing to stop the parties at the Baldwin. With the rum fleet only three to twelve miles offshore, there was first-class whiskey readily available, and this attracted people to Beach Haven. The Baldwin Grill simply became a café where booze was served in teacups, and an experienced manager from an Atlantic City nightclub was hired to run the operation. A raised dance floor was put in front of the old fireplace for shows with professional dancers, singers and impersonators. The revenue poured into "Club Baldwin."

Little Egg Harbor Yacht Club had had close ties to the Baldwin ever since the club organized there in the Assembly Room in 1912. Little Egg's annual Yachtsman's Ball, held in late August in the main ballroom, always had a theme to it, and one of the most memorable was in 1927, when everyone dressed in costumes limited to the colors black and white. More than a hundred attended, attired as judges, waiters, tramps, nuns and dominoes. There were black cats and white

Lynn Photo

By the mid-1930s, the Baldwin's porches had been enclosed. By the 1940s, the hotel was showing its age. Gone were the Baldwin's trademark minarets; when one toppled in a storm, the others were taken down.

cats, convicts in stripes and little French maids. One reveler came as a black-and-white can buoy and another as a bottle of Black and White Scotch. There was an elimination dance in which each couple showed off their trickiest steps until the judges had a winner. The twenties were fun at the Baldwin.

After it passed out of the hands of the Bairds, the hotel went through a succession of owners, winding up in the twenties and thirties being owned and managed by Erving and Jessie Townsend. In June 1931 they built a popular miniature golf course on Atlantic Avenue on the east side of the hotel where the tennis courts had been.

In 1940, Charles Yocum and his wife, Beryl, took over the hotel and developed a loyal following. With the Engleside closed in 1940, the Baldwin had no more competition in what was becoming a slow market. The era of the big hotel was ending, and the Baldwin, now past sixty, was beginning to show its age. One of the tall minarets had fallen in a storm, and the rest had to be removed and capped, greatly altering the outward appearance of the place. It was at about this time that the Yocums and their friends and guests began facetiously to refer to the old place as "Dracula's castle."

During the war years and immediately after, the place was livened up with the music of Freddy Herman, who had started out there in the late thirties. Herman, the Quaker City Maestro, played the violin while his group did sweet and hot numbers on the accordion, piano, bass viol and drums. They were on from nine to one every night, and brought about a resurgence of the old Baldwin spirit.

Then a costly fire swept through part of the hotel on the afternoon of August 9, 1947. It started in a second-floor room over the dining room in the east wing when nearly all of the 275 guests were at the beach. Ten local fire companies showed up, aided and directed by about fifty Philadelphia fire chiefs who, ironically, happened to be in Beach Haven for a convention that weekend. The fire started at two o'clock, and when it was over at four, the damage totaled seventy-five

The Baldwin caught fire on the windy night of September 24, 1960, and went up in the New Jersey coast's most spectacular blaze. With the era of the big shore hotels over, the Baldwin was not rebuilt. Holy Innocents Episcopal Church stands at the site today, a fitting ending since the hotel's original owners donated the money to build the original Holy Innocents church.

thousand dollars. Forty-four ocean-view rooms had to be closed, and the dining room that ran along the east side of the building was a ruin. After the fire, the hotel remained open with guests dining in the ballroom, but the Baldwin continued to lose money as costly repairs ate up profits, and finally, it was sold in December 1953 to pay taxes and liens.

Abe and Cora Korb of Perth Amboy, New Jersey, picked up the Hotel Baldwin, furnishings, equipment and whole two-acre block for forty-two thousand dollars. It had 155 usable rooms and seventy-five baths when the Korbs took over at the end of the summer season of 1954. The property was managed by Nate and Lena Levison, and the next year activities began to center around the bar, which they named "Dracula's Castle." It was very popular with the college crowd, which was drawn to the wild rock-and-roll of the Morizzo Brothers of Wyckoff, New Jersey. They packed them in for the next four summers, and people continued to stay at the hotel, but there were no special activities for guests. Those days were gone forever.

Near midnight on September 24, 1960, with the hotel deserted and the Levisons out to dinner, a blaze began again in the empty east wing, and this time, driven by gale-force winds off the sea, resulted in the most spectacular fire ever seen on the Jersey coast. Twenty fire companies showed up, some from as far south as Pleasantville and as far north as Toms River. The hotel was destroyed and again, like the Parry House nearly eighty years before, there was no loss of life. The building had been insured only for the amount of the mortgage. The vacant lot was sold the following spring to Holy Innocents Episcopal Church of Beach Haven, and it is now occupied by a church, parish house and brick-walled memorial garden.

No lives were lost in the Baldwin blaze that drew fire companies from as far north as Toms River and as far south as Pleasantville.

Chapter 15

THE MANAHAWKIN AND LONG BEACH RAILROAD

Not until 1872, the year after the twenty-nine-mile Tuckerton Railroad was built on the mainland, was there any alternative to sailing or rowing across the bay to get to Long Beach Island. Steamboat service was introduced that year, when the *Barclay*, a sidewheel paddleboat one hundred twenty feet long and twenty-four feet wide, was brought from Hainesport on the Rancocas Creek, down the Delaware, around Cape May and up the coast to Edge Cove on the meadows east of Tuckerton.

Edge Cove was deep enough for a boat landing, but it was nearly two miles east of Tuckerton. A spur track had been built to connect it to the main line of the Tuckerton Railroad at a point just north of town. At the cove there was a waiting shed and a long wooden dock where the rail passengers boarded the shallow-draft steamboat for the island. For the first two years of service their destination would be Bond's Long Beach House, until the Parry House at Beach Haven was ready for business in 1874.

The paddle-wheel steamboats, with their clanking engines and shrieking whistles, ran across the bay for only a dozen years, but they left their mark on island history. The *Barclay* was followed in a few years by the *Pohatcong*, which was named after a Lenape Indian chief and Tuckerton's lake. The propeller-driven *Haven Belle* was the last of these shallow-draft steamboats to Beach Haven. It ended direct service in 1886 and was relegated to excursions between Beach Haven and Atlantic City.

Edge Cove was a busy place in those years. Clams, oysters and fish were shipped from there by rail to the Philadelphia ferry in Camden. Trains were packed with people in the summer months, and there was always a small fleet of sailboats to compete for passengers and even race the steamboat to the island. There was another sturdy little steamboat called the *Mary*, which

Before the Manahawkin and Long Beach Railroad was formed, island visitors rode the Tuckerton Railroad, facing page, to Edge Cove near Tuckerton on the mainland, then boarded the steam-driven paddlewheeler *Pohatcong* for the trip across the bay to Beach Haven.

was not owned by the Tuckerton Railroad. It delivered passengers to the Columbia and St. Albans hotels at Sea Haven on nearby Tucker's Island, then enjoying its best years.

Visitors to the north end of Long Beach Island, mostly New Yorkers, sailed across the bay from the Pennsylvania Railroad station at Barnegat Pier on the south shore of Toms River. In the summer months there was a paddle-wheel steamer, the *Hesse*, running from Barnegat Pier to Seaside and to Barnegat City. Later the *Hesse* was replaced by another steamboat, the *Connetquoit*. When these boats landed at the wharf in Barnegat City, guests boarded a horsecar and were taken to Benjamin Archer's big Oceanic Hotel east of the light-

house on a beautiful stretch of beach at East Fourth Street.

The Tuckerton Railroad paralleled a horse-and-wagon road, today's U.S. Route 9, through West Creek, Manahawkin, Barnegat and Waretown. Then, making a wide, northwesterly curve through the pines, the single-track line ended in the town of Whiting in north-central Ocean County, where connections were made for the train that crossed the state between Camden and South Amboy.

The town was named for Nathan C. Whiting, who came from Connecticut in 1852, purchased an extensive tract of woodland in Manchester Township, erected a steam sawmill and manufactured lumber. Shipping it to New York and

The Pennsylvania Railroad built the Beach Haven depot, above. In the summertime, trains with private rail cars and as many as eight passenger cars rolled south on the island, facing page, top. A detail from a 1909 U.S. Coast & Geodetic Survey chart shows the tracks of the "P. and B.H.R.R." ending in Beach Haven, and across the bay, the old spur track to Edge Cove, from where steamboats would depart, can be seen.

Philadelphia by train, he prospered greatly and founded the settlement he called Whiting. Railroaders always referred to the town as "Whitings." It was more than likely a possessive because of Whiting's huge holdings in the area, much in the manner that the south end of Long Beach used to be called Holgate's or Bond's. At any rate, Whitings with an "s" is the way it was spelled on all railroad tickets and schedules and so it remained, at least for train people. Whiting, incidentally, disposed of all his properties in 1873

and returned in poor health to New Haven, where he died in 1883.

In the peak summer months of the 1870s and 1880s, as many as two hundred passengers a day were making the transfer at Whiting to ride the Tuckerton Railroad, and still the only way over to Long Beach Island was by steamboat and sailboat. This style of transportation was to continue for a dozen years, with the Tuckerton line bringing more and more people to the shore each season. But travel across the bay was difficult in foul

weather when schedules were upset. The steamboats shut down every autumn, and it was impossible to keep regular sailboat service in the winter. The logistics of supplying the burgeoning hotels was a problem, and so a railroad across the bay to the island — not a new idea — became a topic of consuming interest.

As early as 1871 a piece in *The New Jersey Courier* noted that the Manahawkin meadows would be the best location for a railroad bridge across the bay:

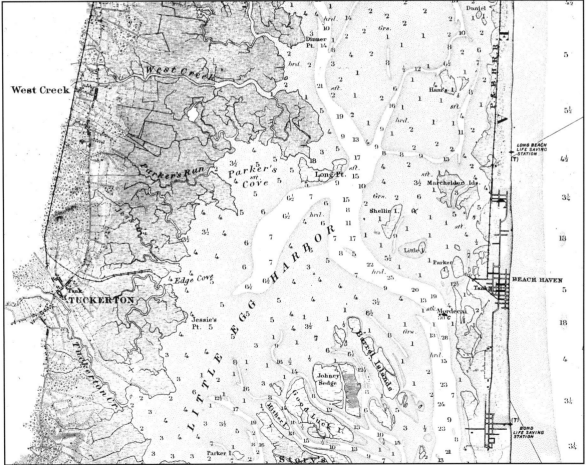

There is a big future in store for Manahawkin. The long, straight, wide street [Bay Avenue] commencing at Kinley's Hotel and stretching away down to the bay shore is not to end there, but will be continued over to Long Beach. Once on the beach, it will continue along the meadows, creeks etc. up to Barnegat Inlet and south to Bonds. [Beach Haven and Barnegat City did not yet exist.]

The big engine passed through here last Saturday afternoon, October 18, 1871, for the first time all the way through from Whitings to Tuckerton.

One of the principal promoters and backers of a scheme to get a railroad to Long Beach Island was William Hewitt, an entrepreneur who wanted to develop an area he named Waverly Beach, where there was no steamboat connection. He approached the operators of the Tuckerton Railroad, but they had neither the capital nor the inclination to undertake the job.

Hewitt then went to the operators of the giant Pennsylvania Railroad and, enticing them with investment front money of $43,800, got them to begin construction of a wooden trestle bridge in 1885. It crossed a mile of open water just east of Manahawkin and used the Bonnet islands as natural steppingstones the rest of the way across the bay. Then a drawbridge, which had to be cranked open by hand, was built over the boat channel between Cedar Bonnet Island and the present borough of Ship Bottom.

Meanwhile, ties, rails and gravel were brought across the bay by raft, and a rail line from Barnegat City to Beach Haven was begun. This new route up and down the island would be called the Manahawkin and Long Beach Railroad, and the Pennsylvania contracted to have the Tuckerton Railroad run it at thirty cents a mile. The Pennsylvania Railroad would still own it, provide extra cars and engines in the summer months, and pay all the maintenance costs.

The railroad line across the bay was completed in early June 1886, and the first engine reached Barnegat City on the twenty-eighth of that month. The completion of the line into Beach Haven was delayed because of a big salt pond and a creek on the route in Waverly Beach at Fourteenth Street in today's North Beach Haven. A wooden bridge was built to cross it, and on July 24, the first engine and cars of the Manahawkin and Long Beach Railroad rolled into Beach Haven.

The delay in completing the line into Beach Haven does not mean that the terrain was any better elsewhere on the island. In the years the railroad ran north of Ship Bottom, there were at least fourteen trestle bridges over glades and low places on the nine-mile stretch to Barnegat City. These cuts were natural and allowed ocean high tides to run freely across the island into Barnegat Bay. Consequently, there was seldom any erosion during storm tides. There were, however, several times when one or more of these small bridges washed away and had to be rebuilt.

℘ ℅

On that long-ago summer morning when the first engine of the Long Beach Railroad chuffed triumphantly into Beach Haven, the hotels emptied to celebrate the occasion. The scream of the engine's whistle, its clanging bell and hissing clouds of steam answered by the cheering crowds ushered in a new era of swift, comfortable trips to the seashore. But there was another effect. July 24, 1886 marked the beginning of a change in the physical appearance of the island.

Long Beach Island was still a wild and beautifully desolate stretch of bogs, bushes and sand dunes. Outside of Beach Haven, which was scarcely a dozen years old, and Barnegat City, not much older than that, there were no streets or roads anywhere. These two resorts at opposite

In Beach Haven, trains turned around on Y-shaped tracks in the broad bayside meadows, above. Although the parent Pennsylvania Railroad built station houses in Barnegat Light and Beach Haven, some small communities like the one at Beach Haven Terrace built their own, facing page, top. Otherwise, the desolate stops on the island line were marked by spare waiting sheds of galvanized iron with red tin roofs.

ends of the island had horsecar service to their major hotels, and graded, but not-yet-graveled streets, and narrow, wooden boardwalks. Some of the Life Saving stations in the sixteen miles between the two resorts were connected by twisting, rutted sand trails, but there was no road the length of the island but the railroad, and so it would remain until the building of the automobile bridge twenty-eight years later, in 1914.

Besides bringing in more people, the railroad changed the island by bringing in gravel for land fill — tons and tons of it from the mainland, where it was loaded by hand into gondola cars. Streets in Beach Haven were laid by pouring the gravel over a bed of eelgrass and salt hay. In time the roads became packed solid by the passage of heavy wagons. Bogs, ponds and creeks were filled in.

And ironically, Beach Haven, which billed itself as the "only practical seashore resort in America" because its ocean winds and distance from the mainland kept it free of pollen, suddenly found itself polluted almost overnight with ragweed and goldenrod. The seeds and plants had been carried in the carloads of gravel from the mainland, and within a decade the borough council was offering a bounty of two cents a pound to eradicate the troublesome plants, now growing in every street. It took years to get them under control.

The train made more money hauling freight than it ever did carrying passengers, and every gondola full of orange gravel helped to offset losses. Low areas were filled in for future development and to get rid of mosquitoes. The process of dumping and spreading was easier than loading the gondolas on the mainland, where workers dug the fill with long-handled shovels from Cox's gravel pits near West Creek.

Carload after carload of gravel had to be dumped in the train's roadbed, which at sea level was subject to tidal washout. The Long Beach

Railroad was fortunate to have as its parent the powerful and affluent Pennsylvania Railroad. The tiny Tuckerton Railroad, which served only as manager, could never have afforded to maintain the bridges and track. It was a common sight during storm tides, especially in the Manahawkin meadows, to see a brakeman out on the cowcatcher feeling for the rails and ties with a pole as the train inched through deep water toward the bridge.

In the early years, cattle roamed the north end of the island and sometimes stood on the track and refused to budge. There were also frequent brush fires caused by sparks when the train burned wood with soft coal. It was all part of the adventure of traveling to a beautiful, unspoiled part of the coast.

The north end of the island, with its tiny sea grass industry and its single fishery, did not have enough cargo to make freight service profitable. Worse yet was the steady decline in the number of passengers. The big hotels near the lighthouse had seen better times in the old steamboat years than they did after the railroad came. One reason was the severe beach erosion endangering the resort. Another was the fact that Barnegat City was a stronghold of the temperance movement, making it less fun for the sporting crowd who enjoyed the excitement of the Hotel Baldwin, the clubs and the whole social tone of Beach Haven. Finally, there was tragedy. Several cases of typhoid fever, one of which was fatal, struck one of the Barnegat City hotels around 1905, ruining business that season. The automobile road to Barnegat City was completed in June 1920; three years later, the Long Beach Railroad ceased all operations on the north end of the island.

Passengers coming to the island on the modern railroad stopped horse-and-cart traffic, above, as the train approached Manahawkin Bay and headed toward the trestle. The railroad bridge tender rowed to work and closed the trestle when the train approached to keep the schedule running smoothly, left. Potential summer cottagers were lured to Brant Beach by canny developer Harold McLaughlin who built an attractive waiting station at his new resort, facing page, top.

Beach Haven continued to thrive as a resort, but it relied on the railroad less and less. The growing number of private automobiles and a new bus company stole passengers from the rail line while a trucking firm started taking away the freight and fish business. Passenger service on the railroad, which peaked in 1920, was all over in one short decade. It was freight service only after 1930 and just one trip a day.

By then, the railroad bridge across the bay had gone so long without repairs that it was actually too dangerous for passenger traffic. On November 17, 1935, a powerful northeast storm destroyed more than a mile of trestle just east of Manahawkin and washed the wreckage eight hundred feet south onto the causeway bridge, where cars had to drive around it. The last freight train had left the island the night before.

The Pennsylvania Railroad had lost more than a million dollars in the forty-nine years of its operation on Long Beach Island. Today there are only a few structures left to show that a railroad had ever been here. The three station houses, the only ones ever built, are still standing. One, at Third Street in Beach Haven, and another, at Eleventh Street in Barnegat Light, were both built by the Pennsylvania Railroad and later converted to private dwellings. The third one, now a residence and retail shop in Brant Beach, was built by a real estate firm to encourage development in the area. At all the rest of the stops on the line, train passengers had to make do with wooden waiting sheds. Painted gray with red tin roofs, the sheds stood on the west side of the track and had no doors; in winter, people waiting for the train were exposed to the fierce Atlantic winds. The Harvey Cedars waiting shed was a bit more elaborate, resembling a small Cape Cod. After the rail service died, it was eventually moved and is now the first floor of a private home.

Just like adults, children dressed up when they rode the train between Beach Haven and Philadelphia, above. When the train approached the Manahawkin meadows just before crossing the bay to the island, passengers slammed windows shut to keep out the swarms of gnats, mosquitoes and greenhead flies that appeared at various times of the year, facing page, top. Island rail travel came to an end in 1935 when a November northeaster washed out a mile of track, the longest span of the trestle over Manahawkin Bay.

There is one other legacy from the days of the railroad on Long Beach Island: the series of wide areas in the boulevard every mile or so up the island as far as Surf City. Now used as parking areas for local businesses, they were not, as has often been supposed, the sites of former stations. They were shunt tracks for donkey engines and hand cars when scheduled trains were coming through on the single track of the main line. The actual stations were often several blocks away. When Long Beach Boulevard was built on the island in 1914, it had to go around the shunt tracks. When all the tracks on the island were removed in 1936 and the boulevard straightened, the bypasses were left in place.

Chapter 16

THE PEAHALA GUNNING CLUB

Peahala Park, a mile south of Brant Beach, is today a small summer community of some four hundred houses and a half-dozen businesses. A section of Long Beach Township, it starts at Eighty-eighth Street, and within its southern borders at Ninety-sixth Street are two movie theaters and a supermarket. These eight blocks, so fully developed now, were once a part of the hunting preserve of the Peahala Gunning Club, one of nearly a dozen private gunning clubs that flourished on the island for twenty-eight years between the coming of the railroad in 1886 and the building of the automobile bridge in 1914.

The club was started by a group of west Jersey sportsmen from Burlington and Mount Holly who for many years had been the guests of Captain Thomas Jones, the owner of an unpretentious boarding hotel for fishermen and hunters on the site. In the years after the Civil War, this narrow part of the island was known simply as "Tommie Jones'," just as Holgate five miles to the south was always called "Bond's" after the innkeeper and genial host. Tommie Jones' old, barnlike hotel was located at what is today the intersection of Eighty-ninth Street and Beach Avenue.

In 1882 the men from Burlington County bought Jones' building and open land, including Daniel and High islands in the bay, and formed the Peahala Gunning Club, limited to a membership of fifteen. In newspaper interviews in 1903 and again in 1920, club members claimed that the word "Peahala" came from an Indian word for "some kind of waterfowl." There is no proof of this etymology anywhere other than their belief that it was true.

To be invited to the exclusive Peahala Club in the 1880s and 1890s was a mark of social distinction. When the Long Beach Railroad came to the island in 1886, the Pennsylvania Railroad, its

N.R. Ewan (both)

In 1900, Peahala Gunning Club members posed on their shady, oceanfront porch, above. At right is the former clubhouse, built around 1860 as Captain Tommie Jones' boardinghouse. On the facing page, the railroad tracks and waiting shed, located at today's 90th Street, are seen from the club's dock on the bay.

parent, made the Peahala Club a scheduled stop on its way to Beach Haven and built a waiting shed there. It would be located today on the west side of Long Beach Boulevard at Ninetieth Street.

Jones' old place served as a clubhouse for ten years until a new one was built a few hundred feet south on a high dune commanding a splendid view. It was a tall, three-story building of white clapboard with green trim. Big double-windowed dormers jutted from its hipped roof. There were nine bedrooms filled with bunk beds on the second and third floors. The club reception room, with its bar, fireplace, soft leather chairs and enormous pipe organ, was imposing. The dining room and the solarium were on the oceanside, and from the upper decks the island

Bill Kane

The clubhouse was destroyed in 1940 to make room for a real estate development. On a calm night in early June, firefighters stood by as the building was set ablaze.

endless games of poker and bridge, and there were cookouts and beach fires every night..

Beach parties were a favorite recreation of the Peahala Club people because it was the best way to escape the mosquitoes. Starting in the early afternoon, the men would dig a big hole in the sand and fill it with wood from wrecks, and when they had a pit of red coals, in would go wheelbarrow loads of seaweed to steam clams, potatoes and corn. Chicken was fried in big, long-handled iron skillets. There were games of quoits and leapfrog and king-of-the mountain with a lot of rolling down the sand dunes. There were foot races at low tide, once as far as the tall pavilion at Surf City and back — all before eating, of course. Afterwards, there were toasted marshmallows and singing accompanied by banjoes, which everyone knew how to play. There is a note in the club register for August 16, 1922: "Rain again. Couldn't cook on the beach. Ate in the dining room. Pfui."

After 1930 the club fell into disuse as more and more families were buying and building summer cottages of their own. Although it remained undeveloped, the land belonging to the club had long since been sold. The building on its high dune stood all alone for many years, filled with memories.

When plans for a real estate development were made, permission was obtained from the township to burn rather than wreck the building. With firemen standing by on the windless night of June 7, 1940, it was set afire. It went straight up in a crackling red blaze, the club's last bonfire. The charred timbers and foundation stones were buried in a bog. The dunes were leveled, and when the planned grid of streets had been graded and graveled, Sand Dune Lane (Ninetieth Street) and Beach Avenue intersected at the former site of the proud old Peahala Club.

rolled out north and south in endless sand dunes and low forests of beach plum and bayberry. In the distance rose the big hotels of Beach Haven.

Snowden, Rogers, Lippincott, Woolman, Budd, Fenimore — the Peahala Club's membership and guest list has the ring of old West Jersey's farmer-merchant class. Canny and shrewd, they became successful in banking, manufacturing and the law, but never for one moment did they forget how to relax and have fun. The Peahala Club register, kept over a forty-year period, has survived and records their good

times on an island that, but for the mosquitoes, must have been a paradise.

In the register are observations on the weather, comments on the food, details of shipwrecks, and tallies of fish caught and game shot. There are many cartoons, and mention is made of practical jokes pulled and of plays and skits performed. After 1914, when women became more active in the club, Peahala came to resemble an adult summer camp where families who had been socially connected for generations went to have fun. Children stayed at home. There were

Chapter 17

THE CORINTHIAN YACHT AND GUN CLUB

For eighty years there stood in Beach Haven, on the northwest corner of Marine Street at Beach Avenue, a handsome house in the bungalow style so popular at the turn of the century. It had characteristically broad verandas on two sides and a long, gently sloping, dormered roof from the peak of which jutted a remarkably thick chimney.

The front door, shaded by the wide roof, opened into a big living room with a twelve-foot ceiling. Every visitor's eye was drawn immediately to the north wall of the room. There, at about the center of the house, stood the most unusual open fireplace ever seen on Long Beach Island. From its enormous hearth of poured black concrete there rose, to a height of fully seven feet, a mantle of white mortar, all three sides of which, right up to the ceiling, were harmoniously decorated with artifacts reminiscent of early New Jersey marshland gunning and the male camaraderie associated with the sport. During construction, these items had been pressed into the wet mortar, and when it hardened they remained fixed. Prominently displayed in the mortar over the mantelpiece were half models of a square-

rigged ship and several different kinds of duck, goose and shorebird decoys, all beautifully carved and painted. Crisscrossed among them were old fowling pieces, cavalry sabers and eel spears. Filling in the spaces between these larger pieces were scores of black and yellow clay pigeons, little tobacco pipes of white clay, red and green shotgun shells, poker chips, playing cards fanned out in a royal flush, silver dollars and whiskey flasks, oyster shells, an alarm clock and hundreds of brass cartridges. It was a perfect example of found art, and the effect was overwhelming.

The building with this remarkable fireplace as its centerpiece was built in 1904 as winter quarters for the Beach Haven Gun Club, founded the previous year by John S. Dickerson of Philadelphia. The club's activities normally centered around the nearby Hotel Baldwin, whose owner, James Baird, was himself a club member, but the Baldwin closed in late September and did not open until June. At the new clubhouse, the fireplace was used for both heating and cooking in the bitter cold months of the gunning season.

In 1907 the club changed its name to the Corinthian Yacht and Gun Club of Beach Ha-

ven, New Jersey, to provide, they said, "for the needs of the growing number of amateur boatmen whose interests were not being well served by the better-established Beach Haven Yacht Club." The latter's membership was composed entirely of professional boat captains and their clients. By bringing the amateur boating crowd into the gun club, the original members were not only adding people who shared the same social background, they were also adding money to their coffers.

This deliberate broadening of the membership enabled the club to immediately add a second floor and to put in cement walks, tennis courts and acetylene lighting. A new, ten thousand-dollar plant had just been built in Beach Haven, and already there were sixty-five streetlights around town, but only a handful of houses could afford the lighting. Since the Corinthian was not very close to the water, members built a narrow boardwalk over the sand and across the meadows to their boat moorings in a big cove at nearby Pearl Street. At the cove, they had a caretaker with a gasoline motor launch to take them to their boat moorings. It was a three-block walk, but it was

still closer than keeping their boats at the Beach Haven Yacht Club on Dock Road.

The name Corinthian was chosen for its noble connotations. Besides describing the highest order of classical architecture, the name also referred to Corinth, a seaport that had been the wealthiest and most powerful city in ancient Greece. The membership adopted a burgee with a navy-blue cross on a white field and a blue rock or clay pigeon in the upper-left quadrant near the hoist. The blue rock had been the symbol on the burgee of the former Beach Haven Gun Club. As a yacht club, the Corinthian was very small, and it could hardly compete with the Beach Haven Yacht Club, ex-

The Corinthian Yacht and Gun Club's unique fireplace, a mosaic of found art, dominated the main social room. The building was enlarged in 1907 as the Beach Haven Gun Club became the Corinthian, facing page, top. On Saturday mornings in July and August, trap shooting was held in the fields south of the clubhouse and proved to be very popular with women.

cept, perhaps, in social prominence. Unabashedly aristocratic in tone, the Corinthian had a membership of thirty, all summer residents, mostly cottagers.

There was a ladies auxiliary, the first of its kind on Long Beach Island, and among the women was many a father's daughter who had grown up with guns and was skilled enough to join the men at traps. They went bird hunting with them and took turns shooting at targets on the beach. Most of them, however, seized upon the opportunity to use the clubhouse for bridge parties, tennis and teas. This would not have happened at the more democratic but also very male-oriented Beach Haven Yacht Club, where women seldom felt welcome.

Gunning, shooting and social activities were the top priority of the Corinthian. Every other Saturday morning in July and August there were trap shooting contests in an empty lot near the clubhouse. Gentlemen in summer hunting togs and neckties pointed their long-barreled Winchesters and Parkers as the blue rock skimmed across the sky. A staccato "pip, pip, pip" echoed off the shingled towers of the Baldwin, and the haze of black powder smoke drifted over the sand hills of south Beach Haven.

These were the golden years of sport gunning on Long Beach Island, before the coming of the automobile and the passage of the Federal Migratory Bird Act of 1914, which outlawed the thoughtless extermination of shorebirds and the shooting of ducks in the spring migrations. Birds were shot simply for target practice, just as porpoises were killed by men firing high-powered rifles from the beach while admiring crowds looked on.

But the members of the Corinthian Gun Club were above such behavior. Like the Peahala Club, the Corinthian was a forerunner of Ducks Unlimited in practicing conservation. But the club could not survive in a restrictive climate of laws that now limited the gunning season to a fraction of its former length, nor could members cope with the steady pace of real estate development that was making trapshooting dangerous in Beach Haven.

In 1911 the Baldwin built an annex with winter accommodations for gunners. The hotel was far more comfortable in freezing weather, and once the original purpose of the Corinthian had been subverted, the club folded. It was also too far from its boat moorings on the bay to be a successful yacht club; furthermore, Frederick Ostendorff was building a huge garage on Pearl Street, right on the route of the club's boardwalk. The clubhouse was sold to the Fraternal Order of the Moose, which held it until the middle twenties, when it became a private dwelling. Each successive owner preserved the fireplace.

The Corinthian, however, paved the way for the founding of the Little Egg Harbor Yacht Club, to which every member at once transferred. At the new club's initial meeting at the Baldwin in 1912, Charles Beck, who had been president of the Corinthian, was elected commodore. One of the first items of business after setting up a racing schedule for the season was the formation of

The ladies auxiliary at the Corinthian used the clubhouse for teas, bridge parties and tennis, a tradition carried over into the Little Egg Harbor Yacht Club which absorbed the Corinthian's membership in 1912.

a ladies auxiliary, an obvious legacy of the Corinthian. Their first meeting was at the Beck home, "the Farm" on Liberty Avenue. A clubhouse for the new yacht club in the meadows between Berkeley Avenue and Ocean Street and just opposite Mordecai Island would not be built until 1916, but when it was, all the old social traditions of the Corinthian were continued.

In later years the old Corinthian clubhouse was jointly owned by four families, who put it up for sale in 1984. Because it stood on two buildable lots, it was bought by a contractor as an in-

vestment. When it was learned that the house and its unique fireplace would be torn down, younger members of the families selling the building staged a party and pried everything of value out of the mantle. Then one bright, Saturday morning in April, almost eighty years to the day that the Corinthian had been built, a big diesel cat chewed the old clubhouse to pieces. It had been perfectly sound. The rubble of splintered wood and the brick and cement of that impressive fireplace were hauled off to a mainland landfill. Two duplexes stand on the property today.

Chapter 18

THE AUTOMOBILE AND "THE LURE OF LONG BEACH"

Automobiles arrived on the island several years before there was a way to drive them across the bay: They were brought in by train on flatcars. Model T's putted along the beach at low tide among the scattered Life Saving stations, and big Packards crunched the gravel in the wide streets of Beach Haven. But it was all for sport and play. There was nowhere to go but back home on the train in September.

The only road north out of Beach Haven was a two-mile-long cart path, an extension of Beach Avenue. It skirted deep bogs above Fifth Street and then crossed a wooden bridge over a sluggish creek at the Hotel Waverly on East Thirteenth Street before finally ending at U.S. Life Saving Station #21 at Beach Haven Terrace. South of town, below the Corinthian Yacht and Gun Club and the Hotel Baldwin at Marine Street, there was another narrow sand road which ran for two miles past the Beck Farm to Bond's Life Saving Station. From there it continued another three miles down Tucker's Beach to the little wooden bridge across the slough over to Sea Haven on Tucker's Island.

On the mainland the situation was a little better; at least most of the towns were connected by graveled roads. From out of Camden, Moorestown and Mount Holly, daring motorists in goggles and dusters braved the undulating old carriage and toll roads through the pines to the little village of Manahawkin. There they would park their machines at a garage near the railroad station and take the train to Beach Haven. Sailing connections were always available for those who did not wish to take or wait for the train.

Credit for the idea of building an automobile bridge across Manahawkin Bay and the driving force to bring it to reality goes to a man with an unusual first name, Maja Leon Berry, a prominent lawyer and judge on the Ocean County bench. It was while riding in a Pullman car, as the train slowly crossed the bay, that the idea occurred to him. Berry was with his good friend, Charles Beck of the Beck Engraving Company of Philadelphia and the Beck Farm. The two men discussed the idea of building an automobile causeway parallel to the railroad trestle. With no schedules and no waiting, it would be faster than the train. That was the beginning. The year was 1912.

Within a month they had called a meeting of potential investors at the Hotel Baldwin, and Beck launched the undertaking with a personal check for five hundred dollars. The Long Beach Turnpike Company was formed with Beck as president, Ezra Parker as vice president, and W. Mercer Baird, owner of the Baldwin, treasurer.

Despite the lack of roads, it was clearly evident that the automobile was on its way. There was excitement in the air. Frederick Ostendorff, a longtime resident of Beach Haven and former Philadelphia restaurateur, began to build the biggest garage on the coast between Asbury Park and Atlantic City, a massive brick structure with a capacity for the storage of two hundred automobiles. With hydraulic lifts and every modern service, Ostendorff's Garage, at the corner of Bay Avenue and Pearl Street, was the wonder of its day.

Judge Berry continued to work behind the scenes. With his political connections, he was able to get state, county and municipal authorities to work together to build a main road on the island and the access roads to the bridge. It was a major undertaking. The train towed long lines of gondola cars filled with gravel from the pits on the mainland, and laborers spread and graded it. These local men and their families lived in houseboats on the meadows and followed the work down the island for nearly three years until it was finished. The narrow, two-lane highway ran from Ship Bottom to Beach Haven just east of the railroad tracks and cost sixty-three thousand dollars. Building a road from Ship Bottom to Barnegat City would not begin until 1920.

The causeway over the Manahawkin meadows and across five thousand feet of open water to the first of the Bonnet Islands was built parallel to the wooden railroad trestle, just eight hundred feet south of it. Where they crossed over the channel between Cedar Bonnet Island and Ship Bottom, both bridges were side by side. It took all of eighteen months, but everything was ready for opening day on June 20, 1914.

It was a pleasant Saturday morning when the 103 beribboned and decorated motor vehicles which had been congregating since dawn in

More than a hundred cars putted across the new causeway in June 1914, top, but drivers headed for the opening day celebration in Beach Haven didn't pay a toll as they would in later years for the drawbridge, above. In an earlier era, the beach at low tide, facing page, was the island's only real north-south road. Horses still had their purpose as workers spread and graded gravel carried from the mainland in gondola cars for new roads and real estate development as the wetlands were filled.

Manahawkin began their stately procession across the new causeway. The bay was filled with small boats. Horns and claxons blew. Whistles tooted and engines backfired. At the entrance to the island, by a huge triangular flower bed and a big American flag, the driver of each car was handed a slim, blue book as a souvenir of the day. It was the 1914 edition of *The Lure of Long Beach* by George B. Somerville, the first written history of the island.

Every house on the parade route was hung with flags, flowers and bunting as the long line of cars proceeded south to Spray Beach and Beach Haven for the greatest celebration since the arrival of the railroad twenty-eight years earlier.

As the hundred-plus cars proceeded down the island, a great fleet of small boats sailed across the bay. Everyone would converge on the Engleside Hotel for speeches by Augustus Keil, president of the Long Beach Board of Trade, Governor James F. Fielder and state Senator Thomas Mathis, who led the parade. Dignitaries and guests in wicker chairs lined the long porch while the Long Beach Military Band played Sousa

marches. At two o'clock, there was a luncheon for two hundred people in the hotel dining room.

After lunch, the crowd moved to a baseball game at the newly graveled diamond on the vacant lots between Fifth and Seventh streets east of Beach Avenue and just south of the new school building. Automobiles formed a huge semicircle in the outfield, and drivers and passengers watched the game from there and from the beachfront.

The game was played between the Beach Haven and Tuckerton teams, with the home team losing, 13-2. Before it was over, the crowd was thrilled by the arrival of a hydro-aeroplane flown from Atlantic City by a Chicago man named E.L. Jaquith, who performed aerial acrobatics over the field and beach and then landed in the bay. At 7:30, before the night ended in a spectacular display of fireworks, there was a testimonial dinner at the Hotel Baldwin during which prizes were

awarded for the best-decorated car and cottage. First prize for the best-decorated car went to Frederick Ostendorff of the cavernous Ostendorff's Garage, with the best-decorated house award won by former borough mayor Joseph Shonders.

Each dinner guest also received a copy of *The Lure of Long Beach*, only eighty pages long and with some thirty photographs. Little is known about the book's author, George B. Somerville,

In Beach Haven Terrace, the Wilson family was among the motorists celebrating the new causeway's opening and posed at Maryland Avenue while en route to Beach Haven, where state and local dignitaries presided over a gathering at a bunting-bedecked Engleside Hotel, facing page.

except that he was introduced to knowledgeable old-timers and was given access to records and documents through Charles Beck, whose engraving company printed the book. Beck's son-in-law, journalist Edgar Smiley Nash, actually provided most of the material from his own writing, and the Board of Trade published *The Lure*.

After opening day, the book sold for fifty cents until the first edition ran out. It was not reprinted, and the rights to the book fell into Beck's hands, probably because his son-in-law may have had more to do with the writing of the book than

did Somerville. Whole passages from it can be traced directly to Nash's short-lived 1907 newspaper, *The Breeze*.

Twenty years later, Charles Beck asked his grandson, Charles Edgar Nash, to revise and update the Somerville book, still the property of the Board of Trade. Nash was in his early thirties then, writing technical manuals for Bell Telephone, and had the skills for such a project. He took on the task with enthusiasm; having spent all his childhood summers at Beach Haven, he knew and loved the history of the whole island.

Keeping much of the book's structure, Nash added several new chapters, tripling the length of the original and putting in twenty photographs of his own. Somerville's name was dropped from the title page. Despite the use of the same title, format and chapter headings, three-fourths of the 1936 edition of *The Lure of Long Beach* was Nash's own writing, and the parts that he retained from the 1914 edition are mostly his father's work from *The Breeze*.

Nash was a good writer and an accurate one who was fortunate to have a firsthand source in older family members who recalled early island history. He wrote several travel books and numerous articles over the years, including a long-running column called "More Lore of Long Beach." In 1974, Nash wrote a twenty-four part series for the column on his grandfather's farm on Liberty Avenue in Beach Haven.

The old causeway is the one common link in the collective memories of those who can remember the island of the 1950s and earlier. The rumble of the boards, that first whiff of salt air, that thin line of lights across the water after dark, the broken clams dropped by sea gulls, the whitecaps level with the road in a north-easter are all images and sensations shared by motorists to Long Beach Island for forty-five years, from 1914 until 1959.

At the inland waterway channel between Cedar Bonnet Island and Ship Bottom where they were only a hundred feet apart, both the causeway and the railroad trestle were drawbridges that had to be turned to one side by the bridge tenders with a T-shaped key in order to let large boats pass. It was a slow and cumbersome process, but after 1920 when the state took over the operation and maintenance of the causeway from the Long Beach Transportation Company, the automobile bridge was improved by changing it to a bascule or lift bridge. The railroad bridge remained unchanged, but the tender always kept it in the open position until just before the train was due.

The longest single span of the old causeway was the mile-long trestle bridge from the Manahawkin meadows to the first of the Bonnet islands where a bulkheaded and graveled road was laid to connect with another, shorter bridge to the next island and then to the drawbridge. In those early days, motorists were astonished to find crushed and broken clam shells littering the boards of the longest of the three bridges. Sea gulls bombed the bridge with clams at every low tide, and the broken shells were a hazard because primitive tires were vulnerable to the sharp edges. A couple of times a week, an attendant swept the bridge with a long-handled broom.

It is, of course, not unusual for sea birds to drop hard clams from great heights to break the shells and get at the meat, but they do not always succeed. Bird watchers have noted gulls dropping the same clam as many as twenty times on hard sand at low tide. Until the solid, wooden causeway bridge was built, there were very few hard surfaces other than boats, a few docks and some shed roofs. Roads were still made of gravel and were much too soft.

The first sea gull assaults on the causeway bridge began about 1919 with the start of large-scale dredging operations. After 1924, the problem worsened with the digging of the "Mathis Channel" along the west of Little Egg Harbor Bay. The construc-

Sea gulls routinely bombarded the new wooden causeway bridges with clams. The sharp edges of the broken shells easily punctured primitive automobile tires and had to be constantly swept up.

As the concrete piers of the new causeway bridge rise in 1956, motorists continue across a tide- and wave-swept causeway, a common, if frightening, driving experience during northeasters and spring tides.

tion of this much-needed channel was the result of a bill in the state Legislature introduced by Senator Thomas Mathis. When passed, the bill allocated one hundred fifty thousand dollars for dredging a new channel from the drawbridge at Cedar Bonnet to Beach Haven, a distance of six miles. It would be a hundred feet wide and six feet deep at low tide.

Few boaters today realize that before the 1920s any craft with a deep draft had to use the natural channel that wound from Cedar Bonnet, across to the mainland, down to Parkertown and then back across to Beach Haven. There was nothing but shallow water along the island side of Little Egg Harbor Bay north of Beach Haven. Not only would the new channel

be better for boatmen, shortening the distance between Beach Haven and Ship Bottom, but all that mud thrown up on the meadows would create more land for new homes.

Digging this channel over the next several years also was a bonanza for the gulls who found millions of clams dredged up in the mud and sand at all stages of the tide. The birds carried them in their beaks right to the bridge. The roads on the island were not paved with concrete until 1932, but by then most of the dredging was finished. As traffic increased on the bridge, the gulls went elsewhere with their clams. By this time, automobile tires were tougher, and that lone sweeper with his broom went on to more important tasks.

For two decades after the causeway opened, a motorist could look to the north and watch the train cross the bay. In a bad storm in November 1935, the mile-long rail trestle broke apart and washed up against the causeway, now the only means across the bay. For the next twenty years, traffic backed up at the drawbridge and then clattered over the low, wooden bridges, but in 1956 the old causeway was dwarfed by huge concrete supports of a new steel bridge being built a hundred feet to the south. Three years later, the old causeway, so familiar to all, was gone. The wooden bridges were removed, and all that remains of the old span are parts of the roadway on Cedar Bonnet Island and on the mainland in Hilliard (Mud City) as an extension of East Bay Avenue.

Chapter 19

THE HOUSEBOAT COLONY AT BEACH HAVEN

As late as 1910 there was only one side street west of Bay Avenue in Beach Haven and that was Dock Road, which had started out as a canal. The entire bayside was deeply indented with coves and in the biggest of them, between what is now Centre and Amber streets, there was a gathering of houseboats in the meadows each summer large enough to be called a colony. The people who lived in the boats, nearly all from the mainland, were the families of captains and crewmen in the fleet of the Beach Haven Yacht Club, then one of the East Coast's biggest centers for sportfishing.

Lured by the seasonal work, these men from Parkertown, West Creek and Cedar Run had been bringing houseboats over to the island since the 1880s. At first they towed them with sailboats, but after 1910 most baymen had garveys with noisy "one-lunger" gasoline engines. By June, their well-established little floating community was lined up along the meadows or on them. At night their kerosene lanterns could be seen from uptown, where townspeople wondered how anyone could live out there in such thick clouds of mosquitoes.

There were obvious discomforts, but the colony enjoyed its freedom and its friendships.

The boats were fairly close to each other, and they varied in length from twenty to fifty feet. Most were oblong, wood-and-tarpaper cabins with flat roofs on a flat-bottomed cedar hull. Their fore and aft decks were screened over to make porches which were cool and pleasant. Other boats were more ornate and, depending upon the taste of their owners, looked just like little cedar-shake houses with peaked roofs and shutters. Some were little more than canvas stretched over wooden hoops like Conestoga wagons without wheels. The really big houseboats moored at the yacht club could bunk fifteen or twenty men and were towed out to the islands and used by gunning clubs in duck season.

Inside most houseboats the long cabin was divided by a partition running fore and aft. On one side there were tables, chairs and a kerosene cook stove or a potbellied coal-and-wood burner. Metal stovepipes stuck out of every cabin roof. One side of every boat was partitioned off into one or two bunk rooms. All windows slid sideways and were well-screened. On the screened afterdeck of every houseboat was a wooden privy or outhouse, a convenience which was to be the colony's undoing.

There were rowboats, garveys and sneakboxes tied up everywhere, and houseboaters used them to carry buckets of water for cooking and cleaning from the taps on the yacht club wharf. Women and children going shopping or strolling in town would wait for low tide and, carrying their shoes, would slog across the marsh. Since no one had an icebox, foodstuffs were purchased only as they could be used, and all milk had to be in cans. There was, however, an unlimited supply of fresh fish, clams and crabs.

There were houseboat colonies elsewhere on the island, anywhere there was work. West of Bay Avenue for most of the length of the island, there was little solid ground. It was all meadow and marsh indented by several large coves, and in these coves, especially the deep one at Seventh Street, there were numerous houseboats. Swedish and Norwegian fishermen and "West Crickers" from the mainland lived in these floating homes, usually accessible by long, rickety, undulating boardwalks built on skinny pilings sunk into the meadows. The walkways ran up to the edge of the graveled roadbed of the train.

On the first cold, clear morning in September, with the sky a deep blue and the heather

South of the public dock at Beach Haven, a houseboat colony of boat captains, their wives and families, and island workers anchored in the meadows each summer and enjoyed simple pleasures, like the late afternoon sun hitting a cabin top.

turning purple in the marshes, the houseboats would start heading back to the creeks on the mainland. Scattered all over the bay, they would sometimes anchor and wait for a better wind or a change in the tide. They had all the time in the world.

But time was really running out for this way of life. There had been complaints for many years that the houseboaters, who paid no taxes and were not a part of the town, were creating a health problem. The twice-daily tide and the broad waters of Little Egg Harbor Bay could not handle the sewage generated by the houseboat colony. An ordinance went into effect on June 20, 1926, banning all occupied houseboats from Beach Haven waters, and the rest of the island soon passed similar legislation.

From the distance of time, the freedom of those early houseboaters, whose lifestyle has so nearly been forgotten, is enviable. Some of their boats, tethered to the land forever by the inflexible lines of public utilities, imperishable cedar hulls buried in gravel or hidden by cinder blocks, are still recognizable on the bayside streets of Long Beach Island. Although no longer mobile, these former houseboats are still used as residences and enjoyed by proud owners.

In 1912 some of Beach Haven's fashionable summertime hotel guests, here with a uniformed porter from the Engleside, stroll the town's earliest boardwalk. The ornate acetylene street lamps were installed in 1907.

Chapter 20

THE BOARDWALK AT BEACH HAVEN

In the spring of 1917, Beach Haven's brand new boardwalk ran for a mile and a quarter in a smooth ribbon of yellow pine along the oceanfront from the sand hills and ponds of Seventh Street all the way south to the big timber jetty at Holyoke Avenue. Twenty-two blocks long and twenty feet wide, twice as big as its predecessor built in 1898, it was a major drawing card for Beach Haven. Its solid two-by-four planking rang to the footsteps of the crowds who had motored down from Camden and Philadelphia to see it.

It was actually Beach Haven's third boardwalk. The first was short-lived and little more than a wooden pathway between the oceanfront bathhouses of the two major hotels. It had been built in 1896 at the suggestion of Robert B. Engle of the Engleside to connect his bathhouses with those of the Hotel Baldwin four blocks away. It was only eight feet wide and lay right on top of the former dunes that had been leveled years before to provide ocean views for summer people. Although the original purpose of the walk was to keep guests from tracking sand into the lobbies, it proved to be even more popular for strolling and socializing.

Believing that a project of this nature was a municipal responsibility rather than a private one, Robert Engle, now a state senator for Ocean County, pushed for a bigger and wider walk in 1897. Citing the pleasures of the famous Atlantic City boardwalk, which was then twenty years old, Engle persuaded the town councilmen to scrap plans to enlarge the Beach Haven School and start at once on a new boardwalk.

Widened to twelve feet and considerably lengthened, the new, publicly financed walk was designed to be built on pilings on the beach rather than on the flattened dunes. There were ambitious plans to run it from Fifth Street on the north to Essex Avenue on the south, a distance of one mile, but when it was finally built the next year it started at Sixth Street on the north and went only as far as Amber Street. The town ran out of money at three thousand dollars, but in one more year there was enough revenue to extend it to Marine Street as far as the Baldwin bathhouses. The 1898 walk was now a half-mile long and so it would remain until it was torn down in the autumn of 1916 to build a new and better one.

In its first ten years, the boardwalk, like the rest of town, was lit by kerosene oil lamps set atop wooden posts. A lamplighter filled and lit each one every night and cleaned them as often as necessary, and they stayed on until they burned out around dawn. In 1907, Beach Haven built a ten thousand dollar acetylene plant, and then both the old boardwalk and its successor built in 1917 were ornamented at every block with gas lamps hanging from tall, gracefully curved, wrought iron standards. The gas for all the lights around town and on the boardwalk was turned on and off at the gashouse, but each lamp still had to be lighted by hand with a long pole strung with a battery-charged wire. The lamplighter, with his pole and his batteries in a shoulder pouch, walked swiftly around to each lamp making sparks to ignite them while the gas was flowing. The lamps were shut off simultaneously at dawn.

The 1898 boardwalk was one of the great symbols of Beach Haven's golden era during the Edwardian period. Each summer seemed more exciting than the one before. The hotels were packed to their very doors and the Pennsylvania Railroad was running extra cars on weekends. When the automobile arrived on the island in 1914 over the newly built causeway across the bay, everyone was certain that there was no limit to the growth of this marvelous resort. It was time for a new boardwalk.

After several meetings, the borough accepted a bid of twenty thousand dollars, and work began in the fall of 1916. The old boardwalk was torn down; then the new pilings, set twenty feet apart to double the width of the walk, were sunk into the sand east of the dune line from Seventh Street to Holyoke Avenue, a distance of a mile and a quarter. The stringers were in by December, and everyone waited anxiously for the train that would deliver the thousands of twenty-foot two-by-fours for the planking. They arrived after the New Year in several flatcars.

Since all the side streets ended at Atlantic Avenue, the contract included narrow wooden approaches across the sand to the edge of the boardwalk. Like the one it replaced, the 1917 boardwalk had no railings and never would for all the years of its existence because they had been placed under a separate contract to reduce the cost. The borough did, however, put in benches at frequent intervals and street lamps at every block.

Railings were deemed unnecessary because the walk was normally no more than a foot or two above the sand, posing no real threat to anyone except at the southern end where erosion left the walk dangerously high, sometimes by as much as seven or eight feet. It shuddered with each dizzying rush of the waves at high tide. As early as the fall of 1917 when the structure was less than six months old, engineering professor Lewis Haupt of the University of Pennsylvania was hired to design and build a flying buttress or sea wall of wood pilings along the beachfront from Belvoir to Essex avenues. Unattractive but necessary, the barrier worked for only a decade before the southernmost seven blocks of the boardwalk, from Belvoir to Holyoke Avenue, washed out in a storm.

In the forty-six years — from 1898 until 1944 — that Beach Haven had its two boardwalks, it is remarkable that for such a desirable location there was so little commercial development on it. There was nothing at all on the old boardwalk, and as for the new one, it had no businesses until 1920 and then fewer than six enterprises, even at its peak in 1941, the summer before the war.

The boardwalk stroller, starting at the north end at Seventh Street, would find no structures in the ocean block east of Atlantic until Second Street, where there was an ice cream parlor followed by an amusement arcade at Centre Street, a dress shop at Amber and nothing more for three blocks until the Baldwin bathhouses at Marine Street, where there were a Japanese novelty shop and a hot dog concession. The sixth and last enterprise on the boardwalk was The Sea Chest owned by Nat and Betty Ewer at Berkeley Avenue, opposite the ocean fishing pier one block from the end of the walk at Belvoir.

When the first boardwalk was built in 1898, kerosene lamps softly illuminated the half-mile stretch. The lamps had to be filled each day and lit each evening.

In 1917, a wider and longer boardwalk fronts the ocean block which shows little development. Other than the bathhouses of the Baldwin and Engleside hotels which dominate the town's oceanfront, there are only a few boardwalk businesses, including an ice cream parlour, an amusement arcade and a dress shop.

The first store on the new boardwalk in 1920 was the Japanese Novelty Shop of Haidee Nakamura, who leased space in the east end of the Baldwin bathhouses at Marine Street. Nakamura sold fancy wares of silk and bamboo, little dolls with porcelain heads, incense, wind chimes and firecrackers. It was only here that one could buy the handsome glazed chinaware hand-painted with images of Beach Haven landmarks, sets so eagerly sought by collectors today. Rhea Britz, who specialized in amber jewelry, had a tiny gift shop on the south side of the same build-ing, which in the late twenties became a cold soda and hot dog place operated by Joe Sprague while he managed the Baldwin bathhouses.

In the fall of 1922, Lilly Schlingloff built a two-story house on the boardwalk at Second Street and opened a tearoom and ice cream par-

Earl C. Roper

Built in 1924 off Berkeley Avenue, the municipal fishing pier was popular with anglers until the Hurricane of 1944 washed it away.

In the Baldwin bathhouses in 1920, Haidee Nakamura opened the Japanese Novelty Store and sold wind chimes, incense and firecrackers as the first business on the boardwalk, above, left.

lor called Madame Lilly's. The town then built a first aid station on the beach at Coral Street and erected two large pavilions, one them on the beach at Centre Street. By 1924, a T-shaped municipal fishing pier extending two hundred feet from the boardwalk was constructed at Berkeley Avenue and opened in July.

The Engleside Hotel had beachfront tennis courts and, unlike the Baldwin, never leased space in its bathhouses, but immediately to the south of them on Amber Street, a New York firm dealing in fine ladies apparel, evening gowns and accessories opened a two-story building in May 1925. The shop in its front room was run by Rose Myer, whose good taste could be counted on. Everything came down from New York: the skirts and jackets with the padded shoulders, the broad-brimmed hats, and the casual sports clothes and handbags that could last a lifetime.

In the 1920s, after a cycle of severe northeasters eroded the beaches, a series of jetties called hurdles were installed to protect the boardwalk's southern end, above, but the design failed. In a 1928 September gale, the seven southernmost blocks of the boardwalk, from Belvoir to Holyoke, washed away, facing page.

Nothing was cheap or tawdry. Myer called her shop Maison Mae.

The only place for amusements — and really the only bit of honky-tonk on the whole Beach Haven boardwalk — was the popular Downing's Skee-Ball Arcade at Centre Street. Here the hollow roll of the wooden balls mingled with the constant crack of electric target rifles, the dinging of bells and the cry of the barker. It was on the beach near Downings that the "world's largest checker board" was built in the summer of 1937, sixteen feet square with red and black discs eighteen inches in diameter moved by players with long poles.

The last shop added to the boardwalk, a trim little flat-top with portholes along both sides, was The Sea Chest gift shop of Betty Nash who, newly graduated from Ogontz College and seeking a career, convinced her grandfather, Charles Beck, to buy property and build the shop at Berkeley Avenue in 1937. She ran The Sea Chest for two years and was joined by her new husband, Nat Ewer, who shared her talent for merchandising. Together the Ewers made a career of selling the classically beautiful gifts that became their trademark.

In the early years of the first boardwalk, all the ocean blocks between Atlantic Avenue

eastward to the leveled dunes were undeveloped sand lots with narrow wooden ramps but no streets. The only buildings on the oceanfront were the bathhouses of the Engleside and the Baldwin. Bathhouses are seldom seen now, but in their day they performed a useful function closely tied with custom and with the history of the bathing suit.

In the 1890s, a visitor to Barnegat City remarked that it was probably the only resort on the coast of New Jersey where one might see people walking along the side streets to the beach in bathing attire. Such lack of formality would never have been encountered at any other New Jersey resort where ocean bathers were required to cover up with long robes when not on the beach.

A decade later, a Philadelphia reporter staying at Beach Haven was astonished to find cottagers surf fishing in their bathing suits as if, to him, there was something indecorous about it. Actually it was no longer unusual in Beach Haven and elsewhere on the island to see summer residents on the streets and boardwalk in bathing suits at a time when such attire was still considered improper and even proscribed at other resorts.

Why, then, if rules were less strict at Beach Haven, did the town still have bathhouses? For one thing, day trippers needed them since it was illegal to change in an automobile or on the streets, a rule that was strictly enforced. However, the real reason for the existence of bathhouses was that although cottagers might do it, guests at the Engleside and Baldwin were forbidden to wear bathing attire walking to and from the hotel and beach. The problem was sand. Not only did it get tracked into the hotels, but it also clogged up the drains, and where would the wet bathing suits be hung to dry? There was only one solution.

Each of these hotels owned and operated its own bathhouses for the convenience of its guests and anyone else as well. Bathers were charged fifty cents a day or three dollars a week for the use of a small, walk-in locker containing only a bench on a slatted wooden floor and hooks on the walls but no shower or running water. A husband and wife could share one for five dollars a week. The bathhouses were used only as changing rooms and were kept locked, but all valuables were placed in the custody of the bathhouse manager.

Bathing suits in those years were made of thickly seamed, dark wool, usually trimmed in white. Even on a hot day, they took several hours to dry, and they also collected a lot of sand which the hotel plumbing simply could not handle. Most people owned more than one suit, and part of the bathhouse manager's job was to hang up the wet ones and have them back in the proper locker for the next day's use, along with a clean towel.

The Baldwin bathhouses lined the ocean block at Marine Street between Atlantic Avenue and the boardwalk. The long, narrow structure ran east and west and had cedar-shake sides and roof. It was partitioned down the middle with fifty lockers on each side; men used the north side and women, the south. There were only two shower stalls at the east end, one for men and one for women, but there was no hot water, the sole purpose being to wash off sand. Bathing suits had to be kept on while showering since walking back to the lockers in a towel was not permitted. The Engleside bathhouses on Amber Street at the boardwalk were similar in size and operation.

The 1917 boardwalk shall always be associated with the Beach Haven of the years between the two wars, when the great transatlantic zeppelins arriving at or leaving Lakehurst thrummed overhead on summer afternoons and fires dotted the beach at night, a time of print dresses, floppy hats and spectator shoes, an era that came to an abrupt end with Pearl Harbor. That first wartime summer of 1942 was very different. For security reasons, the lights were turned out all along the oceanfront. There was no surf fishing and no beach fires from sunset to sunrise. The New Jersey National Guard came to Beach Haven and camped on the baseball field. With the Coast Guard, they patrolled the beaches and boardwalk at night.

The shops remained open, but most good things were in short supply "for the duration." By 1944, the danger from enemy submarines and boat landings had passed, and now only the seaward side of the lights on the tar-scuffed boardwalk was painted black. The war, it appeared, would soon be over and things would return to normal, but then came one of New Jersey's worst storms.

The hurricane of September 14, 1944, destroyed the fishing pier, boardwalk and every structure on it except the Baldwin bathhouses. There had been five businesses and every one was a total loss. Only the Ewers pulled together and reopened the next summer, but in a different place. Betty and Nat's new Sea Chest was on the ground floor of the Baldwin, and within a few more years they bought an old sailing schooner, had it towed from New England to Beach Haven, and converted it into a gift shop and a popular attraction on Long Beach Island, the Lucy Evelyn.

After that storm, the worst one to hit the island in over a century, there was nothing left of the boardwalk but a long, parallel row of old chestnut pilings. The decking had been lifted in

In 1898, the earliest boardwalk kept wealthy cottagers and vacationers above bothersome sand, facing page, top. In the late 1930s, a wider boardwalk, bottom, was still the place to see and be seen. The lamps lining the 1917 boardwalk, this page, were powered by the town's acetylene plant, the first of its kind on the island.

huge sections, some with benches and lamps attached, and scattered in the side streets of Beach Haven. The boardwalk could have been rebuilt, and the topic was heatedly discussed at every borough meeting as late as the spring of 1946, but it came to no avail. It would cost almost eighty thousand dollars to rebuild only four blocks of it. Unfortunately, all of the salvaged decking had

been sold to Atlantic City to repair its own ravaged walk, and new material had become prohibitively expensive.

They're all gone now, those massive, wooden beachfront structures, the towering gingerbread pavilions at Harvey Cedars and Surf City, the fishing piers at Ship Bottom and Beach Haven, and even the little boardwalk at

Beach Haven Terrace, but it is that beautiful, mile-long Beach Haven boardwalk that is haunting. Memories of it fade like the receding tap of hard leather heels on thick boards, and are as ephemeral as zebra shadows in the sand on a late August afternoon or the halos around those old goose-necked lamps on a foggy spring evening.

Chapter 21

THE POUND FISHERMEN

Lynn Photo (above); Bill Kane (right)

Like these men from the Crest Fishery, on the facing page, pound fishermen launched their skiffs at dawn to tend the nets a mile or two off the beach. On their return, above, the men pulled the heavily laden boats up onto the beach with horses and, in later years, with tractors.

The technique of catching roving schools of fish in a trap or a pound has been used for thousands of years in rivers, shallow lakes and bays, but practicing this type of fishing two to three miles out in the ocean's depths had to wait for modern technology. Once there were steam pumps capable of sinking long poles into the ocean floor so that nets could be hung on them, a new industry was born. The first commercial pound nets operated off Sandy Hook and Long Branch in the 1870s. There were none off Long Beach Island until at least 1886 when there was a train to haul the fish to market.

The industry was most active on Long Beach Island in the 1920s and 1930s, when there were five major pound fisheries in operation. Beach Haven had the Sun Fishery and the Beach Haven Fishery. A few miles to the north there was Tonnes Bohn's Crest Fishery, and in Ship Bottom, across the road from each other at the entrance to the island, the Barnegat City Fishery and the Surf City Fishery, which had moved there in 1923 when train service was discontinued on the north end of the island. Each of these five companies owned and maintained at least four or five pound net installations out in the ocean, working them from April through November.

The pounds were set up two to three miles offshore in about thirty-six feet of water. To hold the heavy nets, thirty or forty huge poles of North Carolina hickory, nearly ninety feet long, were used. Half of them stood in the sandy floor in a straight line running perpendicular to the shore

for sixteen hundred feet, or about five city blocks. A series of long, weighted nets reaching to the bottom were strung out along these poles to form what was called the "leader line." The remaining poles were grouped to form the pound, an enclosure fifty feet square with a big net hung to form a pocket. The pound net had a bottom to it and a narrow funnel opening, which the fish could enter but from which they could not usually escape. Fish swimming along the coast would encounter the barrier of the east-west net. Instinctively heading for deeper water to get around this fencelike obstruction, they would be

led into the heart-shaped funnel net and finally into the pocket.

Each morning at daybreak a crew of usually seven men launched a thirty-two-foot skiff into the surf. Hand over hand, they guided it under a thick line strung from a pole on the beach to another one set into the sand bar just beyond the surf. Once they were over the bar, the gasoline engine was started up.

There was no way to know what would be found in the heavy nets until they were slowly drawn up. Sometimes there were so many fish that a return trip was necessary, and sometimes there

The poles from which the pound nets hung were North Carolina hickory, 80 feet in length. With long-handled nets the men scooped out the fish and threw them, flapping, into the bottom of the boat, facing page, top. On their return, the crew prepare to pull their pound boat onto the beach.

were very little. The fish were scooped out of the pound net with long-handled dip nets and dumped flapping into the bottom of the boat. They would be sorted and put into fish baskets later. The nets were then lowered for the next day's catch. At times there were giant sharks or devil fish that could ruin a net but which the men brought in as crowd-drawing curiosities. Other large fish were valuable; an eight hundred-pound tuna could be sold and the profits divided among the men. As many as a dozen boats from the island fisheries went out every day except Sunday, in good weather and in bad.

The return of the fully laden boats to shore at around seven or eight A.M. always brought people down to the beach. It was a thrilling sight, especially in rough seas, to watch them roar the engine and ride the boat in under clouds of gulls. The instant the wide-beamed skiff hit the sand, six of the crew would jump into the surf in their hip boots and, clinging to the sides, would steady the boat until a heavy towline could be attached to the bow. Then, with gumwood rollers on planks placed under the skiff's flat bottom, the boat was pulled up above the tide line with a block-and-tackle rig and a tractor or, in the early years, by horses. A single boat could hold eighteen thousand pounds of fish.

The men would climb back into the boat and sort the fish into two-handled, slatted oak baskets, each with a capacity of fifty pounds. From time to time a nice kingfish, sea bass or bonito would be tossed onto the sand to an eager girl or boy who would run it home to mother for breakfast. The loaded baskets were transported in a flatbed truck to the fishery icehouse, where the catch was packed into big barrels weighing two hundred pounds when full. Each was covered with burlap nailed around the rim and lined up on the platform for shipment by train to New York's Fulton Fish Market. After 1935, trucks

Warm mornings before shore breezes picked up were the best times to work the pounds, above. After the six-man crew skillfully rode the boat into the surf, facing page, gummed rollers set across wood planks helped workhorses pull the boats above the high tide line.

were used to transport the fish, which were packed into well-iced wooden boxes.

Nearly all of the pound boat crews and the other men who worked for the fisheries were Scandinavian, mostly Norwegian. There were a few Portuguese and many North Carolinians, who, it was said, had followed the trainloads of hickory poles up the coast to the pound nets. Nearly half of the men were single and lived over the packing sheds in barracks-type housing or dormitories with a galley, a messroom and usually a full-time cook. During the fishing season the men were roused at 4:30 A.M. for a huge breakfast of eggs, pancakes and mountains of sausages and pork chops. Their midday meal, after returning from the pounds and sorting the fish, was the big one, with platters of steaks, hams, roasts and every kind of fish. Supper was

light, usually sandwiches which the men made themselves.

There was more to the job than just fishing. Long afternoons were spent tarring and repairing the nets, which had to be cleared of seaweed and replaced every few weeks. Poles loosened in storms had to be reset with a water pump and a jet spear. For all of this the men were paid about sixty dollars a month, which, with room and board, was very acceptable in those days.

In the winter, pound fishing was suspended. With the work force reduced, many of the men found jobs on tugboats in Philadelphia, but it was Long Beach Island that most of them called home. The pound fishermen worked hard and they played hard. With their laughter, their drinking songs, and noisy, foot-stomping, hand-clapping dances, they filled tiny bars like the Hav

Inn, the Hudson House, Mom Riese's, the Port Hole, Hans' and Kubel's. Those were happy years.

The industry, which reached its peak in the thirties, continued to operate through World War II. The Hurricane of 1944 devastated the pound nets and poles, which had become very costly to replace as the prices of everything but fish skyrocketed. Then the fish populations dwindled to a fraction of what they once had been. There was no sound explanation for this although some blamed the draggers for tearing up the bottom while others said it was oil from all the tankers torpedoed during the war. The Crest Fishery formed a consortium of investors, betting that the slump was just part of a cycle and also hoping for a rise in fish prices. They hung on, buying up boats and nets from companies going out of business until the Crest, too, ceased all pound fishing in 1956.

Chapter 22

CAMP MIQUON

J. Leonard Mason, supervisor of wrestling and boxing in the physical education department at the University of Pennsylvania, decided in 1924 that Long Beach Island, much of it still a bayberry-covered wilderness sixty miles from Philadelphia, might be a good place to start a boys' camp. There were big dunes, miles of clean beaches and a wide, shallow bay teeming with fish and crabs and absolutely perfect for boating. Mason chose Brant Beach because of the extreme narrowness of that part of the island. It was a three-minute walk from ocean to bay, ideal for a camp.

In the early twenties there were about thirty or so scattered cottages in the one-mile stretch of Brant Beach, which had a post office and its own train station. The little, well-planned community of mostly summer residents was only a dozen years old and had been started by Henry McLaughlin, a bank trust officer and lawyer. In 1911, he had sunk an artesian well and built a water tower. The belt from the water pump could be switched to an electric generator so that for a few hours every evening Brant Beach cottages glowed with the first electric lighting system on the island.

Mason had been running the successful Camp Neshaminy in Bucks County, Pennsylvania, since 1920, but the area was becoming much too settled for him so he moved his whole operation to Brant Beach and called it Camp Miquon. He bought two blocks of oceanfront property between Fifty-sixth and Fifty-eighth streets and built a big bungalow on pilings. The campers stayed in tents on the beach that first

year, the way they had been doing at Neshaminy, but it was too sandy, so Mason had six sleeping cabins built atop pilings on the beach. On the bayside just across the railroad tracks was a beautiful natural cove that gave Brant Beach its name. Here Mason built a long dock for the many boats needed by the camp.

In the sixteen years of Camp Miquon's existence there were never more than fifty boys at a time. It was a small camp, but it was also very expensive and very exclusive. There were two, four-week cycles from late June until the end of August, and the cost for a four-week stay was $150, an exorbitant sum then, enough to rent a house at the shore for the season. The boys, who ranged in age from eight to sixteen, were mostly from well-to-do Philadelphia families more likely to be traveling in Europe than summering at the Jersey shore.

Mason believed in lots of fresh air. The camp's cabins had pyramidal, cedar-shake roofs and were screened from floor to ceiling on all four sides. When it rained, a weighted canvas was lowered on the weather side only. Eight to ten boys of various ages and two counselors slept in the cabins, designated A, B,

A Bit of Nature Study on Gull Island

A brochure for Camp Miquon glowingly described the camp's interest in young boys' "health and all-around proper development," including a daily rest period, wholesome food, nonsectarian services each Sunday, and the "cheerful personality of a real camp mother" meant to soothe the homesick pangs of first-time campers.

Camp Miquon
By the Sea

BRANT BEACH (Ocean County)
NEW JERSEY

[FOR CHRISTIAN BOYS—6 TO 18 YEARS]

FOUNDED 1920

DR. AND MRS. J. LEONARD MASON
Directors and Owners
440 South Fiftieth Street
Philadelphia, Pa.

Life Saving and First Aid

C, D and E. Nearby, also on pilings, there was a wash shed with two long rows of showers and sinks that drained into the sand. The latrines were in the big house where there was indoor plumbing.

The counselors Mason employed were all unusually talented young men. Some were fine athletes like his own sons, one of whom was a champion boxer. They were recruited through an old-boy network at Haverford, Swarthmore and Lafayette colleges and Mason's own University of Pennsylvania. They knew seamanship, riflery and horseback riding and how to play all kinds of games, sports and musical instruments. Some were widely read and could tell the boys frightening ghost stories while they sat around a beach fire under the stars, toasting marshmallows.

It was a quasi-military camp, with emphasis on naval etiquette and close-order drills. The boys had sailor suits for formal occasions, but most of the time they wore blue shorts, sneakers and a white polo shirt. The day began and ended with bugle calls, and wherever the boys went, whether to the boat docks on the bay or to the movies at the Colony Theater twenty blocks to the north, they went in columns of two, march-ing and singing old military songs. The return marches were in the dark; there were no street lights then and the counselors carried flashlights.

Mason emphasized sailing and seamanship, and the camp fleet was only two blocks away on the bay. Tied up at the long dock were canoes, rowboats, catboats, Perrines and sneak boxes, enough boats for every boy in the camp. On rainy days campers sat in the big assembly room over-looking the ocean, practicing knot tying, sema-phore and Morse code or preparing for their annual minstrel show, which was one of the highlights of the season.

Meals were served in the screened porch on the west side of the main house, where Mason and his family and guests ate with the campers at long picnic tables. The cook and his wife were from Maryland, and they frequently served fried chicken, corn bread, lots of vegetables, and wonderful pies or the crabs and the fish the boys caught every day. Afterwards there were travel talks and informative lectures given by Mason's wide circle of faculty friends, and often there was music. Mason's wife, Marian, played the piano by ear, and everyone sang old favorites and college songs.

After Mason received his doctorate in physical education in 1929, he was always addressed as Dr. Mason, but he was more affectionately known to campers and counselors alike as "Big Chief." He was as multitalented as any of his counselors, a judo expert and an authority on sand sculpture. He outdid himself when the campers put on their annual minstrel show in

Ben Crane (above); Corcoran Darlington (below)

Campers practiced naval etiquette, but here naval cadets use camp facilities after Labor Day, 1934. Every August the camp held popular minstel shows, below, attended by many islanders.

August, which was always well attended by neighboring cottagers. Dr. Mason would perform with his Indian clubs, a sport at which he had been twice a national champion. He was also a lover of the Scottish ballads of Harry Lauder and would sing "Roamin' in the Gloamin' " at the drop of a hat.

Only one untoward incident, a fatal plane crash, ever marred the sixteen happy summers of Camp Miquon. It occurred under such poignantly sad circumstances that in the telling and retelling of it over the years some essential facts were lost, even as to the time and place.

It happened in the summer of 1936. Nine-year-old David Eynon was one of thirty-five campers that season. Young David's father, a prominent Philadelphia physician, was chief of surgery at Chester General Hospital. Dr. John S. Eynon had a private plane, and on weekends he was in the habit of buzzing the camp while his son was there, usually dropping small packages containing money or a message.

On Saturday afternoon, August 15, Eynon circled low over the camp to drop fifty cents in a weighted handkerchief to his son and then, banking out over the ocean for a return pass, he made another drop; this time it was an affectionate message to David. He was now only

feet above the camp, flying north up the beach for one more turn before heading over the bay and home to Pennsylvania. But he was not to make it. Lacking sufficient altitude, the plane nosedived into the big dunes at Forty-eighth Street with a shattering crash. Dr. Eynon and his one passenger were killed instantly.

Along with all the other campers, David heard the crash and watched in horror as exploding bits of wood, aluminum and fabric from the bright yellow monoplane rose high above the mountainous dunes ten blocks to the north. As the debris fluttered downward, the next sounds were the shouts of widely scattered people on the beach running toward the site of the crash.

David and the other campers were held back by Dr. and Mrs. Mason. Someone retrieved from the sand another weighted handkerchief containing a scrap of paper, Dr. Eynon's last message to his son. It was only one line. "I love you, David — Dad."

Despite his father's tragic death and its association with the camp, David insisted on returning the next year. He, like all the other boys, was happy there and much of it had to do with

In 1936, just after he dropped a note to his son, camper David Eynon's father died when his plane crashed into dunes near the camp. In stalwart Miquon style, the youngster insisted on returning the next summer.

Meet Us at the Old Ship's Wheel Boys!

the way Mason ran the camp. From the morning plunge in the ocean and setting up exercises until the stories just before taps, the whole day was structured. The portly but very active Dr. Mason, strikingly handsome with his great mane of white hair and his yachting cap, was the power behind the camp, but he was getting ready to retire. Despite its high costs, the camp had never been more than marginally profitable, nor was there anyone to fill Mason's shoes. His two sons and two daughters who had been so helpful had finished college and moved on to careers of their own. The summer of 1940 was the last for Camp Miquon.

Two years later, with the nation at war, the oceanfront was under guard and blacked out at night. In August, Dr. Mason, still on the university faculty, died suddenly of a heart attack while at work. He was 61. The camp property was listed for sale, but with a war on there were no takers. The beach sleeping cabins were sold at auction the following year, and the Hurricane of 1944 wrecked any camp buildings that had not been sold and removed. The partially damaged main bungalow was sold after the hurricane, moved to Fifty-sixth Street near the bay, and converted into a private residence.

Today not a trace of Camp Miquon remains at the oceanfront. Two of the cabins that were removed in 1943 were taken to the bayside near the Brant Beach Yacht Club and three others to the south side of Delaware Avenue in Beach Haven Terrace, where they remain to this day, all in a row and easily recognizable by their pyramidal roofs. Another one was moved to Beach Haven between Glendola and Holyoke avenues on the edge of the bay and became the home of the late historian and writer Charles Edgar Nash. He had its wooden sides encased in pink and yellow bricks from the chimney of the Engleside Hotel, which had just been demolished. Nash's landmark structure on its pie-shaped lot lasted until 1986, when it was torn down to erect a new home.

Chapter 23

HARRY COLMER OF THE MOVIES

Beach Haven's first multipurpose building was its little wooden schoolhouse on the north side of Third Street. In the 1880s and 1890s it was also the first Catholic mission church and eventually, in 1913, the first movie house and dance hall. When it was built and dedicated as a school on May 1, 1885, the resort was only a dozen years old. Until then, the town's four or five children had been taught in the parlor off the lobby of the Beach Haven House, a hotel on the northeast corner of Bay Avenue and Centre Street. They were taught by Lilly Bates, the daughter of the hotel's owner and the first paid teacher in the new school.

Third Street soon became the busiest side street in town. It was on the route of the horsecar, the tracks of which ran from the train station past the schoolhouse and down Beach Avenue to the Hotel Baldwin. The school building also was used by the town government for monthly meetings and for other civic occasions. During the summer months, mission priests traveled from Lakewood to the island to say Catholic masses in the schoolhouse twice every Sunday and holy day.

After the present Beach Haven School was built on Eighth Street in 1912, the old school stood vacant for a year until Sid Verts, a Philadelphia

electrician, bought it. Verts, who represented the Beach Haven Amusement Company, began to show movies four times a week. Although moving pictures were just beginning to catch on, Verts wanted to sell out.

At about this time another electrician from Camden, Harry Colmer, came to the island to do a contract job for the Beach Haven Water Works. He liked the town, moved his family there and was attracted to the movie business, especially the technical end of it which he understood perfectly. Colmer and a local man named Leon Cranmer bought the building and the business from Sid Verts and his stock company. After a balcony was installed, it held fifty persons. When Colmer and Cranmer opened, they charged ten cents for children and fifteen cents for adults.

Colmer named the movie house the Colonial theater, which soon drew crowds for such popular fare as Mack Sennet comedies, Bronco Billy westerns and *The Perils of Pauline.* Public electricity in Beach Haven was at least a decade away, so the projector was hand-cranked. The power for the lamp came from a gasoline-driven Lathrope generator with a big fan belt. The generator was outside on the east side of the building, and the exhaust pipe was buried partly

underground to muffle the noise of the machine. The silent films were always accompanied by the spirited piano playing of Freda Joorman Cranmer who, during the exciting parts, would get to her feet and, leaning forward, drum away at the keyboard for maximum effect. After the evening show, the chairs were folded up and there were country dances to piano, banjo and fiddle music with a caller.

By the twenties, the movies were so popular that a bigger theater was needed. Colmer and Cranmer bought the northwest corner of Bay Avenue and Centre Street and, in five weeks during the spring of 1922, they erected their new moving picture house. The four sides of the building were constructed in the Firman Cranmer Lumber Yard across the street; once the frame had been erected, they were hoisted up against it by means of a gin, pulleys and Firman Cranmer's automobile. The new movie house was ready for the grand opening on the Fourth of July weekend, when a four-piece orchestra played at each evening performance of Cecil B. DeMille's adventure epic, *Fool's Paradise.*

Shortly after the new theater opened, Cranmer decided to get out of the business. He had plans to buy a service station, and later started a

The moving pictures had a new venue in 1922 when Leon Cranmer and Harry Colmer, right, built the Colonial theater in Beach Haven. Colmer bought out his partner and eventually opened two other theaters.

bus line to Camden in competition with the Long Beach Railroad. Colmer bought out his partner and became the sole owner of the business, employing his family in nearly every stage of the operation. In the winter months during the twenties, they moved back into the little theater on Third Street because it was easier to heat and the off-season crowds were smaller.

In the thirties, before air conditioning, Colmer solved the heat problem by dragging several hundred-pound cakes of ice up a tin chute into galvanized troughs under big wall fans in the front of the theater. On hot summer nights the fans blew a fine, chilled mist over the delighted audience.

In the late twenties, a real estate company seeking to develop Brant Beach built a big theater at Thirty-fifth Street. While waiting for the land boom that would not come in time for them, the company's investors were forced to unload the theater, and Colmer bought it. It became the Colony theatre, the second theater in his chain. Colmer had the only movies on the island, and since there were no other theaters on the main-

land between Tuckerton and Toms River, he decided to expand and bought an old opera house in Barnegat. He named it the Park theater and began to show movies there.

With three theaters on the circuit, the logistics of the whole operation became staggering. There were four or five heavy cans of film for each movie; since there was a different movie in each theater every night, they had to be transported by automobile after the movies closed at midnight and arrangements made to meet with the film distributor in Manahawkin so everything would be ready for the next night's showing. In addition, handbills and ads had to be delivered, and posters and signs had to be changed. Colmer was up until nearly dawn seven days a week.

If Colmer never went to bed before four A.M., it was said by those who knew him well that he never went to bed hungry, either. He was a giant of a man, six feet four and over three hundred pounds. He was a frequent patron of Jacob Britz's ice cream parlor, located across from the Colonial on the southwest corner of Bay Avenue and Centre Street. In the twenties, before Britz's became a tavern, Colmer was a regular customer. He had a weakness for Minnie Britz's peach pies and often devoured a whole pie in one sitting. Everyone enjoyed his extremely dry sense of humor; his observations on life were funny but so unique that his friends could not recall a single one of his many throwaway lines.

But it was his immense height and girth that most moviegoers remember. Many a wisecracking teenager found himself scrunching down in his seat in terror when the aisle boards creaked at the approach of Harry Colmer. The Brant Beach theater got hot on summer evenings and, with the emergency doors open on the east side for ventilation, the mosquitoes would get

In World War II Beach Haven, movie audiences clapped at every sighting of an American flag at the Colonial Theater. The National Guard unit stationed in town came in uniform, at the ready for air raid alerts. If an alert siren sounded, they'd stream out the exits, their gear clinking and clanking.

through the screen doors. Colmer lumbered up and down the aisles with a half-gallon flit gun, spraying the doors and walls.

Two generations of moviegoers on Long Beach Island benefited greatly from Harry Colmer's excellent credit rating and cash-and-carry policy with film distributors. Colmer was always able to get first-run movies. He took a lot of B-pictures along with the major films, but in those days people went to the movies every night no matter what was playing. It was the only entertainment on the island at a time when no show would have been complete without a Leon Errol or an Edgar Kennedy comedy, a newsreel and, of course, a cartoon and the prevues. Not only did the movies change every night, but the price was right, too. All through the war years and into the

early sixties, the price of admission was twenty cents for children and fifty cents for adults.

During World War II, movie audiences clapped enthusiastically every time an American flag appeared on the screen, and the six o'clock show began with a playing of "The Star-Spangled Banner," during which everyone stood at attention. Coastguardsmen and soldiers came to the theaters in uniform. In Beach Haven, where a unit of the National Guard lived in tents on the ball field at Pearl Street, the troops came to the movies with helmets and guns and cartridge belts in case there might be a surprise drill after dark. At the sound of the alert, they would all get up and leave with much clinking and clanking, but the movie went on.

Certain places came to be associated with the movies. Next to the Colonial was Webb's, with

its enameled white front and sizzling hamburgers for the after-theater and after-bar crowd. The Colony in Brant Beach had the Shinn-Dig and Agnes Shinn, who never forgot a child's name in thirty years. It was a great place to play pinball and buy candy before the movie.

Harry Colmer died in 1956; his family ran the movies for another eight years before selling to a company which now operates three theaters on the island, including the two that were built in the era of silent film. The Beach Haven and Brant Beach theaters have been completely renovated, and the original Colonial theater, the little building on Third Street that had been the first school, the first town hall and the first Catholic mission church, is now, after much reconstruction, the Island Baptist Church.

Chapter 24

LONG BEACH TOWNSHIP

In early times, the thinly populated barrier islands of New Jersey had no autonomous political identity. They were governed from the mainland, often by several different townships whose jurisdiction was determined simply by tracing parallel lines on a chart eastward across a bay to that part of the island most nearly opposite. Thus Long Beach Island was governed until the last decade of the nineteenth century by at least five mainland townships.

They began at the south end with Little Egg Harbor Township, which controlled Tucker's Island, Tucker's Beach and the tip of Holgate. The next seven miles of beach and meadows, from Holgate through Beach Haven and as far north as today's Brant Beach, were a part of Eagleswood Township. Present-day Ship Bottom and Surf City were governed by Stafford Township, and from there northward, the island was in the domain of Union (now called Barnegat) and Ocean townships.

By the time there was any serious attempt to make the whole island into a single, self-governing township in 1899, it was too late. Beach Haven had left Eagleswood to incorporate as a borough in 1890. Harvey Cedars and Long Beach

City (Surf City) followed in 1894, declaring independence from Union and Stafford townships respectively, so that Long Beach Township, created by the state Legislature on March 23, 1899, took control of the island from inlet to inlet exclusive of these three boroughs.

Settling for what was left, Long Beach Township found itself divided into four sections of unequal size which, including the four miles of Tucker's Beach, brought the newly formed township's holdings to a total of nearly sixteen miles. Virtually all of it was uninhabited with the exception of Barnegat City and the settlements around the five Life Saving stations of Lovelady's Island, Ship Bottom, Long Beach (Beach Haven Terrace), Bond's, and Little Egg Harbor, which was at Sea Haven on Tucker's Island.

Long Beach Township is today only half the size it was in 1899. Parcels were annexed to Beach Haven Borough in 1903 and again in 1913. Barnegat City left the township and became an independent borough on March 29, 1904, eventually taking the name Barnegat Light in 1948. Ship Bottom-Beach Arlington broke away from Long Beach Township on March 3, 1925, shortening its name to Ship Bottom in 1947. Finally,

in 1936, St. Albans-by-the-Sea (Tucker's Island) had to be dropped from the tax rolls due to the relentless southward drift of Beach Haven Inlet, which had eroded nearly three miles of Tucker's Beach south of Holgate and more than half of Tucker's Island as well.

Of the four scattered sections that make up the territory of Long Beach Township today, three are much the same in size, roughly a mile to a mile and a quarter each in length. Because they are smaller and more identifiable, these sections have acquired their own names of Holgate, North Beach and Loveladies. The fourth section, which lies in the five-mile stretch between Beach Haven and Ship Bottom, is bigger by far than the others but it has no specific name other than "the Township." Within it, however, are no fewer than eleven well-defined little communities, not one of which has any political identity. At least six are variations on the name of Beach Haven, such as Beach Haven Park, Beach Haven Gardens and Beach Haven Terrace, but there is also a Peahala Park, a Spray Beach and a Brant Beach. Brant Beach, one of the largest of these eleven communities, is the site of the Long Beach Township Municipal Building. It is from here sections of the township, from Holgate on the south to North Beach and Loveladies on the north, are governed and policed.

All of the sections and the communities within them have a long history, starting with Holgate, which acquired its name from James Holgate, who owned most of the land south of Beach Haven by the turn of the twentieth century. It was customary long ago to name a part of the island after a current or past big landholder. Holgate's name survived while others like Bond, Jones, Frazier, Smith, Buzby and Horner, once so well-known, faded into history. But it was the arrival of the automobile and the feverish competition to sell real estate that gave the island its variations on the name of Beach Haven. Philadelphia realtors were responsible for this redundancy; Beach Haven had a high profile, while Long Beach Island was often confused with Long Island, New York.

In the 1920s, there was even an attempt to change the name of Holgate to Beach Haven Heights to promote an ambitious real estate venture on the edge of the new Beach Haven Inlet. Later, one part of the development would be called Venice Beach and another the Smith Tract. Some local residents around the Coast Guard station preferred to call the area Bond's, and others called it Beach Haven Inlet, the name that got onto the new water tower in 1939. In the 1950s there was a Beach Haven South below Beach Haven and, until the Great Atlantic Storm of March 1962, a development called Silver Sands. Holgate is the one name that has outlasted them all.

In the history of Long Beach Island, only Beach Haven and Barnegat Light were deliberately planned as resorts to the extent that a grid of streets was laid out and named and investment sought. All of the other communities sprang up around Life Saving stations or old

collection of George Hartnett (all)

Like other early Coast Guard stations, the one in Beach Haven Terrace at Maryland Avenue became the nucleus of a small community, facing page, top. "The Terrace" drew residents with ocean and bayfront structures like this pavilion (top) and fishing pier. Other communities were encouraged by developers like William Ringgold who built the Dolphin Inn in 1886 on 14th Street in North Beach Haven, left.

hotels. The first attempt to deliberately copy Beach Haven in the long stretches between the stations began on a small scale with Waverly Beach in what is now North Beach Haven, a part of Long Beach Township. In 1882, William Hewitt, an Englishman and an active promoter of a railroad to the island, started selling lots on the edge of the creek that was the northern border of Beach Haven and built a hotel there called the Waverly House.

Hewitt enticed the Pennsylvania Railroad to build and manage the Manahawkin and Long Beach Railroad. He believed in the future of the island, working hard to promote Waverly Beach, and he talked some of his friends and William Ringgold, a mortgage banker from Philadelphia, into building the Dolphin Inn, an oceanfront hotel near the Waverly House. Unable to compete with Beach Haven, Hewitt's dream failed, but Waverly Beach inspired Ringgold to start a resort of his own. He sold the Dolphin Inn in 1889 and moved eight blocks north to a bog-filled tract called Cranberry Hill where he built a large house and sold lots to his Philadelphia clientele and friends. Within the year, his daughter had renamed the tiny community of summer cottages Spray Beach, and Ringgold's original oceanfront house was enlarged and became the Spray Beach Hotel.

In 1890 the Pennsylvania Railroad made Spray Beach one of its stops on the run from Ship Bottom to highly profitable Beach Haven. Initially, the railroad had planned more stops but, aside from the Peahala Club and Waverly Beach and an occasional supply drop at Life Saving Station 117 three miles below Ship Bottom, there simply was not enough traffic in the township. In fact, in 1905 there were not many more people living in it than there had been in the nineteenth century.

Station 117, better known as the Long Beach Station, became the nucleus of a new resort called Beach Haven Terrace. Started in 1907 by George H. Smith Jr., William W. Rorer and John Kane of the Fidelity Land Company of Philadelphia, it was ready to greet the automobile age when the island causeway was completed in 1914. For a few years after Bay Avenue was built, it came to a stop at the Terrace because a huge pond at Maryland Avenue forced motorists to detour a block east and drive the rest of the way on Beach Avenue into Beach Haven. Beach Avenue or "Mosquito Alley," then little more than a wagon track, was also the main thoroughfare for Spray Beach.

Until the early twenties, the train was still the primary means of transportation for most potential buyers of shore homes, and Philadelphia realtors ran Saturday morning excursion trains to the island. However, those communities that were developed after 1914 had to make do without a train stop, and Beach Haven Gardens was one of those latecomers. Building lots selling for $150 with $10 down

On the day the causeway bridge opened in 1914, Beach Haven Terrace had a sign to greet motorists using the new boulevard, below. The small community bustled with a post office, general store and bakery.

were advertised in 1926 on a seven-block parcel sandwiched between Beach Haven Terrace on the north and Spray Beach on the south. The tract was developed by G. E. Bliss of Philadelphia, who advised investors to get off the train

at Beach Haven Terrace and walk the five blocks to his office at Twenty-ninth and Beach.

In the mid-thirties, Herbert and Jerome Shapiro developed Beach Haven Park and went on to build Beach Haven West, a major lagoon development on the mainland. James McMurray's Beach Haven Crest grew up near one of the island's several pound fishing operations, the Crest Fishery. Naming real estate ventures after Beach Haven even produced a Haven Beach; the trend ended when builder James O. Brogdon and his wife, Elizabeth, began, in the sand hills north of Beach Haven Terrace, a development of vacation homes called simply "The Dunes." Larger than the island's typical Cape Cods, each home had a roof of a different color. Other developments that did not use Beach Haven as a selling tool included Brighton Beach, started by William C. Smith in 1920, and Peahala Park. Begun in 1940 between Ninetieth and Ninety-sixth streets, Peahala Park retained the name of the old gun-

A panorama of Beach Haven Gardens and Beach Haven Terrace with its Coast Guard station, above, shows the undeveloped land that began to disappear with the development of the 1950s. In the 1930s, Beach Haven Park oceanside lots sold for as little as $150, and the Shapiro name became synonymous with progress.

ning club founded there by a group of Burlington County sportsmen in the 1880s.

Brant Beach was started in 1909 as one of the most ambitious of all the developments outside Beach Haven. From the very beginning it had its own artesian well and water tower and was also the first resort on the island with a generating plant for public electricity. Henry B. McLaughlin, a Philadelphia attorney, was the founder of Brant Beach, but that was not its first name.

The name that McLaughlin settled on was Beach Haven North, but at about that time Waverly Beach chose to call itself North Beach Haven. To give his development a clear identity, McLaughlin came up with Brant Beach, named after its bay beach on a large cove where there was a "brant graveling" that attracted great flocks of the small goose to the area.

Today's Brant Beach runs two miles from Thirty-first Street at Ship Bottom southward forty-three blocks to Seventy-fourth Street. These streets are all numbered, but at Fifty-third they are named as well, with street signs for Mears, Farragut, Sumner, Beardsley, Sigsbee, Paulding and Goldsborough. There are twenty names in all, and they are so unusual that it is unlikely

they would appear anywhere else in the United States outside a naval base. The streets are all named after high-ranking naval officers, mostly rear admirals who established their reputations in the nineteenth century and in the Civil War.

These named streets identify the earlier Brant Beach. The numbered streets from Thirty-first to Fifty-second are part of a development started in 1925 by Philadelphia realtor Robert Osborne in partnership with William Noonan Sr., a vice president of the American Tobacco Company, and Charles B. Deubarrow, a Philadelphia stockbroker. They, too, built houses but their plans included a hotel, a twenty-car garage and a movie theater. Two more hotels and a boardwalk were planned, but the stock market crash in 1929 ended the venture.

At the northern border of Surf City above Twenty-fifth Street, a green and gold sign marks the entrance to "North Beach, Established 1899." That is the date that Long Beach Township was established, but the sign gives no further information about the history of North Beach, a name acquired only in 1949. People who bought land there in the 1930s and 1940s and built beachfront homes knew it as the Frazier Tract.

When Daniel B. Frazier of Philadelphia bought the 165-acre tract in 1911, it was known as the Sewell Tract, a part of the estate of the late U.S. Senator William J. Sewell. Frazier already owned the Harvey Cedars Hotel and was prepared to watch land values rise with the completion of the new automobile causeway across the bay into Ship Bottom in 1914. Unfortunately for people on the island's north end, the only road built from Ship Bottom went directly to Beach Haven. The rest of the island did not get a road until 1920, and by then Surf City and everything north of it had gone into decline, but those who were not waiting to sell land preferred the unspoiled solitude of all those miles of big dunes, bayberry, and flat, treeless meadows.

The Frazier Tract lay vacant for years, a mere passage for motorists to the island's north

Today's North Beach was the wide open Frazier Tract in the 1930s. Fearful that the land would become a state-owned park and public beach, Long Beach Township officials sold ocean-to-bay lots, two hundred feet wide, for $1,000.

end. In 1936 it was seized by the township for tax foreclosure because the state of New Jersey had become interested in the land and planned to purchase it for an oceanfront park. Fearful that such a purchase would undermine real estate values and hurt local revenues with state lands' tax-exempt status, the township listed fifteen lots for sale on April 17, 1937.

Each lot was two hundred feet wide and ran from oceanfront to bayfront. A minimum price of one thousand dollars was set for each section, which was sold to the highest bidder. When all of the lots sold, township mayor Howard Shiffer suggested renaming the tract Long Beach Park

even though there was no longer a chance of the area becoming state property. He liked the name and would later apply it to another undeveloped tract north of Harvey Cedars, today's Loveladies.

Shiffer's suggestion was voted down. The name North Beach was not even considered because the term of "north point o' beach" is used in sailing directions to describe the land on the north side of any inlet. It would have been incorrect for any tract of beach land several miles from the nearest inlet to be labeled as such. Besides, at that very time "north beach" was used to refer to the southern tip of Island Beach just across Barnegat Inlet from the lighthouse.

The Frazier Tract kept its name for another dozen years until a bayside development of twenty houses went up on Starboard Lane. Caring little whether the term was correct or not, the builders and developers chose to call their venture the "North Beach Homes." With plans for the future they pushed the idea of calling the whole tract North Beach, and most people liked it. By then more of the blockwide bayside lots were being subdivided. The completion of the Garden State Parkway was only four years away, and the land rush would soon be on. Frazier had missed the boom by about forty years.

ဆ ၊ၣ

From 1886 until 1935, the Manahawkin and Long Beach Railroad crossed a drawbridge at Cedar Bonnet Island before reaching Barnegat City Junction in Ship Bottom where the train turned north or south. Before the railroad ceased service to the north end in 1920, there had been five scheduled stops at Long Beach City (Surf City), Harvey Cedars, High Point, Club House and Barnegat City.

Club House, the railroad's official name for the township section today called Loveladies, came from "Long Beach Club House," the name of a hotel popular with New Yorkers for half of the nineteenth century. It was built in 1852 as the Atlantic Hotel by a Barnegat man with the unusual name James James. He was a genial and very popular innkeeper and his clientele, mostly sportsmen, always called his place "Double Jimmie's." Around 1868 it became the property of Charles Cox of Barnegat, who changed the name of the hotel to the Long Beach Club House, but it was never a private club at all, and many still called it Double Jimmie's.

When the U.S. Life Saving Service was formed in 1871 and manned station houses were built along the coast, they were all numbered as well as named for each locale. There were seven stations on Long Beach Island and Tucker's Island. Barnegat Inlet, Harvey Cedars, Ship Bottom and all the others were easy choices, but it seemed inappropriate to name a Life Saving station Double Jimmie's or, worse yet, Club House. The only physical feature between the inlet and Harvey Cedars that actually had a name was a tiny island in the bay called Lovelady's Island, where owner Thomas Lovelady of Waretown had built a gunning shack and set up duck blinds.

U.S. Life Saving Station 114 thus became the Lovelady's Island Station, and so a name that might otherwise have been forgotten was recorded on government documents and all coastal charts. The railroad, however, used another name for its timetables and records, officially dubbing the area "Club House." Eventually the old place was abandoned, and train service ended as soon as the automobile road was completed to the north end in 1920. The smaller of the two buildings was moved to Harvey Cedars and became the High Point Inn.

The station was decommissioned in the early thirties at the end of Prohibition and reactivated in 1942 during World War II. Servicemen joked about the name Lovelady's, and at war's end the station was again decommissioned and the name dropped. However, some name had to be given to this township territory and Mayor Shiffer suggested Long Beach Park.

Into the early fifties, Long Beach Park was open land, used only by campers and fishermen; the fires of beach parties could be seen in the enormous dunes. Most people did not even know the area's name and called it High Point, the old name for the northern half of Harvey Cedars. It seemed to have no identity and had only a few homes in the summer of 1949 when the Long Beach Island Foundation for the Arts and Sciences opened on a thirty-acre site across the road from the old Lovelady's Coast Guard Station.

A movement arose to drop the prosaic Long Beach Park and take the name Lovelady's. In 1952 the name of the tract was changed to Loveladies with a new spelling, two years before the Garden State Parkway would bring a wave of buyers for oceanfront lots in this, the last undeveloped area on Long Beach Island.

In 1949, the spare-looking Foundation for the Arts and Sciences was built in Long Beach Park, across from the Lovelady's Coast Guard station. The area was renamed Loveladies by Long Beach Township in 1952.

Chapter 25

THE ISLAND'S HOUSES OF WORSHIP

For most of the 1800s there was not a single church of any denomination on Long Beach Island. Proprietors of the widely scattered hotels usually observed the Sabbath with a ban on cardplaying, billiards, bowling and dancing; fishing, hunting and drinking, considered to be less frivolous pursuits, were rarely interrupted. Clergymen on vacation made themselves available for religious services, but in their absence in the early days anyone wishing to hear a preacher on Sunday had to sail to the mainland.

Not until 1874 after the Parry House at Beach Haven had been built, and the Engleside two years later, were there ever any formal religious services. They were given by visiting clergymen at one hotel or the other, but it was a custom soon to find a more formal setting. A few hours after midnight on Friday, August 12, 1881, the Parry House burned to the ground, an event that inspired the building of the island's first church.

All two hundred Parry House guests escaped uninjured because of the alertness of the Reverend James Lamb, a visiting Episcopal minister from Trinity Church in Moorestown. It was Lamb who smelled the smoke and heard the first faint cries from the hotel kitchen, where the fire had started. Rousing the sleeping guests on both upper floors, he led them through the dark, unlighted corridors to the stairs and to safety outside where many guests joined in the futile bucket brigade.

Charles Parry and his wife, the owners of the hotel, had been among those saved by Lamb's actions, and that evening, a thanksgiving service was held in the parlor of the Engleside Hotel, where the refugees of the Parry House were put up. There would be another special service on Sunday morning led by Reverend Lamb, who had become an instant hero. During the service Mrs. Parry announced that she would build a church in gratitude for the deliverance of the Parry House guests and, in particular, in memory of her daughter Clara Parry Hilger, who had died in childbirth the previous winter. Mrs. Parry chose the name Holy Innocents Episcopal Church for "All Children in Paradise" who predeceased their parents. Charles Parry was not a churchman, but he was always supportive of his wife's religious interests, and he was very generous with her wishes.

Holy Innocents was built on the northeast corner of Beach Avenue and South Street (Engleside Avenue) in the winter and spring of 1882. The church had been designed by the firm of John Wilson and Sons, the most prestigious architectural firm in Philadelphia. The first service was July 9, when the building was consecrated by Bishop John Scarborough, who called the graceful structure "an ornament to the coast."

When first built, the church stood on the corner of the two streets, but a September hurricane in 1903 toppled its tower and moved the building off its foundations. The church trustees decided to move it eastward twenty-five feet onto a new base, and this time the walls were supported with brick buttresses. The entire cost of rebuilding came to $2,162 and was paid for by Mrs. Parry's granddaughter, Clara D. Hilger. It was her mother who had died when Clara was born.

The church was used only in the summer and fall until 1938 when a winter chapel was constructed just east of the building. The last service ever held at Holy Innocents was on December 15, 1974, when the parish moved three blocks south into a new building between Pearl and Marine streets where the Hotel Baldwin had once stood. The former church buildings were purchased by

In 1882, Holy Innocents Episcopal Church, on the corner of Engleside and Beach avenues in Beach Haven, was the island's first church. The church's design matched the homes of prosperous summertime cottagers. The building is now the Long Beach Island Historical Museum.

the Long Beach Island Historical Museum, and in 1985 the two structures were joined under a common roof. A storage room was constructed between the original church, now an auditorium, and the winter chapel on the east side, which is the main entrance to the museum. The cost of the improvements came to nearly as much as had been spent on the church in its entire ninety-three years of existence.

∞ ❧

In the 1880s, the spiritual needs of the summer population had been met with Holy Inno-

cents seaside memorial chapel and with Catholic masses which were said in the Beach Haven School on Third Street. The Quakers had a meeting house next to the Pharo home on Second Street, but they, too, met only in the summer. A growing population of winter residents had, as yet, no place to go to church.

Heating a large space was a problem to be faced in the winter months, and other structures were too small for a religious service even if a clergyman was available. The big hotels were closed from September until June, and smaller ones like the Ocean House and the Beach Haven

House that did remain open all year for the gunning crowd were also drinking establishments, making them wholly unsuitable.

Most of the year-round population of Beach Haven had grown up on the mainland and were strongly under the influence of Methodism, a faith that had long been established there. Their concern for the proper upbringing of their children led them to organize a Union Sunday School in the waiting room of the brand-new Pennsylvania Railroad station on Third Street at the invitation of the stationmaster. Adults began to attend, too, and then, on a cold February night in 1887, the station, only eight months old, burned to the ground. While it was being rebuilt, Sunday school moved a block east to the town's one-room schoolhouse.

Occasionally a minister from the mainland sailed over and held a Sunday service, and enthusiasm grew, culminating May 5, 1888, in a formally organized Methodist Church group. Still, they had no church until help came from an unexpected source. Dr. Edward Williams, one of the partners in the firm of Burnham, Parry and Williams, bought and presented the tiny congregation with two lots on the east side of Beach Avenue between Centre and Second streets. Part of the land had been occupied by the Parry House before it was destroyed by fire, so Williams and Charles Parry, partners in the hotel, both were prime benefactors of island churches.

Now that the the Methodists had the land and a valid organization, there were loans and donations available to them to build a church through the Church Extension Society of the Methodist General Conference headed by Dr. Alpha Jefferson Kynett, a leading clergyman and reformer of his day. In the thirty-two years of his incumbency he had seen to the building of hundreds of Methodist churches nationwide, and the church at Beach Haven was named in his honor.

Kynett, one of the founders of the Anti-Saloon League which eventually led to the Eighteenth Amendment and Prohibition, died in 1899.

Dedicated in 1891, the Kynett Methodist Church was the first year-round island church. Its pastor was S. J. Gwynne, who sailed over from West Creek each Sunday to preach. Its tall spire, so characteristic of Methodist churches, was a prominent landmark and served as a guide to mariners far out in the bay until a great gale in September 1903 toppled it. As part of the repairs, the church also was moved southward from the middle of the block to the corner of Beach Avenue at Centre Street and put on a firmer foundation. The steeple was replaced with a shorter tower.

The old Quaker meeting house was moved from Second Street to the spot formerly occupied by the church and in 1908 became the town's first library. When the Pharo family built a new library on Third Street in 1924, the library's trustees presented the old one to Kynett Church for a parish house. It remains in that location, having survived the disastrous fire which destroyed the original Kynett Church on Palm Sunday, March 20, 1932.

That setback galvanized the congregation, and the cornerstone for a new church was laid that summer in a well-attended ceremony followed by afternoon services in the Episcopal church. For the next few months, Kynett's Sunday services were held in the Beach Haven Fire Hall, but the new church was ready in a remarkably short time. Its first use was for a Sunday school Christmas festival on Christmas Eve, and regular services resumed two weeks later when the pews were installed. The dedication of the new building was held on August 15, 1933.

ဆ ఴ

The first regularly scheduled Roman Catholic masses also began in Beach Haven, starting in the summer of 1885 in the one-room schoolhouse on Third Street. Priests from Camden and Philadelphia had, from time to time, said masses at private residences around town, but now there were weekly masses during the summer months.

In 1890 priests from Lakewood established a Catholic mission and continued to use the schoolhouse for two masses every Sunday and holy day in July and August until 1893. By then the Reverend Thomas B. Healy, who had assumed charge of the Beach Haven mission, had built a chapel to use in place of the school. Already the parish had been named for St. Thomas Aquinas, but little is known about its beginnings.

Several accounts written at the turn of the century give no indication where the chapel was located or what it looked like. Being temporary, it must have been small and, most likely, north of Centre Street. Records do show that the first mass celebrated in the chapel was on August 13, 1893, and that Catherine Isabella Sprague, daughter of Mary Boylan and Jeremiah Sprague, was the first child baptized there. The resident Catholic population was not large then, probably fewer

The first church to remain open year-round was Kynett Methodist Church, here at its original location on Beach Avenue in Beach Haven. Mariners used the tall steeple as a landmark until it was toppled by a gale in September 1903. During repairs, the church was moved south to the corner of Beach and Centre Street.

The island's Roman Catholic churches were considered missions and did not have full-time pastors. In Beach Haven, St. Thomas Aquinas Church, above, was built in 1899 on Fourth Street and Beach Avenue, a year after the chapel of St. Thomas of Villanova, right, had been built in Surf City with funds from Catholics and non-Catholics.

than seven adults, but the number always swelled in the summertime, and a church for three hundred was planned.

A lot at Fourth Street and Beach Avenue on what was then the northern edge of town was purchased for $450, and the cornerstone for St. Thomas Aquinas Church was laid on June 11, 1899. William L. Butler, a local contractor and the first mayor of Beach Haven, built the thirty-foot by seventy-foot church for four thousand dollars.

Exactly one year earlier and eight miles to the north, the chapel of St. Thomas of Villanova had been built at Surf City with funding from the Thomas Callahan family, Philadelphians who summered on the island. Like the church at Beach Haven, the chapel was used only in the summer months. By 1905 St. Thomas Aquinas Parish pur-

chased a lot on Third and Beach to build a rectory. Father William Gilfillan, who until then had been living at the Hotel Baldwin, was replaced by Father Thomas Joseph Whelan, who built the rectory and eventually oversaw the missions at Surf City and at Barnegat on the mainland. The parish served an area from Waretown to Atlantic County; altogether, there were about 160 Catholics, nineteen of whom were residents of Beach Haven.

By 1928 the two Roman Catholic parishes on the island passed over to the care of the Franciscans of the Holy Name Province of New York, who converted the former rectory at Third and Beach into a friary with a chapel for winter services. By 1937 the churches at Surf City and Beach Haven could not handle the growing sum-

mer population of Catholics, and for the first time masses were offered at the Colony movie theater in Brant Beach. After the war, the Harvey Cedars firehouse and the Brant Beach municipal building were put to the same use for many a summer until 1958, when St. Francis of Assisi Church opened at Brant Beach. In 1965, a new, much larger St. Thomas Aquinas Church was built at Second Street and Atlantic Avenue.

St. Thomas of Villanova Church was also rebuilt that year, and in 1978, one more church was added on the north end of the island, St. Clare's at Loveladies. Besides churches, however, a century of Catholicism on Long Beach Island also brought St. Francis Community Center in Brant Beach, dedicated in 1972 to serve people of all ages and all religions.

In 1890, the year that Kynett Methodist Church was built at Beach Haven, another Methodist church was born at the north end of the island at Barnegat City. Its principal benefactor, Benjamin Franklin Archer, who owned the Oceanic Hotel and was the power behind the resort, commissioned boatwright Enoch Boice to design the church which, inevitably, was built just like a ship. Archer, a strict Methodist from Camden, had hopes that Barnegat City would someday rival Ocean Grove as a religious resort community.

Archer's church would not stay Methodist. In 1912 it had become Presbyterian and would remain so until 1937, when the Episcopal Diocese of New Jersey purchased it and named it after a Biblican fisherman, St. Peter's-at-the-Light. The year-round church still stands at Seventh Street and Central Avenue.

St. Peter's is small with fewer than fifteen to twenty pews, each of them older than the church itself by more than a hundred years. They are of polished natural wood unlike the solid wooden joinery of the walls and ceiling which are painted white in pleasing contrast to the red-carpeted floors. Outside, bushy yews and cedar branches filter the sunlight through the six stained glass windows along the north and south sides. Another two windows are at the back of the church, and all eight of them depict the lives of the saints.

The centerpiece of the church is a triptych of wood standing behind the altar on the west side. It is the work of Lewis Carr, a well-known ecclesiastical artist and sculptor. The center panel shows Christ the Risen King, and the two on either side illustrate episodes in the life of St. Peter.

By coincidence, the very year that Archer's church switched from Methodist to Presbyterian, another island group of mostly Methodists gathered on the beach for an evening song service at

St. Peter's-at-the-Light in Barnegat Light has been a Methodist, Presbyterian and Episcopalian church. It was designed in 1890 by boatwright Enoch Boice, whose nautical joinery can still be seen in the interior.

a new resort community called Beach Haven Terrace. On summer evenings in those years the beach was the only refuge from mosquitoes.

Beach Haven Terrace was only five years old, but it was a thriving little community with a mixture of summer people and permanent residents who needed a place to hold religious services. The gathering on the beach that August night had been spontaneous, but the momentum held and in subsequent weeks the group moved to the lobby of the Clearview Hotel near the oceanfront on New Jersey Avenue, where there was a piano and shelter from the rain.

By the summer of 1916 they had formed Beach Haven Terrace Sabbath Union with Pro-fessor W. Rorer as president and met at his home next to the Coast Guard station on Maryland Avenue, but the congregation was growing and would soon need a church. In 1920 the Reverend Howard Amer of Kynett Methodist Church had raised $1,500 for the Terrace church. With more donations by residents, a lot was purchased and a small chapel was built on the northeast corner of Beach and New Jersey avenues. The first service was held on May 30, 1921.

In 1927 a belfry was added to the tiny building, and the following year it became officially known as the Terrace Methodist Church. By 1931 a kitchen and a community hall were added, and a heating system was installed on the eve of

Although its organizers had met since 1912, Terrace Methodist Church was built in 1927, a tiny chapel at the corner of Beach and New Jersey avenues. Additions and land purchases expanded the church's size.

World War II. All during the war the building, complete with blackout curtains and cots, was used for air raid and first aid drills. The church continued to grow with more additions to the structure and with adjoining property purchased for parking. In 1968, its name was changed for the third time to the First United Methodist Church of Beach Haven Terrace.

ॐ   ☙

Lutheranism traces its origins to the activity of Martin Luther (1483-1546), the leading figure of the Protestant Reformation. Starting in Germany, the new faith spread to Holland and Scandinavia, eventually following the waves of immigration from these countries to America. Lutheranism was well established in Colonial times, but it kept much of its immigrant character, emphasizing the retention of

national languages and customs until the early twentieth century.

Until the middle of the nineteenth century, Lutheranism in America was largely German, but there soon followed a great wave of Scandinavian immigrants. Most of them moved westward to farm the land, but among those Swedes and Norwegians who stayed in the East to follow the sea were many who were skilled fishermen. It was just at this time that the pound fishing industry was starting up along the coast, and there was a demand for strong, experienced men to row the boats out to the nets a mile or two offshore.

By the 1920s and 1930s the fishermen and their descendants had formed the backbone of several small communities on Long Beach Island, especially Barnegat City on the north end, but these families had to go as far as Lake-

wood or Atlantic City to attend a Lutheran church. Such trips could be made only a few times a year, and soon a request went out to the Board of American Missions of the United Lutheran Church in America to conduct a survey on the need for a church.

In the summer of 1939, Reverend Ragnar Kjeldahl was sent to the island. After a meeting in the North Beach Haven home of Nils and Olga Eklund, he learned there was a need for not just one but two congregations, one at Barnegat City to be called Zion and another at Beach Haven Crest to be called Holy Trinity. These separate churches were formed into a single pastorate served by Reverend Kjeldahl until he was called into the Navy in 1943 to serve in the Chaplain Corps.

Holy Trinity rented its first chapel in 1939. It was a rough-hewn structure on a sand lot on the north side of Winifred Avenue in Beach Haven Crest near the fishery. The enthusiastic congregation made an altar out of two fish boxes and an old kitchen table; sprigs of holly decorated the walls, and the cross over the door was made of wood. An old railroad stove took the chill out of the drafty room. Holy Trinity, however, was a congregation blessed with more than its share of skilled carpenters. The men worked constantly on the building and finally, in 1942, the congregation was able to buy the tiny chapel. It would be used for the next fourteen years until a new church on Long Beach Boulevard in Brant Beach was dedicated on June 10, 1956. Later that year the little chapel on Winifred Avenue was sold to the Veterans of Foreign Wars.

The Zion congregation also started in 1939 and had its first services in St. Peter's-at-the-Light; at other times church members met in the town's fire hall, but by the summer of 1942 they had built their own church. It was a tiny place, not much bigger than the makeshift chapel at

Lynn Photo (right)

As the island grew, so did its churches. The seasonal and nondenominational Spray Beach Chapel, above, had its origins in the music room of the Spray Beach Hotel. Trinity Lutheran Church, right, began in a rented building in Beach Haven Crest near the pound fisheries, later moving to Brant Beach. Union Chapel in Ship Bottom-Beach Arlington, facing page, left, was dedicated in 1924 and for a time was called Union Everybody's Church. Members of the United Church of Surf City met in the firehouse until volunteers built a church, far

Beach Haven Terrace, but within the decade a major addition was started in front of the original church. It was finished in 1956, but Zion did not get a full-time pastor until 1977 when the Reverend John E. Pearce arrived.

  ∐   ∑

Of the six island churches that were started in the nineteenth century, only one, the Spray Beach Chapel, can claim uninterrupted use year after year in the same structure. The two Catholic churches at Beach Haven and Surf City and Holy Innocents Episcopal are all in newer, larger

buildings. Kynett Methodist was destroyed by fire in 1932 and rebuilt, and St. Peter's-at-the-Light, while it may be the oldest structure still in use as a church, has been vacant at various intervals over the years as it switched from Methodist to Presbyterian to Episcopal.

Started in the early 1890s in the music room of the old Spray Beach Hotel on Twenty-third Street, Spray Beach has remained a nondenominational summer chapel, fulfilling its original purpose. The idea for a chapel grew out of Sunday school classes conducted in the hotel by

Hettie Ringgold, the wife of William Ringgold, who had purchased a tract of land in 1889 that his daughter named Spray Beach. In the summer of 1894 there were fewer than twelve cottages in the area around the hotel, but there were still enough people to support building a chapel. Most of the inspiration for the project came from Hettie Ringgold.

William L. Butler, Beach Haven's first mayor and best-known building contractor, erected the wood-framed chapel at a cost of nine hundred dollars. Unfortunately, Hettie Ringgold did not

live to see her dream become a reality; she died in May of 1895 and the chapel was not completed until August.

The Spray Beach Chapel is open from mid-May until late September with a different visiting minister each week. The ministers are chosen each year by the board of trustees and usually come from Pennsylvania and New Jersey, but occasionally there will be a visiting missionary from a distant part of the world. Some of the incentive to come to Spray Beach is a free place to stay for a week at the shore, and many ministers have been bringing their families for years.

There are two other nondenominational union churches in Ship Bottom and in Surf City. The Union Church of Ship Bottom, as it was known for nearly sixty years, was built and dedicated in 1924 to become the first house of worship in that town. Before then, as early as 1916, residents and summer visitors met for services

at the old Beach Arlington railroad station until money was raised to build the church at Nineteenth Street and the boulevard. The church's official name for several years in the 1940s was Union Everybody's Church. Reorganized as Grace Evangelical Church in 1982, it is still firmly rooted in the Ship Bottom community, serving some families who as year-round or summer residents are now in their third generation as members.

About the same time a Protestant union movement was starting in Ship Bottom, another was forming in Surf City, also holding services in temporary meeting places like the fire hall or the second floor of the old borough hall at Twelfth Street. The United Church of Surf City became an official congregation, but a decade would pass before it could build a church. Built entirely by volunteers, it was dedicated on September 2, 1934, as Surf City's first and only

Protestant church. The lot on Seventh Street and Central Avenue where it stands was donated by Walter and Irene Pullinger, and the building remains largely in its original condition.

In 1941, in a manner similar to the formation of other churches, a small group of Christian Scientists began to meet in various homes. As their numbers grew, they held services in the Long Beach Township Municipal Building in Brant Beach and by the mid-1950s were able to purchase land to build a church of their own. According to Christian Science precepts, dedication of the one-story building at Tenth Street and Barnegat Avenue in Ship Bottom took place only when the church was debt-free, on August 11, 1968.

        ⅾ   ⇛

The Jewish Community Center of Long Beach Island at Twenty-fourth Street and the boulevard in Spray Beach fulfills social and reli-

The island's Jewish community first observed holy days at private residences or in the Ocean House in Beach Haven and later at the Hotel Baldwin. After the Baldwin burned, the Jewish Community Center was built in Spray Beach in 1961.

gious needs for the island's resident Jewish population and summer visitors. The center has oper-ated on a year-round basis since 1979, and its synagogue services are attended by many from the mainland as well.

The center was built in 1961, but its origins go back a generation earlier to 1941 and can be traced directly to the efforts of Morton N. Kaye, the first person to call together the island's Jewish families who had to go as far as Lakewood and Atlantic City to visit a synagogue or a temple. Kaye, a summer resident of Beach Haven Gardens, felt something had to be done to preserve the Jewish faith and tradition especially among children, and he believed that effort ought to be done close at hand. He struck a responsive chord among Beach Haven's small Jewish com-munity which was nearly as old as the town it-self, having played a vital role in its business life since the 1880s.

The first meetings were held in a small room off the lobby of the Ocean House Hotel on the north side of Centre Street between Beach and Bay avenues in Beach Haven. Just before the na-tion entered the war, Kaye tried to gather as many local and nonresident Jewish people as he could. The meetings for the next several summers were irregular, but the holy days were always ob-served with special services either at the Ocean House or at a private residence.

After the war, attendance at and interest in the meetings picked up. This interest had to do as much with pride in the developments in the new nation of Israel as with the desire for local religious training for children. Just as the need for a larger and better meeting place became a matter of concern, Abe and Cora Korb bought the Hotel Baldwin. From 1955, regular meetings and synagogue services were held in the ballroom of the rambling old structure that had seen so much history in its eighty-some years.

But on a windy September night in 1960, the Baldwin caught fire and was destroyed. By then the leaders of the island's Jewish population, whose new organization had been incorporated since 1955, were deeply committed to having their own place of worship. At a meeting at the Herbert Shapiro home on the bay in Haven Beach during the High Holy Days immediately after the fire, a decision was made to build a synagogue and social center.

The Shapiros donated four lots at Twelfth Street in Beach Haven on the east side of Bay Avenue. The following spring there was a groundbreaking ceremony attended by the island's political figures and several celebrities, including playwright Moss Hart and his wife, actress Kitty Carlyle, who summered on the island in those years. To everyone's dismay, the first piling to be driven went straight down and out of sight. And so did the next two. The lots were directly over an old creek and pond that had once formed the northern border of Beach Haven but had been filled in for nearly fifty years. Since these lots could never support a major building like the center, they were sold and additional monies were raised to buy land at Twenty-fourth Street and the boulevard in Spray Beach, where the center was built and dedicated within the year.

Every religious denomination on the island began modestly, meeting wherever they could in train stations, hotel lobbies, theaters, schools and private homes until their memberships grew and they could afford to build. The Baptists are the latest denomination to follow that progression. They first met in the summer of 1976 when services were held in the Colonial Theater at Bay Avenue and Centre Street and at the Beach Haven fire hall. The congregation called itself the Island Baptist Church; its pastor, the Reverend Michael Jones, also happened to be a builder who appreciated old buildings and knew how to restore them. His ministry and his carpentry skills would dovetail in one of the most historic buildings in Beach Haven, built in 1885, the year before the railroad came to the island.

The long-abandoned building on Third Street between Bay and Beach avenues that the new congregation bought from Elvie Colmer for fifteen thousand dollars had been the first movie theater on the Island. Elvie Colmer's husband, Harry,

Baptists held services at Beach Haven's Colonial theater in 1976 before restoring the town's first schoolhouse and first movie theater on Third Street, above, for the Island Baptist Church.

bought the tiny theater in 1914 and ran it until 1922 when he built a big theater on Bay Avenue.

Even before Harry Colmer's time, the Third Street theater had played many roles. Built as the island's first school, it was a public building and was also used for town meetings and for a summer school to teach illiterate black servants from the Engleside and Baldwin hotels. In the 1880s, before the Methodists built their own church, they held services in the winter months in the little schoolhouse. In the summer it was used by Catholic mission priests from Lakewood who said masses in the building until 1893. Even after Colmer had built his new theater, he still used the former schoolhouse throughout the 1920s in the wintertime when audiences were smaller. At other times during those years, local people held

dances in the building. The single-story, wooden structure remained closed for nearly fifty years until 1981 when the Island Baptists bought it.

There is only one Protestant congregation on the island which does not have its own building, the New Life Assembly of God Church, which meets in the Long Beach Island Grade School in Ship Bottom. With sixteen million members, the Assemblies of God are the largest Pentecostal denomination in the world. They have never had a church on the island, even though an active group began meeting in Ship Bottom as early as 1940. Unable to find the right property, that original group moved to the mainland in the 1970s and built the Cedar Run Assembly of God Church. The New Life Assembly of God has been meeting on the island since 1983.

Chapter 26

THE BEACH HAVEN FREE PUBLIC LIBRARY

The resort of Beach Haven was successful from the moment it was founded in 1874. Almost overnight it seemed, a four-story hotel and dozens of rambling, multigabled cottages rose out of the treeless sand hills of an island that could be reached only by boat.

It took money to do that, lots of it. That money came from an industry that was near its zenith in post-Civil War America, the railroad. Men like Parry, Price, Pharo, Burnham, Williams and the other partners in the Tuckerton and Long Beach Land and Improvement Company were all connected with railroading or with ancillary activities like banking and the law. Parry, Burnham and Williams built locomotives. Pharo and Price were executive officers of the Tuckerton Railroad. All of them were ardent sportsmen who could trace longstanding friendships with each other back to years of fishing and gunning vacations at Bond's Long Beach House on the southern tip of the island. They were no strangers to the area.

These men and their wives were socially prominent, powerful figures in Philadelphia and west Jersey, and most of them were also Quakers. For this reason the first place of worship to be built at the new resort was a Quaker meeting house on the northeast corner of Second Street and Beach Avenue next to the Louella Cottage of Archelaus and Louisa Pharo. The first clerk of the meeting there was, like most of the congregation, a person of consequence. Philip Dunn was president of the First National Bank of Trenton and had a summer cottage nearby on Atlantic Avenue.

The simple meeting house, barnlike in appearance with unpainted clapboard sides, was used only in the summer months. By the middle 1880s many of its original membership began to attend the better-appointed Holy Innocents Episcopal Church, which had been built for the summer community in 1882. In

The Beach Haven Public Library was designed to look like a Colonial Pennsylvania farmhouse. Constructed in 1924 of brick and steel, under the supervision of Philadelphia architect R. Brognard Okie, the library has three working fireplaces and an interior balcony that encircles the second floor.

1905, the meeting house was presented to the town by the Pharo family and moved one block south on Beach Avenue next to Kynett United Methodist Church. At its new location, it would become the town's first library.

Attempts to have a library in Beach Haven had begun as early as the 1880s with a gift of books for the town's children from Dr. Edward Williams, who, along with Charles Parry of the Parry House and the Hotel Baldwin, was a partner in the Baldwin Locomotive Works. The

collection was kept in the home of Samuel Copperthwaite on Engleside Avenue and eventually in one of the Sunday school rooms of Kynett United Methodist Church. After the meeting house was moved, Reverend and Mrs. Alexander Corson of the Methodist church catalogued and organized donations to the library. By the time they left in 1908, it was well on its way.

In 1923 Elizabeth Wilson Pharo, in memory of her husband, Walter, and his parents,

On the ground floor, right, the library's red bricks were originally used as ballast on a sailing ship from England. The library also houses a small museum which is filled with old hotel registers, diaries and official papers of the town's early years.

Archelaus Ridgeway Pharo and Louisa Willits Pharo, a founding family of Beach Haven, offered to build a new library for the town. The building would be located two blocks away from the church on a corner lot owned by her at Third Street and Beach Avenue. The library board accepted the proposal immediately. R. Brognard Okie, one of Philadelphia's finest architects, was contacted by Elizabeth Pharo and modeled the design on a Colonial Pennsylvania farmhouse. Unlike a traditional farmhouse, however, the library would be made entirely of brick and steel with several unusual features, like three working fireplaces, a vaulted ceiling and an interior balcony encircling the first floor.

Tons of concrete were poured and steel girders of the two-story structure were already up by the spring of 1924. Okie moved to Beach Haven and supervised every step of the construction by the local firm of Firman H. Cranmer. Ten railroad carloads of bricks were used to build the solid outer walls, and it was soon evident that the town would have the finest library on the Jersey coast.

As it neared completion in the late fall, the durable beauty of the new library was already drawing praise. The bricks were painted white, and all the windows were hung with shutters of pale green. A sweeping, dormered roof added a grace seldom seen in a public building. Surrounded by a low, white, picket fence and later a well-kept lawn, it added an incomparable dignity to what was in those years the town's main street, Beach Avenue.

At the formal opening on November 29, 1924, it was evident that no expense had been spared with the design of the interior, either. The red bricks in the floors throughout the first level had come originally from England to Philadelphia as ship's ballast, their value enhanced by having been a part of historic St. John's Church in that city. The church had been torn down to make room for the supports of the new Benjamin Franklin Bridge across the Delaware River.

The library is still impressive today. From the main room on the first floor, the great vault of a cathedral ceiling rises fully twenty feet, diffusing reflected sunlight downward without glare. To the left of the main room is a spacious alcove along the north wall. It is used as the children's room today, but fifty years ago it was for women only, a place for the ladies to browse. It opened out onto an airy, screened porch filled with comfortable wicker rockers for reading on summer afternoons. The alcove on the south side of the building was the first children's room and is now the library office.

There are two big, Colonial-style fireplaces on the first floor. One is in the main room, and the other is in the long back room on the east side of the library. In the early years, this was known as the "men's room," where male patrons went for privacy. Today it houses the reference collection and is used for meetings. It is well lit by two tall, French windows, and it, too, opens onto the porch on the north side.

The main reading room with its vaulted ceiling is encircled with a balcony reached by a spiral, stone staircase with thick, flagstone steps. The balcony flooring is oak, as are all of the spindles in the railing. The walls upstairs are also lined with books. One great window on the west side rises ten feet to the ceiling, while the rest are all dormers. On the east wall there is a door where patrons step down into a museum with high, beamed ceilings and a huge fireplace. The museum is small, but it is filled with old hotel registers, deeds, diaries and other relics of Beach Haven's century and more of history.

Robert F. Engle

The steamboat wharf at the end of Dock Road was Beach Haven's gathering spot on summer afternoons in the late 1800s. Here charter captains showed off their docking skills, anglers their catch, and yacht owners their racing prowess as cottagers and residents observed a more innocent seashore unfold before them.

Chapter 27

DEEP SEA FISHING CAPITAL OF THE EAST

There was no more exciting place to be on a late summer afternoon in old Beach Haven than out on the steamboat wharf at the end of Dock Road watching distant sails work their way up the bay. It was the charter boat fleet due in at about four o'clock, roomy yachts and catboats each with a captain, a half dozen or more sunburned anglers and usually a full fish box. Passing the admiring crowd, they would drop sail at the very last instant to glide effortlessly into a slip on the long dock that stretched northward from the Beach Haven Yacht Club or tie up to a mooring: Then it was all over but the cheering and the bragging. Most of the fleet had been down bay near Little Egg Harbor Inlet south of Tucker's Island, and everyone aboard had caught his share which could mean two hundred or three hundred fish per boat.

In the last three decades of the nineteenth century, saltwater fishing drew more visitors to the shore than any other sport except gunning. However, while gunning required knowledge and expensive equipment, anyone could fish. Once a boat had been chartered, the captain provided the drop lines and the bait, and the rest was easy. So abundant were the weakfish, croakers, sheepshead and flounder that one person could catch more fish in two hours than could possibly be eaten in a month. Most of these catches went to waste for lack of refrigeration and many a big fish could have been tossed back to bite again, but no one, much less the captain himself, wanted to return to the dock empty-handed. An overflowing fish box was the surest sign of a good trip, the very best way to stimulate future business.

Charter boat captains came from the ranks of local baymen who discovered when the big Beach Haven hotels were going up and carpenters were making $1.50 a day that a boat owner could command at least three times that figure by taking people out for a day's fishing. The practice caught on very quickly, and boat captains from Tuckerton and West Creek were soon tying up at the Beach Haven steamboat landing to book clients for the following day. By 1878 when the town was only four years old there were forty-four charter boats competing with each other for an ever-growing crowd of summer visitors at the Parry House, the Engleside and the smaller hostelries.

Clearly there was a need to organize chartering at a central location so that each angler knew which boat he had hired and for what date. There was also the matter of boat races in which everyone had a keen interest. There were many private yachts tied up near the public dock, and their owners preferred to have the races properly timed. During the summer of 1881 Charles Gibbons, a cottager; Charles Parry, owner of the Parry House, and a number of local captains organized the Beach Haven Yacht Club. The first sailing regatta was held that same summer over a course that ran across the bay to West Creek, south to Bond's Hotel and north right past the public dock and the cheering throngs, and across to West Creek again. Twice around the course was twenty miles.

Gibbons served as first commodore and Parry lent the money to construct a two-story frame clubhouse at the public dock as the club became a focal point of the community. Around 1886, the yacht club took on the role of policing its members to collectively control chartering prices for the season, and there really was no competition to break the monopoly. Moonlight sailing brought in additional revenue for the charter captains. The yacht club dock was extended farther from the public dock each year, and the clubhouse enjoyed a prominence as the only structure on the very edge of the bay. It was

Robert F. Engle

Before the turn of the century, sailing charters worked the bay. Above, the sheepshead anglers caught disappeared around 1910, and old-timers lamented that they would rather catch one sheepshead than fifty weakfish, which also were abundant. Facing page, anglers and crew of the *Owl* pose with a typical weakfish catch.

impressive but never really fancy.

The clubhouse was just two rooms, one on top of the other. A second-floor porch encircled the building, giving shade to the captains who sat on benches waiting for their parties to arrive or for the phone to ring. Upstairs there was a meeting room and downstairs there were lockers where the captains kept their gear and their whiskey. There was no bar in the club until after 1933.

Ninety-five percent of the fishing was in the bay. In the 1880s and 1890s, Beach Haven boat captains occasionally went out into the ocean to troll

for bluefish, but it was a long trip in those years when the closest inlet was Little Egg Harbor, called New Inlet then. It required a seven- or eight-mile sail just to get around Tucker's Island and out into the Atlantic. Trolling was done with hundred-foot hand lines, and anglers wore cotton gloves to protect their hands. At the end of each line was a piece of lead on a wire leader with a sharp hook soldered to the lead. This was the only kind of ocean fishing done in those years.

Before the development and widespread use of the auxiliary gasoline engine around 1905, the

sport of saltwater fishing as practiced in southern Ocean County was done from drifting or anchored sailboats anywhere on the bay. Hand lines attached to oblong wooden frames were perfectly suitable in the days before the saltwater fishing reel had been perfected. After 1910 reels became less subject to rust, but the linen fishing line had to be unwound after each use, washed in fresh water and dried or it would rot. Bamboo poles were occasionally used.

Most bay fish were easy to catch with a hand line; even two- to four-pound weakfish could be caught from a drifting boat in this manner. In the early 1920s, about the time the newly formed Beach Haven Inlet was getting to be nearly a mile and a half wide and nine feet deep at low tide at the bar, weakfish in the eight- to ten-pound range, "tide runners," suddenly made their appearance. The whole method of catching weakfish changed. The bamboo pole and drop line which anyone could use was upgraded to a higher quality of rod and reel.

After 1905, more and more charter captains put engines into their boats if only to make it easier to dock. The newness of engine power was also attractive to potential customers, making them feel more secure. The bay started to get noisy, and there were captains who blamed a bad day's fishing on clanking motors. It was just at this time that the Beach Haven Gun Club expanded its membership with a name change into the Corinthian Yacht and Gun Club and undertook to preserve the enjoyment of sailing craft and competitive racing.

The supremacy of power boats over sail, especially evident as engines improved during and after World War I, enabled sport fishermen to take advantage of a wholly unexpected turn of events. In 1920 a winter storm reopened an old inlet two and a half miles below Beach Haven. Within a short time it was deep and wide enough to be navigable, saving boaters considerable time getting out into the ocean. By 1922 it was superior to the older Little Egg Harbor Inlet and had acquired the name Beach Haven Inlet.

Among the first charter captains to use it regularly was Tom Jones of Beach Haven. While trolling for blues, charter captains would occasionally catch a forty-pound tuna on the same lure. The tuna landings intrigued Jones; he thought there had to be a natural feeding ground for these bigger fish somewhere nearby, and he began to carefully plot each of his trips on a chart.

In August 1923 after some unprecedented catches in the same general area, Jones took careful soundings and discovered something that commercial trawler fishermen had been aware of for some time: the existence of a sand ridge on the ocean floor about thirty-five miles out. The average depth at that distance is one hundred feet, but at the ridge it suddenly rises to a depth of about sixty feet. Commonly known today as Barnegat Ridge, this series of huge submarine dunes is about ten miles long and a mile wide and may have been an island in the last ice age when the ocean level was considerably lower.

In the twenties, some captains called it the Nine Fathom Bank because ocean depth rose to nine fathoms or fifty-four feet on a floor ranging from thirteen to twenty fathoms. Along its slopes countless squid and other small fish were fed upon by tuna, false albacore and other game fish. The course to reach it from Beach Haven Inlet was east-northeast for about two hours; the big fish were best caught by trolling at speeds of seven to ten miles an hour.

Fewer than twenty-five tuna were taken during that August when Captain Jones first discovered the ridge. The next year more than a hundred were caught, along with great quantities of bluefish, false albacore and bonito: The same lure could be used for all of them. Most tuna caught were bluefin weighing between twenty-five and one hundred pounds, and anglers seldom came back without fish. The usual tally was eight to a dozen in a mixed catch. These were golden years for the Beach Haven Yacht Club when the resort became the East Coast capital of "deep sea fishing," an expression that usually evoked images of novelist Zane Grey pulling in the big ones off Catalina.

In 1930 the yacht club, nearing fifty years, found itself in a curious position because nothing had ever been done to secure its existence. In addition, the clubhouse itself was found to be a squatter on land belonging to the Joseph Taylor estate. Rather than purchasing a secure title for ten thousand dollars, the club trustees moved the building two blocks south to Engleside Avenue on bayfront land belonging to Max Schoenberg; a new permanent dock, able to accommodate fifty power boats, was installed without even missing the season. By 1932 the trip to "The Ridge" had become a way of life. Boats were getting larger, averaging thirty-five to forty feet. Cruising at nine knots, they could make the trip in just under three hours. If they left at dawn, trolling began at about eight o'clock. When they returned late in the afternoon, the streets were packed with automobiles as family members and the curious went down to the docks to see what had been brought in. Fish was handed out to any-

one who asked; the idea was to show off what you had caught. Huge rays, sea turtles, hammerhead sharks and even dolphins were on display – anything to draw a crowd. Every charter captain knew the value of showmanship.

Throughout the 1930s, bay fishing continued to be as good as it ever was in the old days, with sometimes hundreds of weakfish to a single boat, but the emphasis at the club was on ocean fishing. Great schools of tuna had moved in to a range of twelve to eighteen miles and were attacking any kind of lure paid out to them. The summer of 1938 was the best anyone could ever remember for big game fishing. Never before had so many white marlin, wahoo and other tropical fish been seen in these latitudes. That the Gulf Stream was moving closer to shore was only one of the many theories to explain the unusual catches, but no one knew for sure. In the first two weeks of August, five white marlin weighing about fifty pounds each were caught. This was unusual, but it was nothing compared to what was to happen on the afternoon of August 30.

Ward Wheelock of Haverford, Pennsylvania, aboard the *Eleanor* captained by Watson "Kinky" Pharo, caught the first blue marlin ever taken off the New Jersey coast. It was hooked five miles off Beach Haven Inlet and brought to gaff after a battle of one hour. The giant billfish weighed two hundred pounds and was ten feet, seven inches long. It was mounted and hung on the wall at the yacht club and in February taken

These weakfish taken on one outing were typical of catch numbers in the early part of the century. Facing page, the old Beach Haven Yacht Club dock ran north and south because it was easier for sailboats to use the tide to glide into the dock and tie up.

to the Sportsman's Show in New York, displayed in the space leased by the Borough of Beach Haven to advertise itself as the "Deep Sea Fishing Capital of the East."

The next year began with great expectations. Once more the tuna seemed unlimited, most of them averaging forty pounds, but it was billfish that every angler hoped to hook. Captains and crew scanned the sea with binoculars searching for the spikelike twelve- to eighteen-inch black dorsal fin, which on a sunning blue marlin looks much like a periscope, a dreadful harbinger of the dark days so near at hand when Hitler's wolf packs would roam the coast. While 1939 may have been another good season for tuna, no one was able to get a marlin with hook and line. A few big ones got caught that summer in the pound nets a mile or two offshore, but that did not count.

The 1940 and 1941 seasons were slow and filled with rumors of gas rationing. Fishing parties were nervous about submarines and the number of anglers dwindled as the cost of fuel rose. Even before the attack on Pearl Harbor, the Coast Guard was authorized to confiscate party and charter boats and the bigger private boats for nearshore patrols. Although owners were reimbursed, they were out one boat for the duration. Some of them joined the Coast Guard Auxiliary and went on patrols with the military in their own conscripted boats. Others were enterprising enough to wrangle their way into a "fish for defense" program designed to offset meat rationing. It was fun, it was patriotic, they were able to get extra gasoline coupons for their efforts, but it was still only bay fishing. With the exception of pound fishermen, no other boaters were permitted in the ocean for almost three years. The atmosphere at the Acme Hotel bar on the docks was dismal. When boat captains talked about the "good old days," they meant 1938. Wartime restrictions undoubtedly crippled charter fishing at Beach Haven, perhaps permanently, but it was not the only disaster. That was yet to come.

The Hurricane of September 1944 destroyed thirteen boats at the Beach Haven Yacht Club. By the time the war was over the following August, it was clear that charter boat fishing would never get back to what it had been. Most of the older boats needed constant repair, and good ones were simply too expensive for any newcomers to the trade. Those who still had serviceable craft found themselves overworked and oftentimes praying for foul weather.

By the mid-1950s there were still fish coming into the dock, but activity slowed as older captains retired without being replaced. The club became more of a social organization as fewer new members actually owned boats. New marinas like Howe's Boat Basin near the site of the old clubhouse began to fill up with private boats, many owned by anglers who had fished from charter boats in the thirties. The appearance of strong, nearly maintenance-free fiberglass boats changed the economics of chartering. Smaller craft were now available, but the initial cost of a bigger boat, the kind needed for chartering, was simply too high for the average young man who wanted to enter the field.

Twenty-five years had passed since Kinky Pharo had astonished the fishing world with his blue marlin when another record was set July 13,

1963. Jack Ranier aboard Mount Holly lawyer Harold T. "Piney" Parker's *ABC* caught a 385-pound broadbill swordfish forty miles southeast of Beach Haven, the biggest fish ever caught with hook and line off Long Beach Island. The head with its great four-foot sword was mounted and still hangs on the west wall of the Beach Haven Marlin and Tuna Club, an organization of private boat owners and their friends that began as a splinter group of the Beach Haven Yacht Club in the 1940s.

In the early 1960s, scientific researchers from Massachusetts' Woods Hole Oceanographic Institution taking sonar soundings of the Hudson, Wilmington and Baltimore canyons some seventy to eighty miles offshore announced finding incredibly rich marine life. These huge underwater extensions of the Hudson and Delaware rivers, almost halfway to the Gulf Stream, were formed in geologic times by millions of years of

The Philadelphia Inquirer *(above)*; Barry T. Parker *(top)*

Before powerful boats and electronic equipment found the haunts of every fish, it was the golden age of gamefishing. On his sport boat *ABC*, Harold T. "Piney" Parker chased broadbill swordfish and marlin. After World War II most sportfishing was from private skiffs like the first *ABC* seen at left in 1947 in Little Egg Harbor Bay after a trip "outside."

erosive waterflow over dry land. Now deep beneath the ocean, they attract summer populations of big game tropical fish when warmer waters from the Gulf Stream spill over into the canyons. Here was the haunt of the fabled blue marlin and the swordfish, the yellowfin, big eye and albacore tuna, an angler's paradise in northern waters if only there were a way to get there.

Coincident with this discovery was the development of the large, thirty- to fifty-foot, sportfishing cruiser equipped with every conceivable fishing device – tuna towers, outriggers, downriggers, gin poles, fighting chairs and full electronic gear like sonar, radar and Loran, all of it unavailable before the war when old-time captains relied on a compass and watch to find their way to and from favorite fishing grounds. A whole new fishing era had begun, reaching its peak in the 1960s when gas prices were still low, boats were few and foreign commercial fishing boats were rarely seen.

A trip to the canyon in those days was the ultimate fishing experience. It always began in darkness at the dock with a take-out cup of coffee from Joe Sprague's Diner. Stepping lightly onto the transom of the *ABC*, the *Anthracite*, the *Dolphin II* or the *Offspring*, hushed voices were soon cut off by the start-up cough and nasal rumble of the engines. Lines were cast off. There was a slow pulling forward out of the slip, a turn out around the last pier of the marina and then south, careful to make no wake. Once in the channel the shadowy figure at the controls up on the flying bridge opened the throttle. The bow rose, the stern sank and a great wide trough of white water rolled out toward the north as gulls darted and slid across the gray clouds of mist and spray from the exhaust. The old Beach Haven water tower stood alone in the red dawn of a perfect August morning, waiting. There was never anything like it.

Today the trips to Barnegat Ridge and the canyons begin in much the same way, but the return is vastly different. There is no crowd of onlookers at the dock. Marinas are surrounded by cyclone fences with guard shacks at some of them. A single piece of electronic gear may be worth more than a charter captain in the thirties paid for his entire boat. There are very strict weight limits for just about every game fish, and often even the big ones are tagged and released. Many owners live aboard their boats in the summer months. The Beach Haven Yacht Club still meets, but it is a social organization without a clubhouse or a dock: In 1985, the clubhouse was pulled down to make way for condominiums. Only the Beach Haven Marlin and Tuna Club still flourishes, keeping alive all of the old traditions of more than a century of great fishing off Long Beach Island.

No matter what promoters used to lure people to the shore, the beach and ocean drew most vacationers, like this group near the boardwalk at the Engleside

Chapter 28

SAND AND WATER — EIGHTEEN MILES OF BEACHES

Eighteen Mile Beach was just one of the names given to Long Beach in Colonial times when there was a well-defined, deep inlet exactly that distance south of Barnegat Inlet. The inlet seems to have had no name on the charts even though it opened into Little Egg Harbor Bay. By 1800, however, another inlet opened three miles below it at the south end of Tucker's Beach, or Short Beach. In those days all barrier islands were called "beaches." This inlet, naturally enough, was called New Inlet, and the one to the north of it that had played so prominent a part all during the American Revolution and had had no name until now was thereafter referred to as the Old Inlet. Within a generation Old Inlet started sanding up and by 1870 was closed completely, adding several more miles to the length of Long Beach Island. It could have been called Twenty-one Mile Beach.

Old Inlet opened again in February 1920 and within a year or two was given the more appropriate name of Beach Haven Inlet. New Inlet also acquired a better name. It became the Little Egg Harbor Inlet. In between them lay Tucker's Island and a protective sand mass to the east of it that was being called Tucker's Beach. Both were

soon to erode away. Fishing was so good in the newly formed Beach Haven Inlet that the highway was extended south of Beach Haven to accommodate fishermen, who were flocking there to stay in tents. The highway to Barnegat City on the island's north end had just been completed, and when the whole road was measured from end to end or from inlet to inlet it was exactly eighteen miles long, reinforcing the old name for the island. Beach Haven for a generation had been promoting itself as being "Six Miles at Sea." It caught on and was soon applied to the rest of the island. "Eighteen Miles Long" and "Six Miles at Sea" became inseparable advertising slogans for Long Beach Island.

Beach Haven Inlet has moved several miles south since the 1920s, and land has built up behind it to form part of today's Edwin B. Forsythe National Wildlife Refuge. The end of the highway, however, has remained in the same place; for practical purposes, the island is still eighteen miles long. "Six miles at sea" is a slight exaggeration. Even when the meadows on both sides of the bay were covered at high tide in the old days, it was still closer to five miles. But six miles not only sounds better, it has a nice typographical

balance for advertising brochures and signs and has been used for ninety years.

George B. Somerville, whose 1914 edition of *The Lure of Long Beach* was not only a deliberate attempt at promotion but also the first history of the island, was so awed by the huge sand dunes at the new resort of Brant Beach "where the island is no wider than a gunshot from ocean to bay" that he was reminded of Robert Louis Stevenson's tale *The Pavilion on the Links.*

"Links" — always pluralized — is Scots dialect; in the story the term refers not to golf but to the desolate seacoast of northeast Scotland on the "German ocean" where rolling dunes, quicksand and coarse grass set the scene for Stevenson's atmospheric account of love and revenge. The word does, however, have very close associations with the game of golf.

Golf was invented by the Dutch in the fifteenth century and then, for the next four hundred years, found its true home on the links of Scotland. Today, all golf courses in the world are laid out on terrains that, no matter how far inland, are still imitative of a seacoast of big sand hills, and, whether the original meaning has been forgotten or not, the game is still played on links.

Sand, coarse grass and coastal scenery had been a part of golf for so long that it seems fitting that the first — so it was claimed — nine-hole "beach" golf course in the United States was laid out at Beach Haven in the summer of 1922. Beach golf differed from the regular game only in the kind of ball used and the construction of the putting greens. The ball was painted red and made in a way that it would not bury itself in the sand. It also floated, and caddies were expected to go into the ocean to retrieve an overshot ball.

In place of the traditional putting green, half of a small keg, eighteen inches in diameter, was embedded near the water line or behind the dunes with the top of the keg projecting about three inches above the sand. Five of the nine tees were on the tops of sand dunes, some of which rose twenty-five feet above the beach. The island course ran from a big dune at Centre Street just above the Engleside Tennis Club

to the ninth tee in front of the Breakers Hotel on Thirteenth Street in North Beach Haven.

The game was a big hit with the summer colony, and it was considered good form to play nine holes in a bathing suit before the noon bathing hour. There was a great deal of excitement in these years over plans to build a Beach Haven Country Club with an eighteen-hole course around Manahawkin Lake. Several prominent men, including Robert Engle, were involved in the negotiations to buy the land, but it never worked out.

The dunes south of Beach Haven on down to Holgate were as big as any on the island. There were secondary and tertiary dunes — dunes behind dunes — and it was actually possible for children to get lost in them if they could not hear the ocean on calm days. For generations, bathers and campers found privacy in the hollows between these dunes, but in the late 1920s the ocean began to make inroads in the dune line, espe-

cially south of Belvoir Avenue in Beach Haven. Seven blocks of the boardwalk were lost in a winter storm, and the erosion continued despite the building of more timber jetties.

Ocean County Freeholder A. Paul King introduced sand fences as an experiment in 1936, a method used with some success to prevent erosion in Western Dust Bowl areas. This was the first time that slat-and-wire fencing had ever been used to build up sand dunes at the Jersey shore; within a few years fences ran the length of the island.

Even then, most officials realized that the fences were building only piles of sand and not real dunes. Increasing development had reduced the replenishment that oceanfront dunes had always gotten from the west wind. Surface sand was being covered over at a rapid rate. In one more generation, walking on the dunes would be forbidden and, with more and more fencing, beach golf, like camping in the dunes

Bill Kane, facing page (both)

Sand traps, coarse grass, water hazards — Beach Haven had the terrain needed for beach golf, a new craze in the fad-crazy 1920s when guests from the Engleside Hotel, seen in the background, could get in nine holes before the noon bathing hour.

and playing king of the mountain, became distant memories.

Storms, too, shaped the shore. Today only a handful of people in their eighties have any clear memory of the cycle of destructive northeast storms that struck the island in the 1920s, beginning with one of the biggest winter storms of all time, the blizzard of February 4, 1920. This storm reopened an inlet south of Holgate that had been closed for fifty years. Within a month this new inlet was fourteen feet deep and getting wider as it advanced northward, eating away at acres of prime real estate.

The leading expert on beach erosion then was Lewis M. Haupt of Cynwyd, Pennsylvania, a professor of engineering at the University of Pennsylvania and an 1866 graduate of the United States Military Academy at West Point. In a lifetime of service with the Army Corps of Engineers he had studied the effects of water currents on

sandy beaches from the Great Lakes to the Gulf of Mexico and had designed the bulkhead that would save Barnegat Lighthouse in 1921. Haupt immediately ordered building a long, timber jetty at the west end of Lincoln Avenue in Holgate.

Bargeloads of pilings were brought across the bay from Tuckerton and sunk deep into the sand in double rows with a steam-operated pile driver. The solid cedar posts were lapped over with thick planks, crisscrossed with three-foot iron bolts and filled with tons of meadow sod. Even before the project was finished it was clear that the jetty would work as erosion on the north point of beach subsided. To protect Bay Avenue and the ocean beach beyond it, there would now have to be another jetty, this one on the east end of McKinley Avenue. Haupt studied the currents and designed the second jetty with a pronounced hook. It, too,

When vicious northeasters in the early 1920s endangered the Beach Haven boardwalk, University of Pennsylvania engineering professor Lewis Haupt designed a series of jetties to prevent erosion, but a September 1928 northeaster washed away seven blocks of the boardwalk. Other Haupt jetties saved Holgate but probably hastened the demise of Tucker's Island. In Holgate, facing page, surf fishing for "tide runners" became increasingly popular.

worked and by the summer of 1925 it was apparent that the south end had been saved.

The new inlet the storm opened was given the name Beach Haven Inlet, and Haupt's two jetties at Holgate, completed in 1923 and 1924, actually turned the tide. Beach Haven Inlet began to widen and drift southward toward Tucker's Island, where real estate was not so valuable and where no one could afford a jetty. Little Egg Harbor Lighthouse was two and a half miles south of Holgate on the northern tip of Tucker's Island. It fell into the sea in October 1927, and within another twenty years the whole island had disappeared. Haupt's jetties saved Holgate but may have doomed Tucker's Island in the process.

The northeast storms of the next few years also cut into the beaches south of the Hotel Baldwin, endangering the boardwalk Beach Haven had built in 1917. The walkway ran for a mile and a quarter from Eighth Street to Holyoke Avenue, and at every high tide the water swirled dangerously under the southernmost seven blocks. In August 1926 a fourteen-year-old boy, on a dare, jumped from the boardwalk at Glendola Avenue and was swept away and drowned before lifeguards could reach him.

Under Haupt's direction, timber jetties had been constructed all along this stretch of beach both perpendicular and parallel to the shoreline, but they could not withstand the great power of the waves. Seven blocks of the boardwalk from

Belvoir to Holyoke washed out in a September gale in 1928. In sixteen more years, the rest of the boardwalk and its fishing pier would be destroyed in the Hurricane of 1944. Today only a few pilings from the old fishing pier remain in the surf at Berkeley Avenue. As for Haupt's timber jetties, every few years one of them will suddenly reappear following a beach washout, standing nearly seven feet out of the sand in a long, parallel row of cedar posts, usually near the big stone groins.

∞ ∞

Beach camping, once a popular form of recreation, has been gone for nearly sixty years. It reached its peak in the 1920s when the causeway bridge enabled anyone with a car to drive to the

island to take advantage of the remarkably fine fishing at the newly opened Beach Haven Inlet.

A narrow, graveled road had been extended south to Holgate in 1921, and on any summer afternoon parked cars lined both sides. The new inlet was full of fish, especially weakfish, providing sport not seen since the day of the sheepshead a generation earlier. Weakfish could be caught from a rowboat or from the beach but only on the changing tide, so anglers called these fish "tide runners."

With twelve hours between tides, it was only natural for most fishermen to try to stay longer, perhaps several days or a week or two, and many chose to camp out. Camping near the water was fun and it was inexpensive; since the end of the Great War in 1918 there were warehouses all over the East full of cheap and substantial army tents, shovels, cookstoves, blankets and lanterns.

From late spring until early fall, fishermen filed across the causeway in flivvers piled high

with canned goods and war surplus items. All were headed for the beaches of Holgate, which were nearly a mile wider than they are now and ideal for camping. It was only a short walk to the edge of the inlet, which in the 1920s was just south of Cleveland Avenue.

On the beach, life was simple. For fresh water, there was an artesian well nearby at Bond's Coast Guard Station. Anglers fetched it in collapsible canvas buckets and used folding canvas wash ba-

Lynn Photo

In 1905, campers like these in Ship Bottom pitched tents in the dunes, toting fresh water from the nearest Coast Guard station. Beach Haven's Harrison Cottage, facing page, top, had a windmill to pump water; Purkey's Pond in Holgate, one of several on the island fed by natural springs, supplied the Engleside Hotel with ice.

sins back in camp. An iron kettle was used to boil water, and there was always plenty of driftwood available to build a fire. To prepare the day's catch, a broom handle could be wired to a cast-iron skillet greased with bacon or salt pork.

Types of tents varied, but the "A" tent with its single ridge pole supported at each end by uprights was popular. It was roomier than the circular-style tent with one pole in the center. On rainy days, long hours between tides were spent playing cards or trying to sleep; if the tent had been backed into a dune and properly set up, it was usually dry and comfortable. Wool blankets rather than sleeping bags were best because they could be hung on a line to dry, and every camper was advised to have an old overcoat to sleep in on chilly nights. Dried eelgrass made a springy mattress.

Of course, island camping had its drawbacks. In a land breeze, mosquitoes and greenhead flies were so bad that most fishermen wore cotton work gloves. There were gales and storms that could flatten a tent, and then there was the heat, but nice days outnumbered the bad and tenting became more and more popular until 1937, when it was apparent that sanitation was a big problem. There were too many campers, and it was

Beach Haven's wooden water tower was built in 1893. In 1912, it was replaced with a steel tower.

decided that since they, like the houseboaters, did not pay taxes, they would have to go.

While the campers' water came from an artesian well, there has always been fresh surface water of varying quality on New Jersey's barrier islands. This water may not have been potable year-round, but it was good enough for the cattle and horses sent there to roam and breed in Colonial times. One of the largest areas of fresh water then was the Great Swamp, and there were several other low-lying areas, some fed by natural springs that formed ponds which attracted wildfowl by the thousands. Wild cranberries

On the island, several artesian wells were drilled at private expense; the first hotel to have one was Barnegat City's Oceanic, where twin cupolas doubled as water tanks to provide pressure, above. Now found only in Barnegat Light, the island's sand dunes, facing page, once rolled westward in a series of vegetation-covered

grew in a pond in Spray Beach, and Purkey's Pond in Holgate was pure enough, at least in winter, that the ice cut from it was used by guests of the Engleside Hotel in July and August.

Drinkable as the water in these ponds might have been in winter and spring, in the heat of summer it turned brackish as the ponds shrank in size and stagnated under great clouds of mosquitoes. To compensate, all island cottages had some means of gathering rainwater while the big hotels in the early days had water brought over in barrels from the mainland.

For purposes other than drinking, the best source of fresh water lay in great abundance about fifteen feet underground atop an imper-

meable layer of peat moss. It was trapped rainwater that had filtered through the sand and was then pumped up through a hollow pipe stuck into the dunes. In the 1880s many houses had windmills which perpetually pumped this surface water into cisterns.

The first artesian wells were drilled on the island a hundred years ago by a few private individuals who could afford them. As early as 1892 there was an artesian well near the train depot at Passaic Avenue in Harvey Cedars. All visitors remarked upon the statue of a small boy holding one boot upside down in his hand; water ran from the boot constantly. The first hotel to have its own well was the Oceanic at Barne-

gat City where steam pumps forced the water up into tanks in the twin ornamental cupolas atop the roof.

Once tapped, the water from an artesian well runs almost forever. Hydrostatic pressure forces the water to the surface, but a pump is required to lift the water into a tank or standpipe to create the additional pressure to move it any distance. The first big water tank was built at Beach Haven in 1893 after a well had been drilled at a cost of twenty thousand dollars. It was a cedar wood tank on a complex wooden frame, and its height of seventy-five feet provided enough pressure to send water to every house in town, inspiring the creation of many

gardens and lawns. By 1911, however, the wooden tank leaked badly, and the town erected an impressive new steel tank tower that was a hundred feet from its base to the bottom of the tank and another forty-five feet to the flagstaff atop its peculiar lid that resembled nothing so much as a big Chinese coolie hat.

Other tanks and standpipes were built around the island in the next few decades. Until then, residents had no choice but to take a couple of buckets to the nearest artesian well, usually located at a Coast Guard station. This was a way of life for Holgate residents until 1939, when they finally got their tank. There

are no longer any bogs or freshwater ponds on the island. Once the scene of winter skating parties, most of the ponds became municipal trash dumps more than seventy years ago. They have long since been filled in and planted with houses.

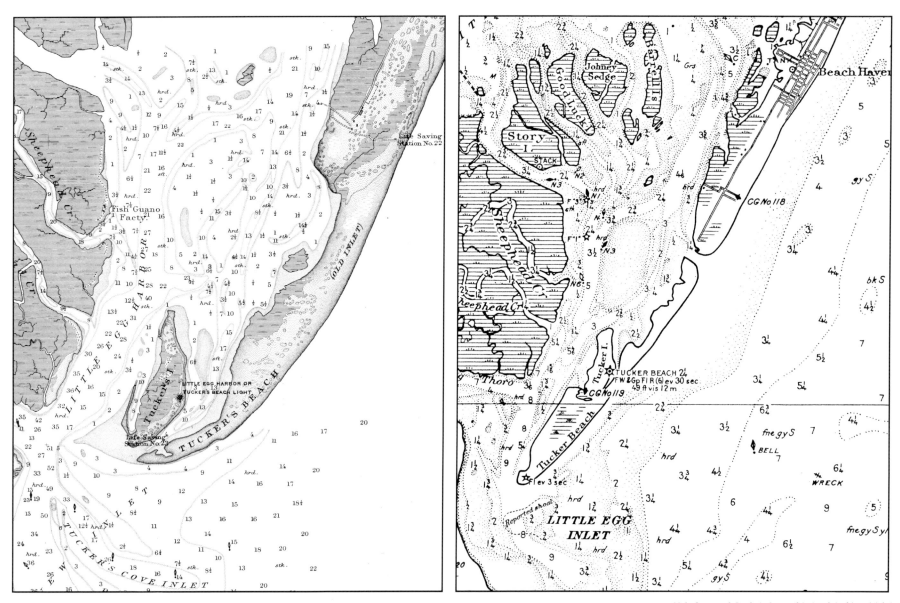

Two charts 47 years apart show changes to Tucker's Island. An 1874 U.S. Coast Survey chart, left, shows Tucker's Beach as a southern extension of Long Beach Island, wrapping around Tucker's Island and separated from it by a slough. A 1921 chart, right, shows the Beach Haven Inlet, a new inlet where "Old Inlet"— noted on the 1874 chart — once closed up. The slough at Tucker's Beach is also disappearing as an overwash of sand connects Tucker's Island with Tucker's Beach.

Postscript

Tucker's Island

Tucker's Island is a perennial favorite among journalists, and over the years confusing information has been published, caused largely by the many conflicting names for what is essentially the same place. Was it Tucker's Beach or Tucker's Island? And what was Short Beach? Was it Sea Haven or St. Albans? Where was St. Albans-by-the-Sea and why was that name used on the Long Beach Township tax maps? Add to this the puzzling changes in the configuration of the area on 150 years of maps; no two are the same. Which was the New Inlet and which was the Old Inlet? What did the slough have to do with making Tucker's Island an island? Wasn't Tucker's Beach really an extension of Long Beach Island? It is time to provide accurate answers to these questions once and for all.

First we must define an island. It is a piece of land completely surrounded by water, no matter what its size. If one end of it is connected to the mainland, then it is a peninsula, not an island. Should an inlet close up between two islands, they become all one. Long Beach Island used to be called just "Long Beach," but it is an island because it has well-defined inlets at either

Sea Haven.

South end of Long Beach. Ten miles north-east from Atlantic City.

Finest Location on the Jersey Coast for Health, Comfort and Recreation.

Trains leave Philadelphia for Sea Haven every day. Fare from Phila. to Sea Haven and back, $2.50.

Sea Haven is separated from the main land by seven miles stretch of salt water, and while there is no finer beach in the world for bathing in both surf and still water, the sailing, fishing and gunning are superior to any other point on the Jersey Coast. There are no land breezes, mosquitos, malaria or fogs, and the pure saline atmosphere is certain relief from Hay Fever and kindred ailments. The U. S. Signal Service Station on the property, affords telegraphic communication to all parts of the country. The Hotel accommodations are unsurpassed.

Several fine cottages are now being built, and

CHOICE BUILDING LOTS

are offered to early buyers at extremely low rates and upon reasonable terms. For maps, prices or other information, call upon or address

The Sea Haven Improvement Co.,
436 Walnut Street, Philadelphia

An ad in the July 26, 1884, issue of *The New Jersey Coast Pilot* touted Sea Haven's sailing, fishing, gunning and bathing, but the failed resort eventually washed into the sea.

end, and it is separated from the mainland by a body of water in exactly the way that Tucker's Beach was in the eighteenth century, when it used to be called Short Beach, before Reuben Tucker ever bought it. It, too, was an island.

Colloquial usage of the terms "beach" and "island" has added to the confusion. Old-time residents of Tuckerton and Manahawkin will say, "He is over on the beach for the day," meaning that he is somewhere over on Long Beach Island, possibly working or visiting, but definitely not on the sand near the water, which is what most people mean when they say "beach." This is how it happened that Tucker's Beach and Tucker's Island came to be interchangeable terms in early accounts and on early maps which clearly show an island that always had an inlet on the north and another on the south until after 1874, when the one to the north closed up. But earlier than that, a process had begun that would cause Tucker's Beach to take on an entirely new meaning.

In the first quarter of the nineteenth century a virtual river of sand drifting down the coast from Monmouth County formed broad shoals in front of Tucker's Island. As more sand was deposited, the shoals formed a huge sand bar that rose well above sea level. When the sand was dry, the wind formed dunes. Plants took seed, and before long there was a whole new beach forming a great hook around Tucker's Island, which was still separated from it by the waters of a partially navigable arm of the bay called a slough. This newly formed beach was called Tucker's Beach even though that had once been an alternative name for Tucker's Island itself. All of this is easily interpreted on the maps drawn in the decades after 1840. By 1874 the accrescent sand which at first made Old Inlet passable only at high tide suddenly closed it, and now anyone could walk the five miles from Tucker's Island up Tucker's Beach to Beach Haven. Tucker's Island and Tucker's Beach no longer meant the same thing.

The arrival of a railroad in Tuckerton in 1871 stimulated resort development in southern Ocean County. Tucker's Island, still separated from Tucker's Beach by the slough, came to be called Sea Haven, probably to compete with Beach Haven, but as a resort it failed in the 1890s. In 1907 a new company tried to develop the lower half of the island into a venture called St. Albans-by-the-Sea. It, too, was doomed to failure, but it remained on the books of Long Beach Township until dropped in 1932. The little community around the lighthouse and the Life Saving station never changed its name. It has been gone now for generations, but it will always be known as Sea Haven.

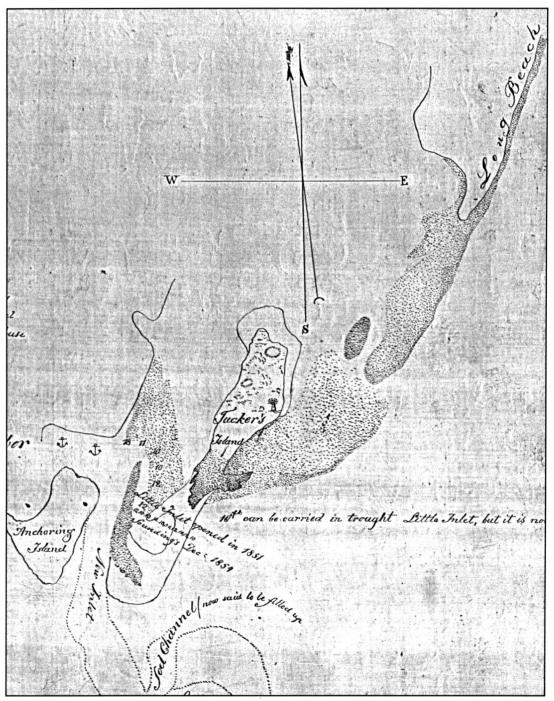

Detail from an April 1853 sketch of Little Egg Harbor Inlet by the U.S. Army Engineer Department shows Tucker's Island with a glowing lighthouse and a couple of hummocks. Although the chart shows Tucker's Island separated from the southern end of "Long Beach," shaded areas also indicate the shoaling that would build up into Tucker's Beach. This extension of Long Beach Island would eventually envelop Tucker's Island.

Index

∞   ∞

Regional works of related interest from Down The Shore Publishing

Six Miles At Sea — A Pictorial History of Long Beach Island, by John Bailey Lloyd, 1990
hard cover, $35.00

Great Storms of the Jersey Shore, by Larry Savadove and Margaret Thomas Buchholz, 1993
hard cover, $42.00

The Lure of Long Beach, New Jersey, by George B. Somerville, 1987 [a reprint of the original 1914 edition]
hard cover, $16.95

Peck's Beach — A Pictorial History of Ocean City, New Jersey, by Tim Cain, 1988
hard cover, $27.00

The annual *Down The Shore Calendar* of New Jersey Shore photographs, $9.95

You may order these titles direct from Down The Shore Publishing, Box 3100, Harvey Cedars, NJ 08008.
(Please add $3.00 shipping and handling per order, and 6% sales tax for New Jersey orders.)
We suggest you try your local bookseller first!